JOHANN STRAUSS AND VIENNA

Operetta and the Politics of Popular Culture

Vienna was always the jewel in the crown of the Habsburg
monarchy, the seat of imperial and royal power as well as the
economic and bureaucratic engine upon which the entire empire
turned. The end of the nineteenth century saw historic changes in
both the city's political infrastructure (with the rise of political
parties) and its outward countenance (with the creation of the
Ringstrasse). This urban transformation was accompanied by the
development of a new and lasting musical genre, Viennese operetta.
No composer was better suited than Johann Strauss to express his
native city's pride and anxiety during this turbulent period. This
book provides an overview of the inception and development of
Viennese operetta, then takes Strauss's works as a series of case
studies in the interaction between stage works and their audience.
It also includes a consideration of Strauss's role as national icon
during his lifetime and throughout the twentieth century. The book
contains fascinating illustrations from the period as well as synopses
of key operettas.

Camille Crittenden is Associate Director of Institutional Gifts at San
Francisco Opera. She has published widely on Johann Strauss and
Viennese culture and on Schoenberg.

CAMBRIDGE STUDIES IN OPERA

Series editor: Arthur Groos
Cornell University

Volumes for *Cambridge Studies in Opera* explore the cultural, political, and social influences of the genre. As a cultural art form, opera is not produced in a vacuum. Rather, it is influenced, whether directly or in more subtle ways, by its social and political environment. In turn, opera leaves its mark on society and contributes to shaping the cultural climate. Studies to be included in the series will look at these various relationships including the politics and economics of opera, the operatic representation of women or the singers who portrayed them, the history of opera as theatre, and the evolution of the opera house.

Editorial Board:
Tim Carter, *Royal Holloway College, University of London*
John Deathridge, *King's College, University of London*
James Hepokoski, *University of Minnesota*
Paul Robinson, *Stanford University*
Ellen Rosand, *Yale University*

Already published
Opera Buffa in Mozart's Vienna
Edited by Mary Hunter and James Webster

Johann Strauss and Vienna

Operetta and the Politics of Popular Culture

Camille Crittenden

CAMBRIDGE
UNIVERSITY PRESS

PUBLISHED BY THE PRESS SYNDICATE OF THE UNIVERSITY OF CAMBRIDGE
The Pitt Building, Trumpington Street, Cambridge, United Kingdom

CAMBRIDGE UNIVERSITY PRESS
The Edinburgh Building, Cambridge CB2 2RU, UK   www.cup.cam.ac.uk
40 West 20th Street, New York, NY10011–4211, USA   www.cup.org
10 Stamford Road, Oakleigh, Melbourne 3166, Australia
Ruiz de Alarcón 13, 28014 Madrid, Spain

First published 2000

Printed in the United Kingdom at the University Press, Cambridge

Typeface Monotype Dante 10.75/14 pt.   *System* QuarkXPress™   [SE]

A catalogue record for this book is available from the British Library

ISBN 0 521 77121 8 hardback

CONTENTS

ILLUSTRATIONS

With the exception of 6.1 all illustrations are reproduced with kind permission of the Österreichische Nationalbibliothek.

ACKNOWLEDGMENTS

Much of the archival research necessary for this study was made possible by a fellowship to Austria from the Fulbright Commission (1994–95). Of the many people who facilitated my work in Vienna, I would like first to thank Norbert Rubey and Dr. Thomas Aigner at the Institut für Johann Strauß Forschung for their encouragement and suggestions. An interdisciplinary approach requires familiarization with many libraries, and the following people made my research much easier than it might have been: in the Wiener Stadt- und Landesbibliothek – Karl Misar in the Handschriftensammlung, Johann Ziegler and Otto Brusatti in the Musiksammlung, and the staff of the Druckschriftensammlung; in the Österreichische Nationalbibliothek – Herr Eppich for his friendly orientation and *Hilfsbereitschaft*, Dr. Günter Brosche and his staff in the Musiksammlung, the staff of the Handschriftensammlung and the Theatersammlung, and the extraordinarily good-natured staff of the Zeitschriftensammlung. I thank Oxford University Press for permission to print a revised version of an article that appeared in *Musical Quarterly* 82, no. 2 (chapter 6) and the Museum der Stadt Wien for permission to publish the photo of Alexander Girardi found in that chapter.

I am grateful for the support of my mentor and colleague Bryan Gilliam, and for the generous advice of series editor Arthur Groos. Thanks go to Victoria Cooper at Cambridge for her sustained enthusiasm and professional guidance. With fond gratitude I thank John R. Palmer for preparing the index, commenting on early drafts, and discussing Vienna and Strauss for more hours than he ever could have imagined.

ABBREVIATIONS AND SHORT TITLES

Abbreviations

NÖL Niederösterreichisches Landesarchiv (Archive of Lower Austria)
ÖNB Österreichische Nationalbibliothek (Austrian National Library)
WSLB Wiener Stadt- und Landesbibliothek (Vienna City Library)
-DS Druckschriftensammlung (Printed Materials Collection)
-HS Handschriftensammlung (Manuscript Collection)
-MS Musiksammlung (Music Collection)
-TS Theatersammlung (Theater Collection)

Short titles

Holzer Rudolf Holzer, ed., *Die Wiener Vorstadtbühnen, Alexander Girardi und das Theater an der Wien* (Vienna: Druck und Verlag der österreichischen Staatsdruckerei, 1951).

Johnston William M. Johnston, *The Austrian Mind: An Intellectual and Social History, 1848–1938* (Berkeley: University of California Press, 1972).

Mailer Franz Mailer, ed., *Johann Strauß (Sohn): Leben und Werk in Briefen und Dokumenten*, 7 vols. (Tutzing: Hans Schneider, 1983–).

McGrath William McGrath, *Dionysian Art and Populist Politics in Austria* (New Haven and London: Yale University Press, 1974).

Schorske Carl E. Schorske, *Fin-de-siècle Vienna: Politics and Culture* (New York: Vintage Books, 1980).

Strauss *Johann Strauß schreibt Briefe*, ed. Adele Strauss (Berlin: Verlag für Kulturpolitik, 1926).

Note to the reader

All translations are my own unless otherwise noted. Where the original German is given, I have preserved the nineteenth-century orthography. English titles of operas and operettas are given in italics where a published translation of the work exists, but in roman where there is no recognized English version.

Introduction

The end of the nineteenth century saw a host of political, social, and artistic struggles within the Habsburg monarchy. Decisions affecting the vast, polyglot expanse of the empire were made in the crucible of Vienna, the imperial and royal seat of power. At the same time, musical life had never been richer in the capital, where performers enjoyed sumptuous new venues in the Court Opera and Musikverein, the Conservatory boasted an expanded faculty and student body, music journalism flourished, and audiences for classical music reached unprecedented proportions.[1] Vienna's fertile musical soil gave rise to a wealth of music in popular styles and genres as well as the standard repertoire heard in concert halls today. With its additional components of text and staging, operetta played a central role in solidifying a Viennese identity, even as that identity was being contested ethnically and politically. Such popular music offers valuable insights not only into the historical circumstances it often addressed, but also into the active and articulate musical life of Vienna.

Indeed, operetta became the expression of a new age in Vienna. Austria had shaken off the dust and shame of its defeat to Prussia in 1866, emerging as a newly established, dualist empire with the *Ausgleich* of 1867.[2] After years of absolutism and economic constraints, Viennese citizens were giddy at the prospect of growth and prosperity heralded by the reforms of Emperor Franz Joseph and the newly elected Liberal Parliament. During the *Gründerzeit*, the period of expansion and development between 1866 and 1873, Vienna saw badly needed industrialization and modernization, bringing the city up-to-date among western European capitals. Although the buildings that line the Ringstrasse today appear as eternal monuments to Vienna's past, that very past was being negotiated and created during these years.[3]

Like the Ringstrasse, operetta reflected the new-found wealth and the Liberal values that created it, for the genre combined aesthetic desire for a new art form with business interest in a profitable new entertainment industry. Anyone with means to do so speculated in the Viennese stock market, and the craze for speculative investments extended to private theaters and to specific works. The theater, in fact, was one market in which all social classes could participate: arriving at the theater hours before tickets went on sale in order to be the first in line, servants often bought up blocks of tickets and then sold them at a profit. Theatrical speculation centered not on spoken stage works or on opera but on operetta and the houses in which it was performed. Operetta authors and composers negotiated with businessmen, selling off various percentages of their royalty rights to eager investors.

This book explores operetta not only as a musical genre but also as a cultural practice popular at a time when musical and social issues were hotly debated. Many who waltzed at masked balls and eagerly awaited each new operetta also influenced political events that shaped modern Europe. Since many of the stage works most success-ful in their own time have failed to "transcend" their historical moment, they offer insights into concerns of the age. Dreams of being memorialized by posterity did not motivate composers of popular music; they wrote for a contemporary audience, hoping for artistic, but also commercial, success. Operettas serve as cultural documents, revealing the Viennese public's concerns, prejudices, goals, and fears at the end of the nineteenth century.

This study focuses on the works of Johann Strauss, a musician central to any understanding of nineteenth-century Viennese music or culture. During his lifetime and since his death a century ago, gen-erations of Viennese venerated Strauss as a totem of their culture. Remembered today chiefly as the creator of the "Blue Danube Waltz" and *Die Fledermaus*, Strauss maintained a high profile in Viennese cultural life for the latter half of the nineteenth century. The social base of his audiences reached far beyond the "elite 2000," the exclusive group of professionals, civil servants, and aristocrats who enjoyed access to the limited number of orchestral concerts in Vienna, such as those by the Gesellschaft der Musikfreunde. Moreover, representatives of the art-music world joined the average member of the listening public as ardent consumers of works by their local musical hero. Indeed, his music continued to inspire and fascinate subsequent generations of Viennese musicians: Mahler mounted the first evening performance of *Die Fledermaus* at the Court Opera; Richard Strauss readily confessed the debt he owed his predecessor for his *Rosenkavalier* waltzes;[4] Webern became convinced of Strauss's genius through conducting his works,[5] and he joined his colleagues Schoenberg and Berg in arranging Strauss waltzes for their Society for Private Musical Performances.[6] The devotion and admiration shown by these eminent composers invites a more detailed investigation into the appeal of Strauss's music.

Championing Strauss as founding father of Viennese operetta has a history almost concurrent with his productions; however, the reasons for Strauss's popularity lie not only in his music but also in the intersection of his career with Viennese musical life and imperial politics. Strauss had been hailed as Vienna's musical ambassador since composing the "Blue Danube Waltz," which premiered during the 1867 World Exhibition in Paris. At this time Offenbach's operettas attracted audiences nightly to Viennese suburban stages. When Strauss began composing operettas a few years later, Vienna greeted his works as their answer to Offenbach, proof to the European community that, despite military losses, Austria still led the cultural world. Strauss's family history and his use of waltzes in his stage works affirmed and celebrated an "essential" Austrian character.

Yet it was not Strauss's musical talents alone that linked his name so inextricably with Viennese operetta, for some of Carl Millöcker's and Franz von Suppé's works were better known and more commercially successful than Strauss's. What Strauss enjoyed, and his colleagues did not, was a close relationship with the social and institutional structures that shaped musical opinion. Highly regarded by the creators and arbiters of art music of his time, Strauss counted as friends and tarock partners such luminaries as Eduard Hanslick,

Johannes Brahms, Hans Richter, Ludwig Bösendorfer, and many other pillars of the Viennese musical establishment.[7] When Hanslick included reviews of Strauss operettas along with those of new concert music or operas in the *Neue Freie Presse*, he bestowed an institutional endorsement on Strauss's music unavailable to other composers of popular music.

These facts should not imply that Strauss's music was interchangeable with that of his operetta colleagues or that the sole difference between them was their social connections. On the contrary, part of the reason Strauss's music found such acclaim in art-music circles was because it, more than the music of his contemporaries, conformed to the criteria of value used to judge art music. By praising Strauss's melodic invention or tasteful instrumentation, Hanslick and Brahms inscribed their critical standards into a genre for many of whose listeners these subtleties were unimportant. The skill necessary for Strauss's achievement, composing music that was sophisticated and elegant yet simple and accessible, has been underestimated. For these reasons, Strauss presents a compelling selection of works to study within the wider context of Viennese operetta and musical life.

This book is organized in two parts; the first (chapters 1 and 2) offers an overview of the sites and circumstances of Viennese operetta. Chapter 1 examines the beginnings of the genre and its roots in Offenbach and in Viennese theatrical and musical traditions, exploring the significance of operetta for Viennese public life and the nature of that public. Chapter 2 discusses the figures most involved in the production of operetta, for these composers, performers, librettists, and directors not only were artistically indispensable but directly contributed to public perception of countless topics, from public policy and religious toleration to fashion and courtship.

The second and larger part of the book examines Strauss and his operettas in a series of case studies. Chapter 3 explores the delicate line he walked between reflecting and creating the Viennese self-image. The Strauss family's music accompanied Vienna's defeats and celebrations throughout the nineteenth century, holding an unprecedented prominence in the city's cultural life. The Viennese used Strauss as a means of representing their city to themselves and to the world, a practice that has continued throughout the twentieth century. Chapter 4 discusses in detail the elements of Strauss's distinctive musical style: prominent violins, refined instrumentation, engaging rhythm, and melodic emphasis on the sixth scale degree (*la*). The circumstances of Strauss's momentous decision to begin composing for the theater, as well as a discussion of *Indigo und die vierzig Räuber*, his first completed effort and the first full-length Viennese operetta, are also of interest here. Strauss grounded this work in local concerns and events, and he used the waltz to represent the Viennese spirit in a variety of settings, often invoking nostalgia for an idealized pre-industrial *Vormärz*.

The nostalgic yearning for a more prosperous time also permeates Strauss's most successful stage work, *Die Fledermaus*, the topic of chapter 5. This work deserves its widespread recognition and admiration, for not only did it fulfill contemporary desires under the pressure of contemporary economic circumstances but it is also the most tightly constructed work of Strauss's long career, filled with elegant melodies and brilliant instrumentation. In it, Strauss weaves a rich web of allusions to his musical forbears and contemporary musical practices. Precisely because this work is so popular, it has become emblematic of Viennese operetta in general. Nonetheless, it departs significantly from the works that preceded and followed it. Its contemporary salon setting and champagne choruses came into vogue again in the twentieth century, but nineteenth-century operetta was far more often set in distant times and places, such as Italy, medieval Germany, or a fictional island.

Along with many of his artistic colleagues, Strauss represented Viennese identity in contrast to some ethnic Other, frequently a minority of the Habsburg empire. This procedure was a timely topic, for increased industrialization and economic expansion brought members of the empire's eastern lands to Vienna, creating tension among the various ethnicities vying for employment, if not leadership, in the capital. Chapter 6 includes a discussion of ways in which

Der Zigeunerbaron thematizes these cultural and political struggles for power and recognition, using dichotomies between urban and rural, sophisticated and coarse, powerful and marginalized, for plot, character, and musical representation.

The final chapter addresses a topic few discussions of late nineteenth-century music can escape, the influence of Richard Wagner. Just as many opera composers felt compelled to imitate or to address in some way the phenomenon of Wagner's music, operetta composers also modified their musical style to accommodate audiences accustomed to the orchestral and vocal styles of Bayreuth. Obvious Wagnerian influences in Strauss's oeuvre limit themselves to two works, the operetta *Simplicius* and his only opera, *Ritter Pásmán*. The title character in the first work resembles Parsifal, and despite Strauss's high hopes for the work, critics derided its combination of comic and serious elements. *Ritter Pásmán* also borrows heavily from Wagner (specifically, *Der fliegende Holländer* and *Die Meistersinger*) and was equally unsuccessful. Although these works failed to win a lasting place in the operatic repertoire, their failure suggests much about the expectations of Viennese audiences and about Strauss's own artistic goals and limitations.

Viennese operetta has enjoyed only a minimal presence in musical scholarship, yet Strauss's stage works prove a remarkably useful corpus for examining many aspects of nineteenth-century life. His composing and conducting careers touched the planes of high art and popular culture in both concert and stage music, an achievement no other musical figure of his time could claim. Moreover, his music continues to attract audiences in Vienna and throughout the world. Aside from musical reasons for evaluating his works more closely, their topicality provides an untapped resource for the cultural historian studying urbanization, anti-Semitism, ethnic relations, and a wealth of further issues relevant to the Vienna of Strauss's day – and our own.

The birth of a genre

At the end of the nineteenth century, Vienna provided an ideal environment for the creation of a new musical genre, the Viennese operetta. Following the conservatism of the Biedermeier period (1815–48) and the neo-absolutism that prevailed after the revolutions of 1848, Vienna opened itself in the 1850s and 1860s to the political, social, and technological advances already underway in the rest of western Europe. Growing industrial development made manufacturing jobs in the city more plentiful and more economically rewarding than agricultural careers in the country. Modernization also increased the size and spending power of the bourgeoisie, who now required service amenities and household staffs to demonstrate their affluence. Immigrants from Habsburg provinces streamed into Vienna in search of employment, creating a more ethnically diverse population than the city had ever known. Within a few decades Vienna grew from a small imperial capital of 500,000 to an important gateway between east and west of almost 2 million residents. The rapid economic expansion and changes in the profile of Vienna's population encouraged, if not required, a new means of musico-dramatic expression.

Despite explosive population growth and intense industrialization, the seat of the Habsburg empire provided an image of calm stability in the figure of Franz Joseph. His coronation in 1848 marked the beginning of a 68-year reign, an unprecedented tenure among modern European nations. As ruler over a geographically immense and multi-lingual empire, he faced increasing obstacles to peaceful rule as various ethnic groups lobbied for autonomy. But the political undercurrents of nationalism and irredentism that eventually threatened to tear the empire apart from within were only just beginning in the last third of the century.

Aside from the temporary effects of a stock market crash in 1873, the city thrived economically with rapid growth in industry, banking, and the railroad.[1] Civic building projects such as channeling the Vienna River, widening streets, and building new roads, bridges, and schools, were all undertaken during the *Gründerzeit* of the 1860s and later. Construction boomed along the newly established Ringstrasse, where monumental public buildings were erected in the Gothic, Renaissance, and Baroque styles in a project of beautification unparalleled in Austria's history. Expansive apartment buildings, both owned and inhabited by Vienna's elite, shared the prime real estate. The chief purpose of these buildings was not utilitarian but rather symbolic, for in them the Liberal bourgeoisie saw reflected their own economic power and cultural sophistication.[2]

The destruction of the city wall in 1857 granted the private *Vorstadt* theaters a new lease on life.[3] As the *Vorstadt* districts became incorporated into the city, their theaters attracted a larger urban audience. Business barons, eager to speculate on theaters and productions, plowed money into both, bringing financial support as well as a willingness to risk novelty. The star system that had developed in concert and theater life in the nineteenth century, exemplified by performers like Franz Liszt, Adeline Patti, and Sarah Bernhardt, finally reached the private theaters as well. Once bastions of ensemble performance, *Vorstadt* theaters would pay extraordinary sums by the end of the century to secure popular performers for their houses. All these economic circumstances and artistic trends directly affected the development of Viennese operetta.

Formally, the genre evolved from a confluence of several traditions, the most direct of which were Offenbach's operettas and spoken Viennese stage works. Offenbach achieved enormous popularity in Vienna during the late 1850s and 1860s, and his operettas provided a natural point of departure for Viennese composers hoping to make the genre their own. Further influences came from contemporary popular music, *Volkslieder* and *Schrammelmusik*, but the farces (*Possen*), folk plays (*Volksstücke*), and comedies (*Lustspiele*) of

Ferdinand Raimund, Johann Nestroy, and Ludwig Anzengruber provided an important narrative model. These dramatic works – performed in the same theaters as operetta and by the same actors –
featured incidental music by Franz von Suppé, Carl Millöcker, and
Adolf Müller, Jr., all of whom became leading operetta composers.
Although Suppé and others had written one-act operettas in the
1860s, it was not until 1871, with Johann Strauss's *Indigo und die vierzig
Räuber*, that the first full-length Viennese operetta emerged.

As the genre increased in popularity, music and theater critics
devoted more attention not only to specific works but also to broader
aesthetic issues. While opera had long received careful critical scrutiny, journalists soon began reporting on operetta as well; Eduard
Hanslick, the unrivalled *éminence grise* among Viennese music critics,
paid close attention to musical developments in the *Vorstadt* theaters.
Hanslick gained a reputation in his own day for barely restrained
pedantry, but he was not alone among Viennese journalists in
his concern for generic categorization. Strauss's *Simplicius* (1887)
aroused much speculation and consternation when it was advertised
without a defining rubric; several newspapers noted the lack of a
descriptive term like "opera," "operetta," or "folk opera," and suggested that it might be a transitional work for the composer, leading
him from the *Vorstadt* theater into the Court Opera.[4] Strauss had
labeled his previous work, *Der Zigeunerbaron* [*The Gypsy Baron*, 1885], a
"comic opera," but although it departed from his previous operetta
style, it was clearly intended for performance at the Theater an der
Wien. He may have hoped this label would gain the work entry into
the Court Opera some day, despite its more modest origins. Only a
few years later Hanslick lamented that "the concept 'opera' is so
broad and so liberal that it encompasses every kind of the most beautiful and most dramatic music."[5]

As broad as the concept "opera" may have become by the 1890s,
operetta had always defined itself against the established genre in
several ways. The table below compares traits associated with each
genre.

Operetta	Opera
Performed in private suburban theaters, away from political centers of power	Performed in Court theaters, subvented and endorsed by monarchy and government, in physical proximity to the Court
Improvisatory tradition continues	Performers adhere to original text
Authority lies with the performer	Authority lies with the composer
Popular music	Art music
Entertainment available to wide social spectrum	Audience composed largely of aristocrats, civil servants, upper bourgeoisie
Plot could be "lascivious," not held to high moral standards, censors more lenient	Proper moral stance must be maintained; here censors were most strict
Women participated in management (Geistinger, Gallmeyer, von Schönerer)	Women involved only as performers
Cross-dressing popular, titillation seeing women in pants	Except for breeches roles, women's bodies remained "appropriately" clothed
Local appeal	International appeal
Value placed on simple melody	Complex melodic, harmonic, and timbral manipulation expected

In some cases, operetta composers deliberately aimed to differentiate their work from opera, while others strove to emulate the high-art genre, hoping that one day their work would be suitable for performance at the Court Opera.

How, then, did the Viennese operetta come to exist as an identifiable genre? Genre theorists have offered various explanations for this process. Frederic Jameson, for one, has argued that *"pure textual exemplifications of a single genre do not exist; and this not merely because pure manifestations of anything are rare, but . . . because texts always come into being at the intersection of several genres and emerge from the tensions in the latter's multiple force* fields."[6] Similarly, Tzvetan Todorov explains that "a new genre is always the transformation of an earlier one, or of several: by inversion, by displacement, by combination."[7] These and other authors stress not only precedents for a new genre but also the importance of the context in which it arose, granting the intended audience significant collaborative power. Jeffrey Kallberg, for example, adopts "an understanding of genre as a communicative concept shared by composers and listeners alike, one that therefore actively informs the experience of a musical work. Construing genre as a social phenomenon requires an investigation into the responses of the communities that encountered a particular genre."[8] Any examination of early Viennese operetta must take into account the intersecting genres, traditions, and expectations that created it. These include the operettas of Offenbach, the heritage of Viennese comic theater, the ubiquity of local folk singers, and the changing tastes of audiences clamoring for entertainment at the end of the nineteenth century.

THEATRICAL MODELS FOR VIENNESE OPERETTA

Offenbach in Vienna

By the mid-1850s Offenbach had found an enthusiastic following in Vienna, where the Carltheater, under the direction of Johann Nestroy, contributed more than any other theater to the growing popularity of French operetta. Nestroy planned a guest appearance of Offenbach's troupe, the *Bouffes-Parisiens*, but the Carltheater's uncertain financial position precluded the visit. Hopeful that a future offer might be tenable, Offenbach refused to grant performance rights for any of his works, but Nestroy evaded the issue in typical nineteenth-century fashion by presenting a pirated production of *Le Mariage aux lanternes* [*Die Verlobung bei der Laterne; Marriage by Lamplight*], translated by comic actor Karl Treumann and orchestrated by Karl Binder from the French piano-vocal score.[9] The success of this production encouraged Nestroy to borrow illegally once again, and he followed it with a version of *Orphée aux enfers*

[*Orpheus in der Unterwelt*; *Orpheus in the Underworld*], playing the role of Jupiter himself.

When Treumann took over leadership of the Carltheater in 1860, he immediately invited Offenbach to conduct three of his operettas with a Viennese cast. The Frenchman received a warm welcome in Vienna in January 1861, when he led productions of *Le Violoneux* [*Die Zaubergeige*; *The Magic Violin*], *Le Mariage aux lanternes*, and *Un Mari à la porte* [*Ein Ehemann vor der Tür*; *A Husband at the Door*], winning acclaim from public and critics alike.[10] Indeed, Hanslick became a supporter of his operettas from that time forward. Feeling increasingly at home in Vienna during the 1860s, Offenbach returned in February 1864 when the Court Opera prepared the premiere of his first opera, *Die Rheinnixen* [*The Rhine Nymphs*]. Although the opera lasted only eight performances before disappearing, it was during this visit that he and Johann Strauss met for the first time. Legend has it that Offenbach then made the fateful suggestion that Strauss try his hand at operetta, but although the two men may indeed have discussed the issue, it was hardly the epiphany for Strauss that later biographers have construed it to be.[11]

Demand for Offenbach's works continued into the early 1870s, and he visited Vienna regularly. In 1871 the humorous weekly *Kikeriki* even cautioned him not to come to Vienna for fear he would be "torn apart" by the four leading theater directors (Friedrich Strampfer, Heinrich Laube, Anton Ascher, and Maximilian Steiner), all seeking exclusive performance rights to his works.[12] His popularity declined somewhat after mid-decade as Viennese composers and librettists sought to distance themselves from French precedents in favor of their own musical and narrative styles. His importance for the inception of Viennese operetta, however, cannot be overlooked.

The success of Parisian operetta and light opera in Vienna was undoubtedly a strong impetus for Viennese authors to try their hand at the genre. (In addition to Offenbach's works, those by Adolphe Adam, Adrien Boieldieu, and Charles Lecocq were also frequently performed.) Although Viennese composers were inspired by their French colleagues, they modified the genre in various ways to suit local tastes. One of the most obvious differences between Parisian and Viennese operetta is the choice of dance genres. The Viennese relied heavily on waltz and polka rhythms, whereas the French preferred the can-can and gallope, if they included dances at all. Offenbach required a smaller cast, chorus, and orchestra than did the Viennese composers, for while Strauss enjoyed access to the full staff at the Theater an der Wien, Offenbach's compositional choices were constrained by the resources available to him in Paris, where, until 1858, governmental regulations limited the number of performers allowed on stage at the *Bouffes-Parisien* to three and the number of orchestral musicians to thirty. By the late 1880s Viennese tastes had evolved to the point where critic Ludwig Speidel, for one, felt that Offenbach's operettas were too thinly orchestrated and used choruses too small to hold the interest of Viennese audiences.[13]

Viennese operetta has been characterized both by contemporary critics and by twentieth-century scholars as more sentimental and romantic than Parisian operetta, which was more ironic and satirical. Whereas Offenbach openly portrays caricatures of government ministers and parodies social mores, Strauss's criticisms are more subtly portrayed and secondary to the romantic story line. Speidel compared Parisian operetta to Viennese in 1888: "The idiotic Kings, feeble-minded Ministers, simpleton Generals, as they schemed in the Parisian operetta, almost all had a satiric look on their face. For [Henri] Meilhac and [Ludovic] Halévy nonsense was a weapon of the wit, while in the Viennese operetta, nonsense is really just nurtured for its own sake."[14] This difference was due, in part, to their respective audiences: Offenbach's Parisian audience of the 1860s was eager to see the Second Empire parodied on stage with quick verbal wit, while Strauss's more ethnically diverse audience of the 1880s could appreciate physical humor and love stories much more immediately. Still, the generalization is flawed for two reasons. First, French operetta composers after Offenbach were also more sentimental and less satiric than he had been. Only because Offenbach and Strauss provide the two outstanding national examples of composers in their genre are they often compared as though they were simultaneous phenomena. Second, Viennese operetta also incorporated parody at various points in its development. Strauss's *Indigo* is replete with parody and was accused of being too much like Offenbach for precisely that reason. Even if the libretti did not include political or social satire, performers often added parody themselves through gesture or delivery style.[15]

Unlike his Viennese colleagues, Offenbach strove to set whole scenes to music, not just isolated numbers; he complained to his librettist Ludovic Halévy that, without situations, the music becomes boring and absurd for the audience.[16] Offenbach worked more closely with his librettists than the Viennese generally did, facilitating a musico-dramatic unity that Viennese operetta frequently lacks. For this trait, he was hailed by Hanslick, among others, as a dramatic composer. Although some Viennese operettas, especially those of the 1880s, include large scene complexes during which the action is furthered through arioso dialogue or melodrama, the genre more often revolves around discrete numbers (couplets, ensembles, finales) separated by spoken dialogue.

The Viennese operetta tradition also differed from Offenbach in its tolerance, even encouragement, of satirical Jewish figures. Offenbach's father was a cantor, and although Offenbach himself converted to Catholicism in 1844, the Jewish traditions and melodies of his childhood remained with him throughout his life. Despite his obvious delight in satire and caricature, he never included or allowed Jewish parodies in his works. Strauss and his colleagues did not shy away from Jewish caricatures and, in fact, were advised by anxious theater directors on several occasions to tone down or eliminate such caricatures from their works.[17]

Despite these differences, Viennese operetta would have been unthinkable without its French predecessor. More than any specific structural or musical influences, Viennese operetta owes its general tone to the French model. The idea of operetta – entertaining scenes linked together through simple melodies and dance numbers – came from France, and although the Viennese operetta was also influenced by operatic and local theatrical forms, its deepest roots are found in Offenbach.

Links to spoken theater

At the beginning of their foray into operetta Viennese composers borrowed heavily from familiar theatrical forms. Although music is the defining element of operetta, the genre shares many features with spoken stage works performed in the *Vorstadt* theaters of its birth. Plays often included couplets (strophic songs) or choruses, as well as musical accompaniment, like dances, marches, or entr'acte music; when the musical portion of these spoken genres was particularly great, they were advertised as being *"mit Gesang"* (with song). Indeed, some early one-act operettas differed little from the common *Posse mit Gesang* or *Lebensbild mit Gesang*. Two leading authors of Viennese *Possen* and *Volksstücke* were Johann Nestroy and Ludwig Anzengruber. Although neither of these authors wrote operetta libretti himself, their works were performed frequently on the stages where operetta emerged. Along with operetta, their works contributed to establishing – as well as criticizing – a public Viennese identity.

Nestroy's works, often set in the Viennese folk milieu, were notorious for their daring political or social critique. One of his most successful works, *Freiheit in Krähwinkel* [*Freedom in Krähwinkel*, July 1848], deals with the freedom of a citizenry against political and religious oppression, an especially apt topic at the time of its premiere. Nestroy's career was firmly established prior to the revolutionary events of 1848 and their aftermath, a time of censorship and absolutism, but he gained renown for adding gestural innuendo to dialogue so that, on the basis of the written text, the censors could not object, although the audience clearly understood the political figure being parodied or the criticism being made. Censorship continued, to varying degrees, until the end of the nineteenth century, and Nestroy's tradition of suggestive, improvisatory gestures persisted on the operetta stage.

Nestroy began his career as a singer in the Vienna Court Opera chorus, and although he ultimately found that his talents lay more in acting and writing than in music, he kept abreast of musical developments and trends.[18] He created parodies of the most popular operas: *Tannhäuser* (subtitled "Comedy of the future with music of the past and current sets, in 3 acts"),[19] *Lohengrin*, and *Martha* ("or the Maid-auction of Mischmond").[20] His parody of *Tannhäuser* (1852), with music by Karl Binder, acquired a following long before Wagner's work reached any Viennese stage (1857).[21] From 1852 until 1860 he directed the Theater an der Wien, where he was engaged as actor and author from 1831 until the end of his life in 1862. His works, characterized by a tone similar to Offenbach's, satirize the government and its employees and implicitly criticize contemporary society and its practices. Although Viennese operetta did not continue his parodic tone, the new genre adopted some of the stock characters found in his plays, such as the dandy, the wealthy businessman, the spunky maid, and the folk from the country. Similar character types may also be found in the works of Nestroy's colleague Ludwig Anzengruber, whose treatment of them is, however, more respectful and sympathetic than satirical.

Anzengruber wrote his most successful and memorable works between 1870 and his death in 1889, thus coinciding with the early development of Viennese operetta. He was the last in the tradition of *Vorstadt* authors, a successor to Nestroy, Raimund, and O. F. Berg (founder of the weekly *Kikeriki*). Like the works of these authors, who lampooned many inanities of Viennese public life, his plays concern moral issues, especially the corruption and power of the Catholic church. During Anzengruber's lifetime many distinctive qualities of the *Vorstadt* disappeared as those neighborhoods were subsumed into the growing metropolis of Vienna, and the atmosphere that had nourished the *Volk* authors was gradually supplanted by the city. Nevertheless, he continued many techniques typical of the *Vorstadt* theater, using asides and eavesdroppers, local dialects, and music and songs – especially entrance songs – to establish characterization. Along with his *Vorstadt* predecessors, his characters' names revealed something of their personality; in *Der Pfarrer von Kirchfeld* [*The Priest of Kirchfeld*], Wurzelsepp ("Wurzel" means "root") digs roots in the mountains for use by a pharmacist, and Hell ("bright"), the clear-sighted minister, argues against the villainous Duke Finsterberg ("dark mountain"). Although the *Volkstück* tradition waned, many of these traits continued in the guise of Viennese operetta.

Anzengruber was supported and encouraged by directors Maximilian Steiner and Marie Geistinger at the Theater an der Wien. There he enjoyed his first success with *Der Pfarrer von Kirchfeld* (1870), a story of religious intolerance (between Lutherans and Catholics) in which Geistinger established herself as a dramatic, as well as a musical, talent. Two of his favorite themes – the land-greedy farmer and illegitimate birth – appeared for the first time in his next work, *Der Meineidbauer* [*The Perjure Farmer*, 1871]. Further successes included *Der G'wissenswurm* [*The Worm of Conscience*, 1874] and his most controversial play, *Das vierte Gebot* [*The Fourth Commandment*, 1877], also works in which Geistinger created the female leading characters. Although he never wrote operetta libretti, his contributions to the Viennese *Volksstück* influenced those who did. His folk tone removes him from Johann Strauss's more urbane style, but other leading operetta composers like Millöcker and Karl Zeller inherited Anzengruber's success in portraying a rural milieu.

EXTRA-THEATRICAL INFLUENCES

Since the old days, Vienna claims three important elements of popular music that speak for the unique musical talent of the Austrians – elements without which any representation of Viennese musical life would certainly remain incomplete. They are military music, dance music, and finally, the folk singers.   Eduard Hanslick[22]

Viennese operetta composers relied on a variety of musical sources for guidance and inspiration as they found their footing in the new genre. Along with Offenbach's works and traditional dance music, two particularly Viennese musical styles contributed to the development of the new genre, folksongs and *Schrammelmusik*. Although this music was originally intended for the enjoyment of the local population, the operettas of Strauss and his colleagues brought these styles to an international audience.

Composers and performers of folksongs exercised a powerful and unacknowledged influence on other contemporary forms of popular music. Often a theater's music director, whose job included providing music for plays and other entertainment, drew on folk music, either directly or indirectly, for inspiration. Although most popular music is ephemeral, existing only as long as its style is fashionable, some folksongs have gained lasting popularity: "Es gibt nur a Kaiserstadt, es gibt nur a Wien" [There's only one imperial city, there's only one Vienna], composed by Wenzel Müller, stayed in the popular repertoire for generations, and the "Fiakerlied" [Coachman's Song], composed by Gustav Pick and premiered by Alexander Girardi in 1885, has remained a public expression of nostalgia for over a century.

Folksongs, performed in local dialect, were usually strophic and often referred to topical events or places. Many offered a sentimental, nostalgic picture of Vienna and its environs, referring to the Vienna woods, the Danube, and the vineyards and wine bars (*Heuriger*) north of the city. The refrain was frequently a yodeling melodic pattern sung to text like "duliäh" or "hoda ruli uli."[23] The Act II chorus in *Die Fledermaus* ("Brüderlein und Schwesterlein") alludes to this style with its refrain of "duidu, la la la," and when Strauss uses "duliäh" as the refrain of *Indigo*'s most popular chorus, "Ja, so singt man in der Stadt wo ich geboren" [Yes, that's how they sing in the city where I was born], he explicitly imitates the folksong idiom. In this number he also follows tradition by referring to Vienna as the place of the characters' birth, for many folksongs emphasize that the singer or the singer's mother was born in Vienna with refrains such as "Muatterl war a Wienerin, drum hab' i Wien so gern" [Mama was a Viennese, that's why I like Vienna so much] and "Das ist mein Wien, mein liebes Wien, so lebt man dort wo ich geboren bin" [That is my Vienna, my dear Vienna, that's how they live where I was born].

The folk singers' art was largely an oral tradition and was not subject to the censorial scrutiny that stage works routinely underwent. Folk singers frequently took advantage of this freedom to express social and political commentary, still thinly disguised by metaphor and allusion. Josephine Gallmeyer, a leading operetta performer and folk singer of her day, explained, "an opera singer sings such high German that you usually can't understand a word; a folk singer, however, sings just what she thinks, so you understand not only what she sings but also a whole lot more."[24] Gallmeyer and others transferred this well-developed art of innuendo and *double entendre* to the operetta stage.

Stage music composers originally borrowed from folk singers, but soon the exchange also worked in reverse. Songs from popular operettas were arranged and publicized by folk singers, much to theater directors' dismay, for the price of a theater ticket far exceeded the cost of an evening in an outdoor café listening to the latest operetta hits, and the singers thereby diminished the potential theater audience. Theater owners had every reason to be concerned about the detrimental effect of folk singers on their businesses: the number of folk-singer societies grew from thirty in 1876 to over seventy in 1890, and police reports showed evidence of more than 19,000 folk-singer productions in 1885 alone.[25] Some theater directors went so far as to press charges against folk singers who popularized songs from operettas to which their theaters owned exclusive performance rights.[26] Members of the folk singers' broad audience included not only local residents of the suburbs where they performed, but also aristocrats and wealthy business families who ventured out occasionally from their new mansions in the city to hear the novelties in *Volksmusik*. When many Viennese singers went to Berlin to participate in festivities at the newly opened *Wintergarten* in 1886, Viennese newspapers portrayed theater directors' joy and relief: "Hooray! We're losing our most dangerous competition!"[27]

Folk singers sometimes worked in collaboration or alternation with local instrumentalists, and one of Vienna's most successful instrumental groups was the Schrammel quartet. Brothers Johann and Josef Schrammel, along with Anton Strohmayer and Georg Dänzer, played two violins, a guitar, and a small clarinet (the "picksüße Hölzl"), creating the distinctive sound of *Schrammelmusik*. Founded in 1878, the ensemble began its career in the *Heuriger* of Nussdorf, a wine-growing suburb north of the city; their repertoire consisted of traditional dances, marches, and folksong arrangements, as well as their own original music. By the late 1880s the quartet had gained sufficient popularity and respect that they were invited to perform in the Viennese institutions of high culture, the Court Opera and the Musikverein. Strauss heard the Schrammel quartet for the first time in 1884 and offered this recommendation: "I hereby declare, with pleasure and confidence, that the ensemble's musical leadership, in execution and presentation, is of artistic significance in the true sense of the word. I highly recommend them to everyone with a sense for the faithful musical representation of Viennese humor and the poetic characteristics of the Viennese folk music genre."[28] These comments coincided with his early work on *Der Zigeunerbaron*, the general tone and instrumentation of which suggest that the Schrammels' music made a strong impression.[29]

Schrammelmusik, like Strauss's works, appealed to all social levels, and just as Strauss was a sought-after entertainer for private balls, the Schrammel quartet likewise became a prestigious addition to private parties. Journalist Julius von der Als explained: "The Viennese *Heuriger* musicians today are no longer beggar musicians. They are welcome in salons and in the palaces of our aristocracy; no intimate party is complete anymore without inviting 'die Schrammeln.' Whoever cannot get the Schrammels must then make do with other musicians."[30] The Schrammel quartet had not existed as long as Strauss's orchestra and could not boast the same musical continuity between generations, but they evoked a similar sense of nostalgia in their listeners by performing traditional folksongs that had been in circulation for years. Indeed, one newspaper described them as "a 'living archive' for the sounding treasures of years gone by."[31]

The name Schrammel has continued its association with Viennese identity throughout the twentieth century. In 1922, Erwin W. Spahn lamented in "O Du arme Stadt der Lieder!" [O, you poor city of songs!] that he "recently went out to where the Schrammels once fiddled. Instead of the sweet Viennese songs, the new jazz blared."[32] The style was revived in the 1960s by members of the Vienna Philharmonic in a group known as the Philharmonia Schrammeln.[33] Subsequent musicians combined traditional tunes with more contemporary popular styles; in the late 1970s, Roland Neuwirth founded a popular music group called the "Extremschrammeln," which began to add rock and blues elements to the traditional folksongs.[34] Neuwirth reorganized his group in the mid-1990s as the Herz.Ton.Schrammeln, an ensemble that toured the United States and Canada in 1999 playing traditional Viennese folk music along with their own new compositions. Although the original Schrammels were not well known internationally, *Schrammelmusik* fulfilled and continues to fulfill a twofold cultural role similar to that of Strauss's music, a gateway for nostalgic recollection and a symbol of Viennese identity.

TRENDS IN VIENNESE OPERETTA: 1865–1900

The earliest Viennese operettas, composed in the late 1860s, closely followed Offenbach's model: short, satirical works requiring a minimum of singers and orchestral forces. Translations of Offenbach's works were quite popular in Vienna, and many composers hoped to share in his success by imitating his style; Suppé's *Die schöne Galathee* [*The Beautiful Galatea*, 1865] was specifically modeled on Offenbach's *Belle Hélène* [*Helen, or Taken from the Greek*, 1864] in style, theme, and scope. Another model for early operettas was the one-act comedies with which they shared an evening's program. Suppé's *Das Pensionat* [The Boarding School, 1860] and *Flotte Bursche* [Carefree Guys, 1863] clearly derived from the local comedies performed alongside them on the *Vorstadt* stage. As Viennese composers gained more experience and confidence, they gradually established traditions of their own.

The first full-length Viennese operettas were set in an exotic utopia (like the island of Makassar in *Indigo und die vierzig Räuber*, 1871), a fictional but realistic land (like the small principalities of Trocadero and Rikarak in *Prinz Methusalem*, 1877), or an actual foreign country (frequently Italy, as in *Carneval in Rom* of 1873 and *Boccaccio* of 1879). Austrian composers felt a special kinship with Italy – not only were they geographic neighbors, but much of northern Italy had belonged to the Habsburg empire until shortly before Viennese operetta emerged.[35] Turkey (*Fatinitza*, 1876) also served as a contrasting musical and social culture, but Asia never held the fascination for the Viennese that it did for Offenbach (*Ba-ta-clan*, 1855) or Gilbert and Sullivan (*The Mikado*, 1885). Although there was an Asian presence in Vienna at the end of the nineteenth century (through visiting dignitaries and theatrical troupes), a Viennese operetta was not set in China until Franz Lehár's *Das Land des Lächelns* [*The Land of Smiles*, 1929].

Operettas of the mid to late 1870s, while still hewing close to French models, were more urban and focused on Vienna. Strauss initiated this trend with the popular *Die Fledermaus* (1874), set in a "spa near a large city," obviously Vienna. Millöcker's *Abenteuer in Wien* [Adventure in Vienna] of 1873 and *Die Frau von Brestl* of 1874 both capitalized on local interest. Nostalgia for Biedermeier Vienna also played a large role in operettas and revues during these years, as the popularity of Millöcker's *Erinnerungen an bessere Zeiten* [Memories of Better Times] of 1874 attested.

Viennese operetta of this decade invariably included a leading woman or a female ensemble dressed in men's clothing. Whether a male character was played by a female actress (Prince Orlofsky in *Die Fledermaus*; Boccaccio and Prince Methusalem in their eponymous works) or a female character disguised herself as a man during the course of the operetta (Fantasca in *Indigo und die vierzig Räuber*) or a male character, played by a woman, disguised herself again as a woman (Vladimir in *Fatinitza*), the decade offered ample opportunity for cross-dressing. Choruses of female "soldiers" were popular for their close-fitting uniforms and the opportunity to march in formation. In the days of tight corsets and long, full skirts, many audience members enjoyed the rare voyeuristic opportunity to see women's legs unveiled. In these respects, Viennese operetta differs from the works of Gilbert and Sullivan, a conscious decision on the Englishmen's part. Gilbert explained:

> We resolved that our plots, however ridiculous, should be coherent, that our dialogue should be void of offence; on artistic principles, no man should play a woman's part and no woman a man's. Finally, we agreed that no lady of the company should be required to wear a dress that she could not wear with absolute propriety at a private fancy ball; and I believe I may say that we proved our case.[36]

During the course of the 1870s, Austrian composers and librettists gradually weaned themselves from the French predecessors that had served them well at the start. A review of Suppé's *Boccaccio*, premiered in 1879, commended the work: "It is gratifying that the French imports of recent years have been superseded by a Viennese work, that local composers offer their French colleagues ever more dangerous competition."[37] Librettist Richard Genée recalled that the Offenbach style of burlesque was no longer appropriate by the end of the 1870s, "and as I then set out to create independent libretti, my efforts were directed toward eliminating the parodic element and the French frivolity from the operetta in order to create a German operetta that, in its essence, would come close to comic opera."[38] Many operetta composers added operatic elements to the existing framework of operetta in hopes of just such an "improvement." A journalist described the typical operetta of 1880:

> Cute songs, ensembles in the style of grand opera, and *Posse* couplets follow each other without embarrassment; one composes according to demand and available resources. Singers who could appear at the opera and comics who have not a tone in their throat must work together, and thus arises that mixed genre that we in Vienna now call operetta.[39]

Hanslick, too, decried the accretion of grand opera elements in operetta, claiming that operetta composers who try to compose in the style of grand opera do it badly, only proving thereby that they do not know how to compose an operetta.[40]

In their efforts to compose in a more serious style, authors in the 1880s rid the genre of the pants roles that had been popular the decade before. Audiences no longer expected the satire and burlesque of earlier days, but rather characters with whom they hoped to identify: virile heroes and demure women. Any hint of androgyny was not suitable for a new nationalist climate in which secure identity and unmistakable differences between the sexes were sought.[41] Female characters themselves also differed in this decade from their predecessors. By the 1880s the earlier typical female character (dominant, witty, influential, energetic) was almost completely pushed into the background. The self-sufficient, scheming Rosalinde and Adele of *Die Fledermaus* (1874) give way to the sweet, obedient Saffi of *Der Zigeunerbaron* (1885).

The leading male role in *Der Zigeunerbaron* is also typical for the time, a strong hero successful in battle. The 1880s witnessed a new emphasis on military might and Austro-German nationalism. A growing national awareness and pride can be seen in reviews of Strauss's *Der lustige Krieg* [*The Merry War*, 1881]:

> Johann Strauss, our characteristic, artistic representative, who is more qualified than anyone to illustrate the lively Viennese life in music, has set an Italian history to music this time. The composer went from the Portuguese land of *Spitzentuch* [*der Königin*] to the Italian of *Der lustige Krieg* – we would, however, like to find him next on his own ground as composer of a comic opera that uses modern material and takes place in Austria.[42]

Strauss gradually complied, beginning with the final act of *Der Zigeunerbaron* four years later. Other operettas of this decade emphasizing German heroism and military strength are Millöcker's *Der Feldprediger* [The Army Chaplain] of 1884 (which takes place in a small Prussian town on the Russian border during the Napoleonic invasions) and *Die sieben Schwaben* [The Seven Swabians] of 1887 (which takes place in Stuttgart during a sixteenth-century war between a local duke and the Swabian league of knights).

The 1880s saw an emphasis not only on German military might

but also on German cultural heritage. The Court Opera promoted a renaissance of German romantic opera, a genre that provided a new model for operetta composers and librettists. The centennial of Carl Maria von Weber's birth brought *Der Freischütz*, *Oberon*, and *Euryanthe* to the Court Opera in 1886. Works by Heinrich Marschner also enjoyed renewed popularity; *Hans Heiling* was frequently performed in the 1880s, while Court Opera director Wilhelm Jahn recovered *Der Vampyr* from the archives, reviving it with great success in 1884. Operetta composers emulated some of the salient musical characteristics of these works; but in addition to horn choruses on- and off-stage and numbers for male chorus (hunting songs, drinking songs, patriotic songs, and the like), the dramatic *Vorspiel* that formally characterized many German romantic operas also became a favorite narrative device for operetta authors.[43]

Wagner's operas, always popular with the Viennese public if not Viennese critics, became commonplace on the Court Opera stage from the 1860s on. All of his works (except *Parsifal*) had been performed there by 1879, a year that saw performances of the *Ring* cycle in its entirety, and these operas remained in the Opera's repertoire thereafter.[44] Newspapers complained openly that Alfred Zamara's operetta *Der Doppelgänger* (1887) was too "Wagnerian," yet it filled the house nightly at the Theater an der Wien.[45] Strauss's *Simplicius* (1888) and Adolf Müller's *Der Hofnarr* (1886) and *Der Liebeshof* (1888) further exemplify contemporary operetta composers' fascination with Wagner and the German renaissance.

After the popularity in the 1880s of German myth, legend, and history, it became fashionable once again in the 1890s to write stage works alluding to current events. Like the *Zeitopern* of a later generation, these works attempted to be modern, witty, and satirical. America became a popular setting for the modern entrepreneurial spirit, characterized by works like *Der Millionenonkel* [The Millionaire Uncle, 1892], *Ein Böhm in Amerika* [A Bohemian in America, 1890], *Der arme Jonathan* [*Poor Jonathan*, 1890], *Das Goldland* [Gold Country, 1893], *Ein Wiener in Amerika* [A Viennese in America, 1893], and *Der American Biograph* [The American Biographer, 1897]. Strauss, too, participated in the modern trend with *Fürstin Ninetta* [Countess Ninetta, 1893], his first operetta following the brief tenure of his only opera, *Ritter Pásmán* (1892). *Ninetta*'s libretto, by journalist Julius Bauer, was highly contemporary and alluded to recent political events; one newspaper dismissed it as a "politisches Witzblatt" (a political humorous newspaper),[46] but sculptor Victor Tilgner congratulated Strauss on the work and noted that the public was surprised at how much they enjoyed it. They thought they had "outgrown" that kind of music, yet the theater took in 1400 fl. on a night during carnival.[47]

Historical, serious topics became passé in the 1890s for several reasons: influential new performers rose to prominence; a series of new theater openings changed the general face of theater life; an Offenbach revival, as well as performances inspired by the death of Suppé in 1895, encouraged renewal of these works; and new names in libretto composition came into play.[48] The librettist of the 1890s was often trained as a journalist rather than as a novelist, playwright, or poet. Among the journalist-librettists were Hugo Wittmann, Julius Bauer, Ignaz Schnitzer (editor of the *Neue Pester Zeitung*), Ludwig Held, Theodor Herzl, Max Kalbeck, Gustav Davis (editor of the *Kronenzeitung*), and Bernhard Buchbinder.[49] These men hoped to modernize operetta and present works relevant to contemporary events and fashions.

An opposite trend was simultaneously in evidence, also a reaction against the perceived excesses of Wagnerism – composers returned to a rustic, folk style exemplified by works such as Strauss's *Waldmeister* [Woodruff, 1896], Zeller's *Der Vogelhändler* [*The Tyrolean*, 1891], and Ziehrer's *Die Landstreicher* [The Tramps, 1899]. These works, set in the countryside around Vienna or in Austria's alpine provinces, used authentic folksongs and imitations of that style. Despite its initial appeal, this music was not rich enough to nurture the operetta through the turn of the century, for after a few lean years operetta composers returned to an urban setting in the first decade of the twentieth century.

THE ROLE OF THEATER IN VIENNESE PUBLIC LIFE

In no other place was the entire texture of life so tightly interwoven with that of the theater as it was in Paris and Vienna.   *Hermann Broch*[50]

The theater was not only a place to enjoy the latest show, to meet friends and family, or to see and be seen; the stage works themselves, along with the performers, became a daily part of Viennese conversation, speculation, and amusement. Indeed, as Broch and others have noted, the public so thoroughly integrated the theatrical experience into their personal epistemology that Viennese public life itself had the quality of an illusion. Broch further explained that, "To a far greater extent than the novel, [the theater] has a social and economic function."[51] Because a theater audience represented a wider socioeconomic span than a novel's readership – the *Volk* rarely read novels, yet they attended their neighborhood theaters – the popular stage acquired greater power to influence and shape public opinion.

The growth of print journalism also affected the relationship between theater and public, for several newspapers were devoted to the affairs of the stage and those who stood in its spotlight. Adolf Glassbrenner, in his 1836 book *Bilder und Träume aus Wien* [Images and Dreams from Vienna] wrote, "The most widely circulated of all Austrian newspapers is the *Wiener Theaterzeitung* [Viennese Theater Newspaper]. Everyone knows that it is read throughout Germany, and [editor, Adolf] Bäuerle is, therefore, a man of great influence."[52] At the end of the century, the *Österreichische Musik- und Theaterzeitung* [Austrian Music and Theater Newspaper] stressed the educational, socializing function of the theater, asserting that "the theater reinforces worldly justice – but a still broader field is open to it alone. A thousand vices that are endured unpunished, the theater punishes; a thousand virtues about which everyone is silent, are praised from the stage."[53] On the other hand, some felt that the theater was failing in its social duty to edify its audiences. Adam Müller-Guttenbrunn, for one, decried theater owners who were more interested in making a profit than enriching the moral lives of their public: "The original noble intention of someone, who wanted to improve the Viennese foundation [*Boden*], morally educating the *Volk* through the theater, has been turned into its exact opposite by his successor; it has sunk into the sewer of Viennese theater life."[54] Theater-goers may not have concurred with the moral lessons taught in the suburban theaters, but the theater's power to affect public life was indisputable.

For this reason, government censors kept a close eye not only on productions in court-subvented theaters but also on developments in the private *Vorstadt* theaters. The censors wrote of *Indigo* (19 January 1871): "Such trash is not suited to fulfill the responsibilities of the stage – as an educational institution. [*Indigo*] seems to be much more an outgrowth of a ruined sense of taste, whose encouragement lies in neither the public's nor the theater's interest."[55] On the other hand, some believed that witnessing extravagent excess in the theater could assuage the urge to overindulge in real life: "Bacchanalian joys, ruinous games, madness thought up by thousands out of idleness, all are avoided by visiting the theater."[56]

The theater's significance as a public presence increased during the politically and socially tumultuous years toward the end of the nineteenth century. In 1894 Hermann Bahr commented on complaints regarding the theater's importance made by political leaders, who could not understand why the rise and fall of a comedy should be taken more seriously than that of a Minister, or why Girardi was more famous than an influential politician: "[The actors] forget what they were and what they could be again: prophets, leaders, architects of the world. They forget that it is their position to interpret life and through these interpretations to send the listeners back to work more engaged, more clever, more aware."[57] Actors are not mere entertainers, in Bahr's view, but sages who could exercise tremendous power in everyday life if they chose to recognize and exploit their influence.

The importance of the stage to the Viennese public at large was noted with bewilderment by a newspaper correspondent from Berlin, who attempted to convey, both to the Viennese around him and to his readers in Berlin, national differences in attitude toward operetta. These comments, written in 1883, must be read in light of two events: first, Austria's humiliating defeat at the hands of Prussia in 1866, the last time the Habsburg empire had relinquished territory; and second, Strauss's recent embarrassment, only two days before, at the Berlin premiere of *Eine Nacht in Venedig* [*A Night in Venice*]:

> For [the Berliners], operetta is an amusement that fills the evening and about which one can speak for awhile at supper; here [in Vienna] the same occasion amounts to an earth-shaking event. When [Anton von] Schmerling battled with Parliamentarians, the Constitution conflict was forgotten over a conflict of [Karl] Treumann with his soubrette [Anna] Marek. Vienna did not concern itself over Rechberg's fiasco at the Frankfurt Royal Convocation because the slaps exchanged by [Franz] Steiner and [Josephine] Gallmeyer absorbed the interest of all.[58]

No other musical genre has rivaled state politics for significance and interest, and no other city than Vienna would grant such privileged attention to "entertainment."

The power of the stage did not elude politicians themselves. Royalty, aristocrats, and members of parliament frequented the Theater an der Wien on a regular basis. When Strauss's first opera premiered at the Court Opera, "one saw the oldest and most respected Imperial Advisors, Presidents, and Justices in the parquet, and between the acts there was an impossibly tangled throng in the hallway."[59] The Emperor himself attended premieres of Strauss's works and encouraged visiting heads of state to do the same. Indeed, the theater was occasionally the site of political persuasion in a very literal sense. In 1875 Franz Joseph attended a guest performance at the Theater an der Wien given by a Hungarian troupe that included Lujza Blaha, the most popular Hungarian actress of the century. At the time of this performance, thirteen Hungarian soldiers were being held in Galicia, awaiting sentencing by the emperor for mutiny. During one of her songs, Blaha fell on her knees and improvised:

> How I would like to speak to the emperor
> And ply his merciful heart with pleas:

Your Majesty in purple ornament
I implore your mercy for thirteen Hungarians!

Even the public that did not understand Hungarian followed the interruption with breathless anticipation. Franz Joseph asked one of his attendants for a translation, then nodded his head in assent to the actress kneeling on stage.[60]

If operetta was frequently weighted with political metaphor, the popular press also represented various political events through operetta metaphors. A cartoon from carnival 1867 shows Prime Minister Ferdinand Beust, a German recently appointed to the Habsburg government, with Charlotte Wolter from the Burgtheater on one arm and Marie Geistinger from the Theater an der Wien on the other (Illustration 1.1). A female figure labeled "Austria" sits alone in the background, and Beust remarks to the women on his arm: "But ladies, please, won't you let me go now? I really must look after the lady for whom I actually came here."[61] *Kikeriki* devoted a full-page cartoon in 1880 to two "ever-recurring" themes: "Every new operetta brings a new chorus of pages and every new ministry brings new taxes" (Illustration 1.2).[62] A year later, a cartoon appeared of Strauss playing his violin in parliament while representatives dance: "Suggestion for rescuing the state: Make Johann Strauss Prime Minister and immediately general contentment will set in" (Illustration 1.3).[63] The faith and support that the Viennese offered Strauss was matched only by the distrust and skepticism they felt for their political leaders.

A few months later a full-page cartoon entitled "Operetta in Politics" presented two uniformed men (German Prime Minister Otto von Bismarck and Austrian Prime Minister Eduard Taaffe) striding away from the crowd before the parliament building. The text captures the rhyme scheme and style of an operetta chorus: "There they whine / those from the infantry, / it doesn't bother / us from the cavalry!"[64] The cartoon probably refers to the Austrian government's decision in October 1881 to impose conscription in Bosnia-Herzegovina, a decree that started a revolt in the area and caused

1.1 Charlotte Wolter, Prime Minister Beust, Marie Geistinger (*Kikeriki*, 14 March 1867)

1.2 Women's chorus dressed as men, representatives filing in to Parliament (*Kikeriki*, 5 December 1880)

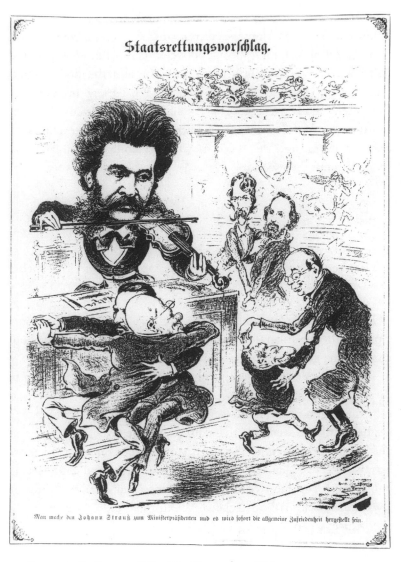

1.3 Strauss in Parliament (*Kikeriki*, 1 December 1881)

bloodshed on both sides before it was enforced. Again in 1885 the political situation was expressed in terms of operetta conventions: "The political metamorphosis between Czar, Battenberger and Sultan was completed as unbelievably quickly as in the modern operetta. At first: Death to this enemy! He'll take Turkey! Immediately thereafter, friends again: Hooray! Deidildiei!"[65] These examples demonstrate that, far from being an evening's escapist entertainment, operetta permeated the ways in which Viennese organized and thought about their world.

OPERETTA RECEPTION

There is no artist in Vienna, and – with the exception of Strauss, Sr. and Lanner – never has been one who enjoyed the same popularity in all levels of society as Strauss.[66]

The operetta stage attracted a wider audience than either the Court Opera or the suburban *Heuriger* and beer gardens. The disparate populations that generally patronized these institutions were more likely to share a physical space and a musical experience in the operetta theater than at any other event. The Theater an der Wien was physically the largest of the *Vorstadt* theaters, and although each theater's aesthetic differed according to its director at the time, the Theater an der Wien tended to offer the most varied repertoire and the most extravagant productions.[67] But despite a large and enthusiastic public, even the most commercially successful operettas did not always meet with critical acclaim. What, then, did critics and audience expect when attending an operetta?

Audience demographics

Whether poor or rich, young or old, peasant or nobility, washerwoman or duchess, prince or worker, Bohemian or German, Hungarian or Croat, all swayed and turned, forgetting sorrows and life in the dance.   *Karl Kobald*[68]

During the first half of the century, *Vorstadt* theater audiences were comprised predominantly of domestic servants who had been born in Vienna and lived with or near their employers. Comedies by Nestroy and Raimund used this milieu as backdrop for and generator of humorous situations. After mid-century, émigrés from eastern and southern Habsburg provinces arrived in Vienna, taking over these jobs and filling new ones created by industrialization and economic expansion. Indeed, between 1848 and 1890 the suburban population rose from less than 200,000 to 536,000.[69] Immigrants settled in the *Vorstadt* areas because of their proximity to industry and their lower cost of living compared to the inner city. The audiences available to neighborhood *Vorstadt* theaters grew along with the suburban population, and many theaters undertook renovations to increase seating capacity. However, the newly arrived generally did not speak German well and even fewer understood Viennese dialect, and this excluded them from the traditional sources of *Alt-Wien* humor.[70] Music, scenery, and dance numbers thus assumed an increasingly important role in their entertainment, paving the way for the success of operetta.

The variety of social classes and ethnicities in the city at large closely matched the composition of *Vorstadt* theater audiences, and many audience members found stereotypes of themselves on-stage. Royalty, aristocracy, businessmen, merchants, and servants all eagerly vied for tickets to see themselves represented in the newest works. Operetta could not have achieved its breadth of popularity and would not have been encouraged to expand its musical resources without this broad spectrum of audience members. A variety of social classes was represented at the Court Opera as well, but they were more differentiated according to where they sat – or stood – in the theater. The established aristocracy and wealthy bourgeoisie bought the most expensive loges and orchestra seats, while merchants and small businessmen filled the parterre and balconies. The uppermost balconies (the "fourth gallery") usually held students and the lower working classes. When newspaper accounts of opera premieres reported snippets of conversation heard from the fourth gallery, they often imitated the dialect of the working classes. Yet students and budding intellectuals sat there alongside coachmen and housemaids in a lively atmosphere. The fourth gallery was "a small state in the theatrical empire, a firmly established group within that ill-defined mass one calls the public. In Viennese theatre the fourth gallery is the court of first and sometimes even final appeal."[71]

Many regular inhabitants of the fourth gallery were themselves entrepreneurs in the theater business: they scalped tickets. The practice of agiotage was widespread in Vienna not only among businessmen but also among servants and skilled workers, who bought rows of seats to be resold at a higher price.[72] This was standard procedure at *Vorstadt* theaters for special performances (premieres, anniversaries, or guest tours); at the premiere of Strauss's first operetta, a newspaper reported: "Tickets to the first performance of Johann Strauss's [*Indigo und die*] *40 Räuber* were traded like casino notes yesterday at the stock exchange. Parterre seats stood at 15 [fl.], loges 60–80, and today the price will probably rise even higher."[73] Before the premiere of Strauss's *Das Spitzentuch der Königin* [*The Queen's Lace Handkerchief*, 1880], the *Fremdenblatt* reported: "For this premiere an agiotage for seats and loges has developed which could not have been better dreamed of during the time of economic upswing, during the *Gründerjahre*. 15 to 20 fl. for a seat, 80 to 100 fl. for a loge."[74] This ritual was also conducted for every evening's performance at the Court Opera.[75] Regarding *Ritter Pásmán* Strauss remarked: "About the 5th performance I can only say that even on the stock market where one can always get an overpriced loge or a seat, there was nothing to be had. The balcony is better sold than ever."[76]

The bulk of Strauss's theater audiences belonged to a higher socio-economic class than audiences in his *Volksgarten* concerts or the café performances of his youth. Wealthier patrons could afford to go to the theater more often, and ticket prices at the Theater an der Wien, where most of Strauss's works enjoyed exclusive engagements, were the highest among the *Vorstadt* theaters.[77] Nevertheless, he reached a broad range of the population with his theater works, for although working-class audience members may have attended an operetta only once while the aristocracy and bourgeoisie attended more often, Strauss's novelties could not be missed. As critic Julius Bauer noted, "A Strauss operetta can be more or less pleasing, but it must be seen and heard by everyone."[78]

Audience expectations

The Viennese public loves to see mirrored on stage the social circles sitting in the audience.[79]

Strauss's audiences expected, above all, to be entertained. They wanted to hear attractive melodies, see exciting dance and chorus numbers, and laugh at comic antics. They expected a happy end, and in that sense the genre did provide an escape from daily concerns, although the manner in which the resolution was achieved often served a moralizing or didactic purpose. Most frequently the resolution involved a return to the familiar social order, either a woman returning to her family or getting married (*Indigo, Carneval in Rom*); or a servant, previously in disguise, returning to his/her social class (*Die Fledermaus, Eine Nacht in Venedig*); or single characters settling down with others of their own nationality (*Der Zigeunerbaron, Der Bettelstudent*). The audience did indeed enjoy seeing its own social circles reflected on stage, a place where they could observe various adventures or transgressions being acted out and then safely resolved without risk to their own domestic security. In an operetta plot, all characters reconcile themselves to their stations in life, a pleasant myth for everyone in the audience.

Viennese audiences were familiar with the differences in repertoire, personnel, and patrons among the various *Vorstadt* theaters, elements that conditioned expectations of what they might see on a given night. Despite these differences, *Vorstadt* stages had lost some of their local distinction and become more urban and uniform in their presentations as a side effect of the destruction of the city wall and incorporation of the suburbs into the city. Since audiences could

now easily travel to other districts, theaters were suddenly competing with entertainment options across the city instead of only those
within their own neighborhood. Each retained its own personality,
but the crossover of directors, staff, and audience created a continuity among them nonetheless.[80]

Audiences soon flocked from the ballroom to the theater to hear
Strauss's novelties, and after many years' experience Strauss knew
instinctively what was required to please them. He explained to his
librettist Ignaz Schnitzer:

> If an operetta is going to be popular, then *everyone* must find something
> in it to suit his tastes . . . And the people in the gallery must also get
> something out of it that they can remember; for these people have no
> money to buy piano reductions, and even less money for a piano, there-
> fore one must present it well so that as soon as they leave the perfor-
> mance something stays in their ear![81]

When Schnitzer sent Strauss a few verses of *Der Zigeunerbaron*,
Strauss warned him that operetta verse need not, indeed it *should* not,
be too intellectual, precisely because of the audience in the gallery.
Besides, he felt, nonsense lends itself better to catchy rhythm.[82]

Audience expectations of operetta were conditioned by personal
musical experience and aptitude. The amateur musician found operetta more accessible than the challenging works performed at the
opera, and the music publishing business flourished, selling arrangements of popular dances and songs from new operettas for enjoyment at home. Music lending libraries also made it possible for a
broad public to acquaint themselves with the newest trends without
spending much money.[83] A guidebook to the city of Vienna from 1892
explained: "The majority of Viennese musical families practice dance
music at home rather than classical music, since understanding the
latter is something reserved for a very few."[84] This dance music may
have been composed as individual numbers or excerpted from recent
popular stage works. As Strauss realized, it was easier for the less
musically educated to remember operetta tunes than recent opera
melodies, especially without the aid of a piano.

Im Carltheater

haben die Besucher während der Aufführung von Strauß's neuer Operette nur den einzigen Wunsch, daß die Bänke hinausgeschafft werden sollten.

1.4 Premiere of *Prinz Methusalem* (*Kikeriki*, 7 January 1877)

Familiarity with the conventions of Strauss's dance music contributed to the physical immediacy of his stage works. For Viennese audiences, attending one of his operettas was a kinetic experience; even if they had not yet danced to the works being performed on stage, one could hardly live in Vienna and *never* have danced to a Strauss waltz. In a review of *Cagliostro in Wien*, Hanslick summarized the atmosphere of a premiere conducted by the composer:

In the foremost orchestra seats, a few listeners who sat too close to the magician began to rise as if electrified. The musical fluid distributes itself lightning fast among the others. They involuntarily keep time with hand and feet, and soon the whole house wants to rise and sing along and fly and sway. The theater becomes a ballroom and everyone yells: Strauss! Strauss![85]

Since most other operetta composers had spent their entire careers in the theater, they did not share with their audience the same extra-theatrical connections to the ballroom that Strauss did. This physical immersion in the work on the part of the spectators continued throughout his career. A cartoon soon after the premiere of *Prinz Methusalem* showed a theater audience dancing wildly, smiling, and waving their arms, the caption explaining that "In the Carltheater the audience has but one wish during the performance of Strauss's new operetta – that the seats could be cleared away" (Illustration 1.4).[86] The gallery was, not surprisingly, the rowdiest portion of the theater, where patrons felt allowed, if not obligated, to express their opinions freely. Indeed, it became customary to hum along with favorite numbers, and on at least one occasion, audience members almost came to blows when one listener wanted to sing along, to the vociferous objections of those around him.[87] For the Viennese, who had become accustomed to expressing a physical response to this music, it required great effort to constrain themselves to conventions of the theater.

Critical reviews from the 1880s and 1890s contribute to these impressions of a largely unsophisticated Viennese audience. Robert Hirschfeld, for example, asserted in 1887 that "one goes to concerts not because one loves the music, but in order to display one's music appreciation."[88] A visitor from Berlin also observed that "the Viennese cannot live on Bach, Beethoven, Mozart and Donizetti; for him Millöcker, Strauss, Ziehrer, Fahrbach and Offenbach are much more suited to his disposition."[89] Composer Albert Lortzing would have agreed: he arrived in Vienna in 1846 to serve as music director of the Theater an der Wien, and although his career as a conductor was successful, his own musical works were less well received. After a disappointing response to his opera *Undine* (1847), he admitted,

> I have had the sad experience to discover that Vienna, Austria in general, is no place for me – as an opera composer . . . The musical taste here is completely corrupt. Only Italian music dominates. German operas, like those by Spohr, Marschner, are given once for the sake of appearances, but disappear again immediately because they don't catch on. Only

dudelei and always dudelei, trillerei, and that in a city where Mozart, Beethoven, Gluck, and others lived and worked.[90]

The Viennese expected not only a varied program, but one that was attractive to the eye as well as the ear. During the financially successful years of the *Gründerzeit*, theater audiences became accustomed to extravagant sets, costumes, and special effects, and *Kikeriki* repeatedly attacked this emphasis on style over substance. One especially telling jab offered a mock announcement of an "ideal" opera performance: decorations, costumes, and set machinery from *Don Juan, Wilhelm Tell, Armida, Sardanapal, Fidelio, Flick und Flock, Freischütz, Zauberflöte, Hugenotten,* and *Prophet,* accompanied by "Blue Danube," "Wine, Woman, and Song," and "Tales from the Vienna Woods" with no mention of performers or plot.[91] Only a year later the management at the Theater an der Wien approximated this combination of luxurious *mise en scène* and Strauss waltzes with *Indigo und die vierzig Räuber.*

Critics' expectations

No other city in Europe could rival Vienna for its wealth of journalism at the end of the nineteenth century; by 1893 the city boasted thirteen major daily German-language newspapers. Music and theater reviews appeared daily, along with the new journalistic genre, the *feuilleton*. This editorial piece was usually printed on the first page, "beneath the fold," and frequently incorporated observations about current social, political, and cultural events, including operetta. The relationship of Viennese critics to the city's operetta was similar to that between siblings: they mercilessly reviewed the genre at home but staunchly defended it against foreign critics. Through the writings of Viennese journalists, almost as much as through the works themselves, operetta became a cultural weapon against perceived infringements by French, Czech, and other national groups.

Operetta coverage was treated seriously, for not only did native efforts merit due consideration, but there was also no wealth of local musical events with which operetta had to compete. Philharmonic concerts numbered only eight to twelve per year, and the Court Opera, where premieres were more rare than at the operetta theaters, usually offered works from the standard repertoire. Hanslick and other music critics prepared themselves thoroughly for the task of reporting new musical events; they requested advance scores of works (and complimentary tickets) from composers, who often made the number of preview scores for critics a point of negotiation with their publishers.[92] Given the sheer number of operetta premieres per year, this practice created an unprecedented degree of contact between critic and composer.

Critics, along with the general audience, expected certain qualities from each new work: the evening should be over within three hours; listeners should be offered a variety of simple, but charming, music; and the work should be suitable for all members of the audience. Hanslick often complained in the press about the low humor and suggestive metaphors heard regularly on the operetta stage. He specifically complimented librettist Ignaz Schnitzer at the premiere of *Der Zigeunerbaron* for writing a "clean" work, free of *double entendres*;[93] and as late as the 1896 premiere of Strauss's *Waldmeister*, Hanslick praised the leading actress for her "tasteful" performance.[94] Other reviewers also commented upon the scantily clad women or those dressed in pants, a popular trend of the 1870s. Paul Lindau, a German critic, paraphrased Goethe when he commented on the Viennese penchant for minimally clothed actresses: "das ewig Weibliche zieht sich nicht an."[95]

Critics often spent a good portion of the review describing the plot; unlike music critics today, who most often need only discuss the standard repertoire, journalists at the end of the nineteenth century were required to introduce and pass judgment upon many new works for their readers each season. After outlining the main elements of the story (during which the librettist regularly came in for harsh words) and discussing individual performances of various actors and actresses, little effort was expended discussing the music itself. They enjoyed pointing out musical similarities to previous operettas or operas and commenting on specific numbers, especially the finales and other highpoints. Journalists were among the select group invited to attend dress rehearsals, and their comparisons of differences between the rehearsal and the premiere can illuminate a composer's decisions regarding cuts and revisions. They reported news (often erroneously) about upcoming productions, works in progress, and gossip about theater personnel. Occasionally, they reported on the audience as well as on the performance, listing names of aristocracy, royalty, and business barons who were in attendance. Critics often determined whether a work would be deemed a "failure" or not, for as personal as their reactions might have been, their opinions exercised great influence over the box office.[96]

Many critics felt obliged to evaluate whether the music was "appropriate" to the genre or not, often complaining that the instrumentation or tone was too excessive for the operetta stage. For most reviewers, especially Hanslick, the maintenance of proper generic distinctions was of utmost importance. Discussing the premiere of Richard Heuberger's *Der Opernball* [*The Opera Ball*, 1898], Hanslick once again outlined the standards that had served as his benchmark for the last 30 years: "[Heuberger] completely fulfilled his goal in *Opernball*, inasmuch as he held this goal always before him: keeping the boundaries of the true Viennese operetta pure. Heuberger lapsed into neither of the most popular mistakes around here: one is called false pathos and the other unfeigned commonness."[97] Other Viennese critics were more generous than Hanslick, but few devoted as much attention to the music as he did. His comments regarding instrumentation, rhythm, and melody reveal more about the work's musical impression than reviews by Ludwig Speidel, Max Kalbeck, Theodor Helm, and other critics better versed in the theater arts.

Reviews never failed to describe the overall effect of the production and the merits of individual performances. Although these impressions are more easily described than the music, they are also more ephemeral, for set and costume designs, theater dimensions, even photos of performers reveal about their original effect only a fraction of what a score reveals about the music. Yet, because operetta composers conceived their works for a specific stage and personnel, these elements are vital to our understanding of various compositional choices. The next chapter will introduce those institutions and personalities most integral to the development of Viennese operetta.

Early Viennese operetta promised untold opportunities for everyone involved in its production. Unlike art-music genres, where the composer had long been the primary, if not the sole, authorial voice, operetta performance practice granted other members of the artistic staff considerable latitude in creating and shaping the final product. Theater directors played an active role as brokers between librettist and composer, matching text with musical style. Leading performers enjoyed enormous influence over their musical numbers, for popular songs then, as today, were more closely identified with the performer than with the composer. That some talented artists fulfilled more than one role – a librettist as composer or a performer as theater director – only further muddled the lines of authority.

Operetta also distinguished itself from its high-art sibling with its orientation toward commercial success. Although some operettas achieved an artistic integrity unmatched by contemporary opera, their immediate goal was to attract a steady, paying audience instead of critical appreciation. As a *Vorstadt*-theater director of an earlier generation, Emanuel Schikaneder, admitted, "my main aim is to promote the box office and to provide what is most effective on the stage, in order to have a full house and good takings."[1] Like other commercial commodities in Vienna's increasingly industrialized culture, operetta was the result of a complicated and lengthy process of production that was itself controlled by myriad social and material factors. It is imperative, even while focusing on Strauss's authorship, to acknowledge the creative personalities with whom he collaborated, giving them credit for their contribution to the genre that became Viennese operetta.

LIBRETTISTS

A textually good couplet can be musically killed by no living or still unborn composer. *Bad texts*, however, kill everything –whether it's a couplet, duet, trio, quartet, ensemble, even a finale well-nourished with trombones and timpani.

Johann Strauss[2]

Viennese operetta librettists came from a diverse assortment of professional and artistic backgrounds, all attracted by the beguiling simplicity of the task and the prospect of financial reward. But although librettists began to receive royalties on performances of their works in the late nineteenth century, no author could sustain a career exclusively through work on operetta libretti. While opera librettists were generally poets and authors by trade (Arrigo Boito or Hugo von Hofmannsthal, for instance), some of the most successful operetta libretti were written by civil servants, businessmen, musicians, and journalists. An examination of their working methods and collaboration with composers illuminates the process of operetta's creation.

Many seasoned theater critics attempted to write libretti, despite the fact that critics of operetta often reserved their harshest judgments for the book. Ludwig Held, Julius Bauer, and Hugo Wittmann are only a few of the journalists who contributed libretti to operettas, none of which enjoyed lasting success. Names familiar today from disparate Viennese musical and social contexts at one time shared a common interest in operetta. Author and leader of the Zionist movement Theodor Herzl collaborated with composer Adolf Müller, Jr. on the operetta *Ein Teufelsweib* [A Devil's Wife, 1890].[3] This creative effort preceded Herzl's engagement on behalf of western European Jews (his book, *Der Judenstaat: Versuch einer modernen Lösung der Judenfrage* [*The Jewish State: Toward a Modern Solution to the Jewish Question*], was published in 1896), and his efforts in operetta were largely forgettable.[4] Max Kalbeck, translator of opera libretti, an early Brahms biographer and, along with Hanslick, one of the most important Viennese music critics, collaborated with Strauss on an operetta set in the Slavic Balkans. Their *Jabuka* (1894) was highly celebrated at its premiere, an event planned to coincide with Strauss's fiftieth anniversary of public performance. It, too, disappeared quickly from the repertoire.

The best-known and most prolific of the Viennese librettists were the duo of F. Zell and Richard Genée. Zell, a pseudonym for Camillo Walzel, was a steamship captain for the Danube Steamship Company and co-director of Theater an der Wien from 1884 to 1889. Genée, a performing musician and composer himself, worked as music director at the Theater an der Wien during Strauss's early foray into operetta and contributed substantially to his success.[5] Between 1875 and 1894, the team of Zell and Genée wrote the text for twenty-three operettas, of which four were composed by Franz von Suppé, three by Strauss, and six by Millöcker.[6]

Strauss often worked at a geographic distance from his librettist, yet he professed to believe in a close cooperation between the two (or more) partners. As he explained to Kalbeck, "In order to take into account all factors of an operetta, both contributors must work within sight of each other's sweat day and night in order to achieve a successful result."[7] Urging Kalbeck to visit soon, Strauss insisted that "the composer must really sleep with the librettist in the same bed so the latter is at his side during the night."[8] When composer and librettist could not work in close proximity, they had to negotiate which element would come first, music or text. For most composers of art-music genres, the idea of someone fitting text to pre-existing music would be unthinkable. However, such a procedure was common practice in the operetta industry.

Correspondence reveals the independent working habits and the practical mindset of leading composers and librettists. Richard Genée reported to Strauss regarding the progress of *Eine Nacht in Venedig*: "Everything I have of the II. Finale, I have texted and filled in the instrumentation."[9] Similarly, composer Adolf Müller wrote to Genée about one of their collaborations:

> The I. Finale will be finished today. At the end I added on a reminiscence from No. 4, "And another song"; naturally another text must come here; that won't be hard if you know the music; this piece – it's not long – is the only one that still needs text – otherwise *everything is*

texted, so you have no more big work with your favorite after-writing [*Nachtextieren*].[10]

Franz von Suppé also expressed frustration in the lack of communication provided by his librettists Moritz West and Ludwig Held: "from April to October, precisely at the most urgent time, I have neither seen nor heard anything from my librettists. My eternal lament for an idea for the second finale, for a third act, for a finished book at all, has remained ignored. And so I continue working ceaselessly in eternal darkness, without knowing if it fits in or not."[11] As these examples demonstrate, the procedure of applying text to finished music was commonplace, eliminating the possibility for anything but remote connections between word and music.

Often librettists worked in pairs, one author contributing the song texts (Genée) and the other the dialogue (Zell), an arrangement that persists to this day in the Broadway musical tradition. Although this division of labor was preferable for the librettists, it could mean trouble for the composer, as Strauss lamented to his brother Eduard: "Working with two librettists is always double the work for the composer. One wants to correct the other and it never leads to improvement. Pure envy in their collaborative work forces the composer either to write everything anew or at least to pull partially different forms and other rhythms out of his hat. In this way one conceives an operetta twice!"[12]

An operetta's failure was rarely attributed to the music; instead a weak libretto often took the blame for poor box office returns. Strauss's only complete failure, *Blindekuh* [Blind Cow, 1878], was rightly attributed to the inane libretto by Rudolf Kneisel, as Strauss's music became popular on its own in other guises. (His waltz "Kennst du mich?" op. 381 was played by salon orchestras for decades, and a modified version of one of this operetta's dances became the world-famous "Sag' zum Abschied leise Servus.") At the same time, audiences and critics more often praised the librettist and performer than the composer for successful couplets, ignoring the composer's role in creating a suitable vehicle for the text. The Viennese tolerated silly texts and fantastic plots more than audiences in Paris or Berlin, where libretti were judged as literary works and were inevitably found wanting.

COMPOSERS

Most nineteenth-century operetta composers served as music directors (Kapellmeister) in the *Vorstadt* theaters, a job that involved composing music for stage productions, rehearsing musical numbers, and conducting performances. Accordingly, these men had gained an intimate knowledge of the inner workings of the theater and the pace of an evening's entertainment before they began composing in the new genre of Viennese operetta. Franz von Suppé, Carl Millöcker, Adolf Müller, Jr., and Richard Genée have rarely been included in music history texts, yet their music was the staple of the operetta repertoire. Because Suppé and Millöcker were, along with Strauss, the leading operetta composers of their age, a brief account of their music and careers will help to illustrate the context in which Strauss's works were created.

Franz von Suppé (1819–95)

In 1835 Suppé moved from his home in Split, then part of Habsburg Dalmatia, to Vienna, where he studied with Simon Sechter and Ignaz von Seyfried at the Vienna Conservatory. Learning German did not come easily for the 26-year-old speaker of Italian, and he experienced difficulties throughout his life understanding Viennese dialect.[13] Suppé's compositional style was informed not only by Italian musical traditions but also by his professional experience in Viennese suburban theaters: in the fall of 1840 Suppé was hired by the Theater in der Josefstadt, where over the next five years he contributed twenty scores accompanying comedies and folk plays; in 1845 he moved to the Theater an der Wien, where he shared the job of Kapellmeister with Albert Lortzing and Adolf Müller, Jr.; and in 1865 he moved to the Carltheater, where he worked until his retirement seventeen years later.

True to his Italian heritage, Suppé's works bear strong musical resemblance to Italian opera of a previous generation. When Gaetano Donizetti came to Vienna in 1842, Suppé spent hours studying scores at his side and accompanied the older composer back to Italy the following year, when he met Rossini and Verdi. Suppé's music, like Donizetti's, features long, elegant vocal lines, accented with flashes of coloratura virtuosity, supported by simple orchestral accompaniments. Both his vocal and instrumental music include more improvisatory, *cadenza*-like sections than that of the Austrians (see Example 2.1). The typically Austrian rising melodic sixth and "yodel"-style melodies based on inversions of the major triad, so common in Viennese music, rarely appear in Suppé's works. Suppé always included more accompanied recitative than the Viennese, and by the time of his most successful work, *Boccaccio* (1879), he had developed a style of writing highly developed scenic complexes involving aria, recitative, and chorus. As critic Theodor Helm acknowledged, "Suppé's serious theoretical training enabled him also to create large forms and exciting ensembles, and to write a finale of ever-increasing intensity."[14] These scenes furthered the action more than the standard couplet could, but their length presented difficulties in repeating any part on demand and in extracting excerpts for individual publication.

Suppé's style is Italianate also in generic preferences; native Austrian dances like the waltz, *Ländler*, and polka appear far less frequently in his works than in those of Strauss and Millöcker. Instead, Suppé, like Donizetti and Bellini, preferred 3/8 and 6/8 meters more suitable for lyrical singing than for dancing. His overtures suggest Rossini's influence: he often repeats an 8- or 16-bar phrase several times, augmenting the instrumentation and expanding the range with each repetition, then, once that crescendo is exhausted, begins another. Overtures such as *Dichter und Bauer* [*Poet and Peasant*] and *Leichte Kavallerie* [*Light Cavalry*] exhibit these features and have remained in the orchestral repertoire for years.

Suppé preferred a darker sound from his orchestra than did the Viennese. Strauss and Millöcker usually created a treble melody (most often given to the violins or flutes), accompanied by bass instruments, while Suppé created a thicker texture by using the middle and bottom ranges also for melodic material, not just accompaniment. This distribution of instrumentation gives Suppé's music a more solid sound as opposed to Strauss's lithe, elegant tone. Suppé often gave the woodwinds and brass more musical material, sometimes allowing them the melody while the strings accompany, an arrangement that occurs far less frequently in Strauss's music. In addition to differences in instrumentation, Suppé's orchestral timbre differs from Strauss's because of the keys he chose. While Strauss's favorite keys are bright and most suitable for strings (G major, D major), Suppé used keys that favor wind instruments and allow for fewer open strings (D-flat major, E-flat major, E major). Over the course of his career, Suppé learned to balance what one critic described as "blaring and screaming Donizetti-isms"[15] with the simpler melodic style of his adopted country.

Suppé wrote several successful one-act operettas in the 1860s: *Das Pensionat* (1860), *Flotte Bursche* (1863), and *Schöne Galathee* (1865). *Fatinitza* (1876), his first full-length operetta, was remarkably successful and achieved over 100 performances. The text, by librettists Zell and Genée, featured a female performer playing the role of a Russian lieutenant, who then disguises herself as a woman – a nineteenth-century *Victor/Victoria*. Suppé's greatest success, *Boccaccio* (1879), initiated the trend of using historical literary figures as operetta characters, a trend Strauss followed in *Das Spitzentuch der Königin* [*The Queen's Lace Handkerchief*, 1880], in which Cervantes plays a leading role. Suppé's two operas, *25 Mädchen und kein Mann* [25 Girls and No Man, 1873] and *Franz Schubert* (1886), premiered at the Court Opera but did not remain long in the repertoire. In addition to his original works, Suppé also contributed several parodies to his theaters' repertories: *Martl, oder Der Portiunculatag in Schnabelhausen* (based on Flotow's *Martha*); *Der Tannhäuser*; *Dinorah, oder Die Turnerfahrt nach Hütteldorf* (based on Meyerbeer's *Dinorah*); and *Lohengelb, oder Die Jungfrau von Dragant* (based on Wagner's *Lohengrin*).

Although many of Suppé's works found success, sentiments of

Example 2.1 Suppé, *Die schöne Galathee* (1865)

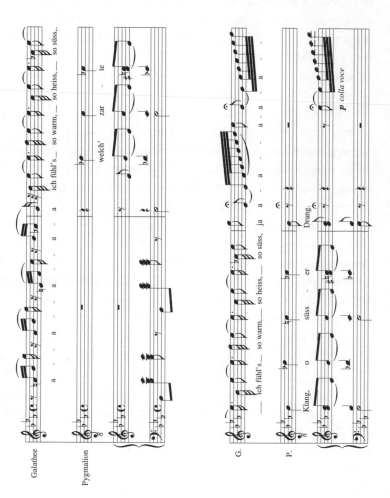

xenophobia affected his reception in Vienna, where he was consistently portrayed in the popular press as an overweight foreigner living in the lap of luxury. One cartoon entitled "Composers' Fate" (1879) showed Beethoven on one side, seated before the piano in a spare room with pages from *Fidelio* on the floor, "for Maestro Beethoven, who often put his thoughts to paper in an unheated room lacking necessities, composing was sour work." The other half of the cartoon showed a large Suppé in a smoking jacket, enjoying a pipe while a bird sings in a cage and a maid brings him a drink, "for Suppé things are going much better" (see Illustration 2.1).[16] Even in the small world of Viennese operetta, Suppé seems to have remained somewhat isolated from his colleagues; he did not vacation in Bad Ischl, as many did, and was never included in the large social gatherings in Strauss's home. But despite the distance from his peers in social situations, he supported the initial professional efforts of fellow conductor and composer Carl Millöcker.

Carl Millöcker (1842–99)

Suppé recommended Millöcker in 1858 for a job as flutist at the Theater in der Josefstadt.[17] Impressed by the young man's talent, Suppé encouraged him to become a Kapellmeister and helped him gain a post at the Landestheater in Graz (1864). Millöcker returned to Vienna in 1867 when he was hired by the Harmonietheater, where he worked closely with Ludwig Anzengruber writing music for his stage works. In 1869 he became Kapellmeister at the Theater an der Wien and conducted countless operetta performances there until his retirement in 1883.

A native Viennese, Millöcker's compositional style is more folk-like than Suppé's: he prefers simple melodies and harmonies, little counterpoint, and instrumentation with frequent doublings. His melodies are colored by the flavor of the Austrian countryside, including the use of drones, the rising melodic sixth, and the cadential melodic line of *fa* falling to *mi* to lend a pastoral, sometimes sentimental quality (see Example 2.2). Millöcker's first successful

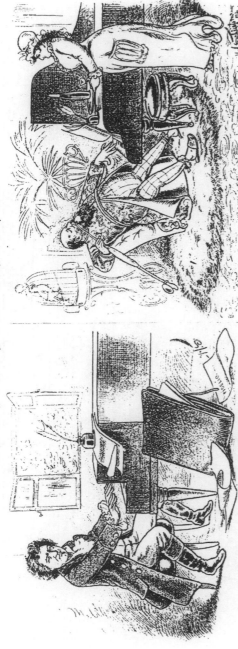

2.1 Beethoven and Suppé (*Kikeriki*, 13 February 1879)

Example 2.2 Millöcker, *Das verwunschene Schloß* (1878)

operetta, *Das verwunschene Schloß* [The Haunted Castle, 1878], suggests his affection for rural Austria in his characters' names, also typical of the Viennese *Volksstück*: Mirzl, Seppl, Andredl, and Traudl. He wrote no overt parodies, and the political criticism typical of Offenbach is largely absent from his works. *Der Floh* characterized his music in 1872: "If one could call Offenbach the musical Heine, then Millöcker would be the Adalbert Stifter of music. So deeply felt, so truly Austrian waft his songs around us."[18] The religious and political implications of these comparisons were unquestionably intentional: Offenbach and Heine as converted German Jews, Millöcker and Stifter as native Austrians.

Millöcker's experience as a wind player led him to grant more musical material to the woodwinds and brass and to choose flat keys more often than Strauss. Overtures by Millöcker, along with those of fellow Austrians Carl Michael Ziehrer (*Die Landstreicher*) and Karl Zeller (*Der Vogelhändler*), tend to be clearly sectional: one dance or song theme follows the next, their different keys often elided only by a common tone or simple pauses. Compared to these overtures, Strauss's and Suppé's impress the listener with their unity of conception and elegance in transitional passages.

Millöcker had years of practical experience in the *Vorstadt* theaters before he began composing operetta, and his stage works clearly reflect this experience. For instance, he writes out recapitulations of refrains or choruses for exit music: a character enters, sings a song, then dialogue intervenes, but before the character or chorus exits, the scene is rounded off with a refrain of the opening music. This musical practice demonstrates an understanding of practical requirements, filling the time necessary to move characters on and off stage, while also providing a sense of musical closure.

Millöcker first made his name as a composer by contributing music to the popular folk play *Drei Paar Schuhe* [*Three Pairs of Shoes*, 1871], but his fame was secured with *Der Bettelstudent* [*The Beggar Student*, 1882], a work that most critics agreed was Zell and Genée's best libretto ever. It premiered on 6 December 1882 with Alexander Girardi in the title role and played nightly for the next two months.

Two Christmas performances (in 1882 and 1883) brought in 2340 fl. and 2366 fl., the largest possible gross incomes at the time.[19] Although Millöcker retired from his conducting post at the Theater an der Wien in 1883, he continued to compose operetta for the theater; some of his more successful works include *Gasparone* (1884), *Der Feldprediger* (1884], *Die sieben Schwaben* (1887), and *Der arme Jonathan* (1890). In all, Millöcker wrote fourteen operettas for the Theater an der Wien and composed music for fifty folk plays. Because of the specifically local flavor of Millöcker's works, he never gained the international reputation that Strauss did, but his contribution to Viennese musical life during his lifetime should not be underestimated. Vienna's "Golden Age" of operetta died with him on the last day of the century.

VIENNESE *VORSTADT* THEATERS

There is hardly an important event in the Court Theater that doesn't have its counterpart in a parody or travesty in the Vorstadt. *Richard Wallaschek*[20]

Until the mid-nineteenth century, the medieval city wall and parade grounds provided a physical demarcation between Vienna's inner city and the suburbs, clearly separating not only the inhabitants but the theaters meant to entertain them as well. Although social classes were segregated by living space, aristocrats and wealthy bourgeoisie occasionally ventured out from their palatial homes in the inner city to enjoy an evening's entertainment among the proletariat. Even after the city wall was razed in 1857, distinctions remained not only between court theaters and suburban theaters but also among the suburban stages themselves. The most influential and historically significant of these – the Theater an der Wien, the Theater in der Josephstadt and the Carltheater – all participated in the development of Viennese operetta.

Since they received no government subvention and were situated away from the geographic and political center of power, *Vorstadt* theaters enjoyed relative freedom from the censors. Here,

the time-honored practice of improvisation continued to be nurtured throughout the nineteenth century. Conventions of extempor-
ized joking and mockery date back to the temporary stages of the
Renaissance Hans-Wurst theaters, where talented performers improvised story and verse on the spot, establishing a lasting tradition of
Stegreifkomödie.[21] Scripts and libretti performed in *Vorstadt* theaters
still required the censor's official approval, and performers on any
stage incurred fines if caught presenting improvised verses.[22] But
scant attention was paid to actual performances, with the result that
improvised language and gesture were likely to include political or
sexual innuendo, while in the carefully monitored court theaters a
more literal performance was necessary.

Unlike court theaters in which the same work rarely appeared two
nights in a row, suburban theaters hoped for lengthy runs of the same
work. The more popular an operetta was, the more consecutive
nights it played. Authors of works for the Burgtheater and Court
Opera undoubtedly hoped to be remunerated for their efforts, but
their careers depended more on favorable critical reception and sales
of publications than on sizable returns at the local box office. Works
with claims to high art also had greater opportunity to reach international audiences, while popular Viennese works (with a few notable
exceptions) relied most heavily upon local audiences for their commercial value and survival in the repertoire.

Premieres of new works were scheduled for specific moments in
the season. The best times were October (early in the season, but
after most Viennese had returned from summer vacation) or January
(when theater business revived after the holidays). Premieres at these
times gave the composer an opportunity to arrange his most successful works for sale and performance at carnival balls. Of course, some
new works filled out the end of the season, but these were less likely
to be successful. Their runs were interrupted for the summer
holiday, a time when many theaters closed for repair and renovation.
As Strauss attested: "Neither theater directors nor the public give any
value to premieres [in late spring]. At this time they only produce the
dregs!"[23] The summer months brought visiting artists and perform-

Table 2.1 Dimensions of Viennese suburban theaters

Theater	Total length	Total width	Auditorium length	Stage depth
Carltheater	29m	15m	17m	10m
Th i/d Josefstadt	20.5m	12.5m	10.1m	6m
Th a/d Wien	45m	21m	19m	13m + 10.5m*

*When the doors at the back of the stage were opened, the stage depth was expanded to almost twice its original length.

ing troupes to *Vorstadt* theaters, and occasionally new operas received premieres here before the Court Opera would risk producing them during the regular season. *Tannhäuser*, for example, was premiered in Vienna on 28 August 1857 at the Thaliatheater, the summer stage of the Theater in der Josefstadt, but did not appear on the Court Opera stage until over two years later, in October 1859.[24]

The three main *Vorstadt* theaters exhibited collective similarities when compared to the court theaters, but each also expressed its own personality through the performers who worked there, the type of work performed, and the audiences who attended regularly. The physical dimensions of the theaters reflect their variety (see Table 2.1).[25]

The Theater an der Wien was by far the largest, a fact that brought advantages (greater possibilities for innovative staging, larger groups of performers, and potentially larger audiences) as well as disadvantages (higher operating costs and increased expense of renovations). The Theater in der Josefstadt was the most intimate, and the Carltheater had the most distinctive and devoted audience. The following discussion will explore in further detail the characteristics of these three theaters.

Theater an der Wien: "A true oasis in the desert of Viennese theater life"[26]

The Theater an der Wien opened its doors in 1801 under the direction of Emanuel Schikaneder and won immediate recognition as the most elegant and technically sophisticated theater in Vienna. Although its management changed frequently during its first decade, the theater hosted premieres not only of stage works but also of concert works central to the canon of Western art music today, including Beethoven's Second, Third, Fifth, and Sixth symphonies, and *Fidelio*. From its beginning the theater offered a repertoire varied in tone and genre; depending on the tastes of the director and the state of the theater's finances, audiences enjoyed comic plays, Italian opera, folk plays, or Viennese operetta on successive evenings.

The consortium running the Theater an der Wien in 1808, led by Count Pálffy, convinced the censors that it was less dangerous for questionable shows to be produced here than on the court stages, thus beginning the tradition of giving works a trial performance before producing them at court, to test not only their political influence but also their artistic merit.[27] Under the management of Franz Pokorny in the late 1840s, the theater continued to rival the Court Opera. He hired Albert Lortzing as Kapellmeister (1846–48) and hosted a guest appearance by Jenny Lind (1847), hoping their work would lend legitimacy to his artistic aspirations. When the popularity of opera declined during the revolutionary year of 1848, Pokorny responded by offering more spoken works; he also changed the theater's name to the German National Theater (*Deutsches Nationaltheater*) at the urging of nationalist students who frequented it, but Pokorny's son Alois restored the original name in 1852.[28]

When Friederich Strampfer assumed leadership of the financially ailing enterprise in summer 1862, a new era began for the theater and for operetta. Under his direction the theater gave Viennese premieres of most of Offenbach's works, a trend that continued under Strampfer's successors. Soon after Maximilian Steiner and Marie Geistinger took over in 1869, *Der Floh* commented:

> The Theater an der Wien is like a good hotel. The audience streams inside because it knows that it will usually get good service. Sometimes something less worthwhile is offered, and then the people also run inside out of curiosity, because they know that the mediocre will also be elegantly served and that they will meet good company.[29]

The social function of attending the theater was frequently more obvious than its musical or artistic value, and the Theater an der Wien's reputation for attracting a fashionable public (at least one that took more pride in its elegance than its artistic taste) continued well into the 1880s. In a short article entitled "The Taming of the Shrew," *Der Floh* explains that directors of *Vorstadt* theaters have not dared to take the draconian but well-meaning measures enforced by court theaters, where hats are forbidden during performances. Under current circumstances, few can see the stage owing to women's elaborate millinery, and the paper sardonically suggests that allowing only women over 24 years old to wear hats would cause many to disappear immediately.[30]

Operetta continued to flourish at the Theater an der Wien through the end of the nineteenth century, and the theater's public valued the institution's long history. Their nostalgia for an idealized past could be better fulfilled here than at the newer theaters, which did not have the same historic resonance. A full-page announcement of a new operetta, *Der liebe Augustin* (by August Klein and Johann Brandl), included a tribute to the Theater an der Wien:

> Du altes Theater an der Wien, duliäh!
> In Dir den lieben Augustin ich sah,
> Du bist und bleibst ja doch die Heimatstätt'
> Von jeder lust'gen Wiener Operett'.
> Zum guten Text von Klein, zu Brandl's Weisen
> Kann jetzt das Publicum nach Altwien reisen.
> O Du lieber Augustin,
> Zum Theater an der Wien
> Alles lauft hin!

> [You old Theater an der Wien, duliäh!
> Where I saw the "dear Augustin,"
> You are and remain the true home
> Of every good Viennese operetta.
> To good texts by Klein, to Brandl's tunes
> The public can now travel to old Vienna.
> *O Du lieber Augustin,*

To the Theater an der Wien
Everyone runs!]³¹

The Theater an der Wien maintained its active support of operetta far longer than any other theater. However, the genre seemed to have run its course by fall of 1889, when other theaters returned to less expensive, less risky genres like the comedy and the folk play. A cartoon of September 1889 shows Franz Jauner (acting director of the Theater an der Wien) dressed as a Greek god, sitting before four theater posters, an operetta being advertised only on that of the Theater an der Wien. The caption explains, "At the opening of the theater season. Only one, the Theater an der Wien, remains the temple for Apollo with the same old operetta story."³²

Less than three months later a cartoon in the same journal pronounced operetta dead in Vienna. It depicts Jauner standing in front of a fog-covered poster for Joseph Hellmesberger, Jr.'s operetta *Das Orakel* [The Oracle], then playing at the Theater an der Wien: "In order to see if the operetta in Vienna has really totally and completely played itself out, I must, of course, ask the oracle – and it seems – it seems to say: yes!"³³ The tone of this comment shows *Kikeriki* at its pessimistic and antagonistic best, but the substance reveals real concern over the fate of Viennese operetta. The late 1880s indeed saw a lull: Offenbach was long dead, and Viennese composers were experimenting with new styles, yielding mixed results at best. If the leading operetta theater could offer nothing better than Hellmesberger's work, critics and public alike had reason for concern.

When operetta failed to attract audiences, the theater frequently extricated itself from difficult financial situations by hosting guest performers. During the second half of the century it offered series of performances by Richard Wagner, Adelina Patti, Sarah Bernhardt, Eleonora Duse, and the renowned theater troupe from Meiningen, among others. These performances were usually scheduled at the beginning or end of the theater's regular season, during which times the public needed extra incentive to attend the theater.

The Theater an der Wien usually refrained from the parodies found in the other *Vorstadt* theaters, but the craze for Pietro Mascagni's *Cavalleria rusticana*, staged at the Court Opera in the fall of 1891, led to a presentation of *Cravalleria musicana*, "a parodistic opera in one single act and various scandalous appearances, by Alexander Weigel. Mascagnibalistic music by *** [Raoul Mader]." Girardi played Duri-Duri Salamucci, and Joseph Joseffy played Alfio, an "emeritus coachman of the Neapolitan tramway, now a cabbie." The music was an original combination of Mascagni's melodies with street songs and operetta melodies. The *Neue Freie Presse* noted that it would have betrayed all theater tradition had Mascagni's opera *not* been parodied by someone.[34]

Viennese operetta experienced a brief revival at the Theater an der Wien in the 1890s with Millöcker's *Der arme Jonathan* (1890), Zeller's *Der Vogelhändler* (1891), and Strauss's *Fürstin Ninetta* (1893) and *Waldmeister* (1895). Yet support even for these works diminished by the end of the century. The Theater an der Wien played a central role again in the "Silver Age" of Viennese operetta, but it would never regain the quality and quantity of repertoire it helped to create in the nineteenth century.

Other *Vorstadt* theaters

Along with the Theater an der Wien, the Carltheater and the Theater in der Josefstadt complete the trio of important *Vorstadt* theaters. The Strampfer Theater, the Fürst Theater, the Thaliatheater, and several other *Vorstadt* theaters came and went, but only these three were leaders in Viennese theatrical life throughout the century. The Carltheater, rebuilt by Court Opera architects Eduard van der Nüll and August Siccard von Siccardsburg in the nineteenth century, was destroyed by Allied bombs in World War II, and an office building now stands in its place on the Taborstrasse in Vienna's II. District. The Theater an der Wien and the Theater in der Josefstadt remain active to this day.

Each theater strove to distinguish itself through repertoire and performers. The Carltheater often featured three or four short works per evening instead of a longer one. Specializing in Parisian works, the theater hosted the first full-length operetta performed in Vienna, Offenbach's *Orpheus in der Unterwelt* (17 March 1860) with Johann Nestroy as Jupiter.[35] In addition to French operetta, the Carltheater devoted more of its repertoire to French comedies and dramas (and their parodies) than did the other *Vorstadt* theaters. *Kikeriki* frequently chided the theater's administration for choosing French pieces over those by home-town authors like Anzengruber and Walzel.[36]

The Carltheater also gained a reputation, especially during Jauner's tenure (1872–77), for its scenic spectacles and sentimental melodramas. One newspaper caricature advertised a fictional "forthcoming play" entitled *Robbery, Murder, and Assault* that included violent scenes of stabbings, spurting blood, and similar gore. The caption read: "Spectacle piece adapted from the French. The management requests that no tears be shed into the parterre. Tissues available at the box office."[37] Despite the perceived lack of artistic integrity, these shows continued to attract audiences after the stock market crash of 1873, a time when all theaters struggled to stay afloat financially. One journal reported in May 1875 that only the Burgtheater and the Carltheater were free from financial crisis; the Burgtheater relied on governmental subvention and long-standing subscriptions, while the Carltheater attracted audiences with "piquant entertainment of various kinds, free of every aesthetic scruple."[38] In addition to violence, the live elephant in Jauner's version of *Around the World in 80 Days* and Lecocq's risqué operetta *La Fille de Madame Angot* [*Angot, die Tochter der Halle*; The Daughter of Madame Angot] repeatedly filled the house.

The anti-Semitic *Kikeriki* and other ultra-German newspapers complained regularly about the Carltheater's penchant for spectacle and its support of non-Viennese authors, complaints based not only upon the repertoire itself but, implicitly, upon the religious background of the audience. For the Leopoldstadt, the district in which

the Carltheater was located, was home to the largest Jewish population of any Viennese district.[39] Before Jauner's engagement, the
theater was directed by the Jewish Anton Ascher (1867–71), a figure
constantly portrayed in the popular press with the exaggerated
hooked nose and small glasses typical of anti-Semitic caricatures.
When theater critics disparagingly juxtaposed the "foreign," "extravagant," and sexually suggestive productions at the Carltheater with
the "native," "simple," and "innocent" offerings at the Theater an der
Wien and the Theater in der Josefstadt, their comparisons reveal the
extent to which religious and political undertones colored impressions of artistic ventures.

The Carltheater experienced difficult times and a frequently
changing directorship in the 1880s, but its success was briefly revived
when Jauner once again assumed artistic leadership in 1895. He
assembled an able operetta ensemble that also made several tours of
Russia. Strauss remarked at the time that, except for Girardi, the
Carltheater boasted a stronger ensemble than the Theater an der
Wien, and Girardi, too, moved there in 1896.[40]

The Carltheater and the Theater an der Wien found their most
formidable competition in the Theater in der Josefstadt, a theater
which, despite its limited physical dimensions, nurtured the early
careers of such renowned entertainers as Ferdinand Raimund and
Wenzel Scholz during the first third of the nineteenth century. When
the theater experienced difficulties competing with Nestroy's
Theater an der Wien in the 1830s, director Franz Pokorny made it a
trial stage for new operas before they reached the Court Opera. *Les
Huguenots*, *La Muette de Portici*, and *Zar und Zimmerman* all received
their Viennese premieres at this theater.[41] Pokorny's tenure became
significant for Viennese theaters in general when he introduced the
practice of paying royalties, a custom that had been standard in
France for some time but not in Austria or Germany. Only years later
did other Viennese theaters adopt his plan for paying authors a percentage of the gross profits.[42] Pokorny touched the lives of later participants in operetta history when he hired Suppé as third
Kapellmeister and Henrietta Treffz, the opera singer who became

Johann Strauss's first wife. Pokorny, Suppé, and Treffz all moved to the Theater an der Wien in 1845 when Pokorny became director of both theaters.

During the second half of the nineteenth century, the Theater in der Josefstadt specialized in pieces of local interest or *Lokalstücke*. These works often featured local dialects, caricatures of Viennese personalities, and allusions to current events. One popular work drawing on Vienna's musical heritage, *Joseph Lanner* (1880), played 117 nights in a row. Other works capitalizing on local flavor included *Alt und Neu Wien* (1865), *Wien bleibt Wien* (1887), *Wiener Schnipfer* (1871), and *Pech-Müller und Pech-Meyer* (1871). Although the Theater in der Josefstadt employed a Kapellmeister and a small orchestra to accompany its spoken works, it did not play a significant role in the musical development of Viennese operetta.

Many *Vorstadt* theaters relied on parody to supplement their repertories, and the Theater in der Josefstadt had provided a home for parodies and counter-parodies since the Congress of Vienna. Grillparzer's play *Der Traum ein Leben* [The Dream, a Life] inspired *Das Leben ein Rausch* [The Life, an Intoxication] in 1822 and *Traumleben oder: Zufriedenheit, die Quelle des Glücks* [Dreamlife or: Contentment, the Source of Happiness] in 1835; the theater responded with *Die Pfeffer-Dösel* [Pepper Shaker] to Charlotte Birch-Pfeiffer's *Pfeffer-Rösel* [Little Pepper-Rose] of 1829; and Wenzel Scholz made his debut in *Die schwarze Frau* [The Black Woman], a parody of Adrien Boieldieu's *Die weiße Frau* [The White Woman]. The tradition continued into the second half of the century when *Drei Paar Stiefel* [Three Pairs of Boots] premiered at Theater in der Josefstadt a few weeks after Millöcker's very popular *Drei Paar Schuhe* [Three Pairs of Shoes] in 1871, and *Der Gigerl vom Land* [The Dandy from the Country] of 1888 at the Fürst Theater was soon followed by *Der Gigerln vom Wien* [The Dandy from Vienna]. The Fürst Theater itself hosted a similar parody of Strauss's work when his *Das Spitzentuch der Königin* of 1880 was modified into *Das Schnupftuch des Königs* [The King's Handkerchief]. On at least one occasion the theater covered its bases by presenting both the original operetta (*Ein Böhm in Amerika*

[A Bohemian in America], by Brunno Zappert, music by Max von Weinzierl) and its parody (*Zwei Böhm in Amerika* [Two Bohemians in America], also by Zappert).[43]

Not only stage works but also well-known performers received satiric homage in the *Vorstadt* theaters. Sarah Bernhardt took such honors with good grace when, after an extended guest performance at the Theater an der Wien in 1882, Josephine Gallmeyer responded with her own *Sarah und Bernhard* at the Carltheater. Gallmeyer had already established herself as a talented parodist in 1874 when she starred in the "parodistic operetta" *Hammlet* [sic] at the Strampfer Theater,[44] a performance that coincided with an Italian theater troupe's performance of Shakespeare's works, including *Amleto, Principe di Danimarco*, at the Theater an der Wien and Ambroise Thomas's *Hamlet* at the Court Opera. Presumably a further response to the Shakespeare series was Friedrich Strampfer's *Der Capellmeister von Venedig*. The Strampfer Theater also offered two parodies of Gounod's *Margarethe*: one, *Eine Faustparodie*, which received poor reviews, and the funnier and distinctly Austrian *Fäustling und Margareth'l*.[45] Along with other Viennese businesses, the Strampfer Theater suffered irrecoverable losses during the stock market crash of 1873, but shortly before it closed in 1875 the theater transformed the extremely popular operetta by Lecocq, *Angot, die Tochter der Halle* (then drawing crowds to the Carltheater), into *Angot an der Donau*, a "parodistic burlesque."

Each of the three main *Vorstadt* theaters evinced a distinct personality, despite frequent changes in direction and personnel, through a combination of repertoire and its regular audience. When actor/director Karl Blasel proposed moving his entire enterprise from the Theater in der Josefstadt to the Carltheater in 1889, a journalist for the *Deutsche Zeitung* expressed skepticism:

> Herr Blasel believes he can move from this theater in this neighborhood to the old Viennese Jewish quarter on the other side of the Danube. The house ghosts of the Josefstadt must go with him, whether they want to or not; the uncritical public should also go. But will it? . . . In the fall, he might as well stand on the streets of Vienna and announce loudly:

'Ladies and Gentlemen! At my behest, the Wurstel-Prater has been moved to Schönbrunn!' The public would laugh at him and not believe it.[46]

Clearly, a theater's identity was achieved not only through choice of repertoire, but also through the expectations of its patrons. This relationship – theater directors on the one hand and paying public on the other – was an active negotiation in which performers and authors served as intermediaries.

DIRECTORS: SHAPING THE THEATER AN DER WIEN

Less visible than the performers, but no less vital to the enterprise of operetta, were the directors who encouraged and facilitated its composition and performance. Motivated more by hopes for profitable box office returns than claims for artistic patronage, the men and women who directed these works played a crucial role in the genre's genesis and development. The history of *Vorstadt* theaters is, in fact, remarkable for the participation of women in the upper echelons of their administration. The Viennese public did not fully accept female directors, who faced frequent mockery in the public press for their unusual responsibilities. But, removed from the restrictions associated with imperial subvention, these stages could allow business sense and creativity to prevail over social convention and tradition. Although many directors worked in several venues over the course of their careers, the following figures all contributed, at one time or another, to establishing an international reputation for the Theater an der Wien as the home of Viennese operetta.

Friedrich Strampfer (1823–90)

Strampfer served at several Viennese theaters, including one of his own (the Strampfer Theater), during his long career. When he assumed direction of the Theater an der Wien in July 1862, the institution was in dire financial straits, and his first few years brought little fiscal success. He made a wise business and artistic decision, however, in hiring Josephine Gallmeyer, an actress who would enjoy years of popularity on various *Vorstadt* stages. He also augmented the theater's reputation and coffers by inviting illustrious guest performers to appear there; Richard Wagner, for one, conducted midday concerts of his own music in 1862 and 1863 to great acclaim.

The Theater an der Wien began its reputation as a leading operetta stage when Strampfer secured the German-language premiere of Offenbach's *Schöne Helene* in 1865; the work was performed on 17 March of that year under the composer's baton with Marie Geistinger in the title role. Indeed, Offenbach had made it a condition of his contract that she be recruited from Germany to lead the Viennese cast. (Gallmeyer left the company out of jealousy soon after Geistinger arrived, thus beginning a decades-long professional competition.) Pleased with the performance, Offenbach granted the Theater an der Wien another twenty-five Viennese premieres of his works until 1882.[47] From 1864 to 1869, the most profitable years under his directorship, Strampfer's repertoire included 46 percent spoken pieces, 40 percent operetta, 13 percent *Feerien* (shows involving magic and myths), and 5 percent operas.[48] These statistics reflect almost entirely evening-length works, unlike the programs of his first few years. He left the Theater an der Wien in July 1869 to the capable partnership of Maximilian Steiner and Marie Geistinger.

Maximilian Steiner (1830–80) and Marie Geistinger (1836–1903)

In the six years that Steiner and Geistinger led the theater, they set a tone for the repertoire that lasted until the end of the century.[49] During their tenure, they not only produced and performed the first full-length Viennese operettas but promoted the works of Ludwig Anzengruber in whom the Viennese *Volksstück* had its last great highpoint; his *Pfarrer von Kirchfeld* (1870), *Der Meineidbauer* (1871), and *Der G'wissenswurm* (1874) became staples of the theater's repertoire and classics of Viennese literature. They hired Carl Millöcker as Kapellmeister in 1869, giving the third of the triumvirate of Viennese operetta composers a permanent position and a venue for his works. Actor Alexander Girardi found his career flourished under the Steiner/Geistinger partnership. Their vision guided the stage successfully through the financial turbulence of the mid-1870s and fostered the early careers of performers who made operetta the influential genre it became.

Marie Geistinger's highly visible position made her an easy target for conservative journals, which inevitably objected to women in leadership positions, and *Kikeriki* published several caricatures of her. One that ran shortly before the premiere of *Die Fledermaus* showed a well-dressed Geistinger with Steiner, portrayed at half her size, hanging on her arm. The accompanying text explained: "In order for Directrice Geistinger to profit from the Russian Stanislaus medal given to Director Steiner as well, she had no other choice . . . but to adorn herself with both the Director and his medal."[50] Although women had been prominent performers for years, it was not until the late nineteenth century in private *Vorstadt* theaters that women thrived in management positions. Still, Geistinger and Alexandrine von Schönerer after her remained the exception to the rule and received little public support.

The Theater an der Wien, like most Viennese theaters, barely survived the stock market crash of 1873 and the ensuing economic depression. Although Geistinger was one of the highest paid performers in the city, her fortune was destroyed in the economic disaster. Only Steiner's good business sense kept the theater from bankruptcy. A cartoon on the cover of *Der Floh* during the summer of 1873 shows Steiner juggling the heads of Johann Strauss, Offenbach, and Geistinger along with three pairs of shoes, a reference to the successful folk comedy *Drei Paar Schuhe*, with music by Millöcker. The paper praised his diplomacy and business acuity, estimating that "if Steiner were director of the World Exhibition, it would now have a profit of 17 million already."[51] The World Exhibition, which opened in Vienna a week before the stock market crashed in May, only intensified the economic misery of the Viennese, embarrassed to have countless international visitors witness the collapse.

Geistinger and Steiner applied in April of 1875 for the management of the Komische Oper, a recently established theater on the Ringstrasse, but their joint application was rejected, as was Steiner's independent application.[52] Geistinger left the management and regular ensemble of the Theater an der Wien that year, and Steiner continued alone until his death in 1880.[53] A cartoon commemorating her departure alludes to *Die Fledermaus* and the change in audience tastes; as a large Geistinger waves good-bye to a small Steiner, she sings: "Even though Strauss still writes so beautifully / The people only want to see elephants!,"[54] a reference to the success of Verne's *Around the World in 80 Days*, in the production by Franz Jauner.

Franz Jauner (1832–1900)

Once described as "the soul of the Theater [an der Wien]," Franz Jauner directed several Viennese theaters at critical periods in their development.[55] His keen business sense, combined with a flair for spectacle, kept the private theaters under his administrative and artistic direction financially viable. Like Schikaneder, his tastes were guided by box office receipts more than artistic elitism; the motto written over the door to his office insisted, "Every genre is allowed except the boring ones!"[56]

Once an actor at Vienna's Burgtheater, Jauner became director of the Carltheater in 1872, when, under his direction, the theater became as much a social center for the upper bourgeoisie as was the Burgtheater for aristocratic/patrician families. Here he cultivated French divorce dramas (the *Ehebruchsdramen* parodied by Adele in Act III of *Die Fledermaus*) and conversation pieces (*Konversationsstücke*). His most spectacular productions were dramatizations of Jules Verne novels; *Around the World in 80 Days* included a snake charmer and a live elephant, and although it was mocked as "a pedagogic farce for mature children"[57] it received 108 performances in the 1870s.[58] After the stock market crash of 1873, operetta returned to the Carltheater's repertoire. This house was one of the few to survive the recession following the economic crisis, owing largely to

Jauner's leadership. His last production there was the premiere of Johann Strauss's *Prinz Methusalem* in 1877, after which he moved to the Court Opera.

Jauner's success at the Carltheater had not gone unnoticed at court, for Franz Joseph invited visiting dignitaries to the theater in the 1870s and supported Jauner's application for the Court Opera directorship. Hoping to rescue the Opera from the debt it had aquired in the wake of the crash, coupled with expenses incurred by the new building (finished in 1869), court officials had attempted to hire Jauner as early as 1875. Although Jauner maintained his position at the Carltheater for almost three more years, he took over administration of the institution from Johann Herbeck at that time. Several journalists, however, expressed disdain for his artistic qualifications. Without naming Jauner, one disparaged his leadership during the economically depressed period of 1875: "The subvented Court theaters generally kept to their old programs, but the leaders of the new opera conceded to popular taste, giving more weight to pompous productions than to the artistic spirit of the performance."[59] In a rare charitable moment Hanslick defended the choice, reasoning that musical decisions are left to the Kapellmeister, not the administrative director, and the ability to manage a theater does not depend on musical talent.[60]

Under Jauner's direction the Opera performed works certain to be popular with the public. In his first season (1875/76), the six most frequently performed operas were Wagner's *Lohengrin* and *Tannhäuser*, Meyerbeer's *Le Prophète* and *Robert le Diable*, Gounod's *Margarethe* (*Faust*), and Ambroise Thomas's *Mignon*.[61] The public clamored for more Wagner, and, unlike previous directors, Jauner realized the importance for Vienna of making peace with the composer. Wagner had been unhappy with the Viennese Court Opera since the early 1860s, when the theater attempted to produce *Tristan und Isolde*, but gave up the project after seventy-seven rehearsals.[62] Partly to facilitate this reconciliation, Jauner hired Wagner protégé Hans Richter as artistic director.[63] Under Jauner's leadership, the Opera offered premieres of *Die Walküre* (5 March 1877), *Siegfried* (9 November 1878), and

Götterdämmerung (14 February 1879) Despite Jauner's reforms and successful new productions, the opera's finances remained poor, and he left the theater at the end of the 1880/81 season.

Jauner began the 1881/82 season at the ill-fated Ringtheater (previously the Komische Oper), and during his directorship Vienna experienced one of the most devastating events in the city's cultural history: on 8 December 1881, only minutes before the curtain rose on Offenbach's *Les Contes d'Hoffmann* [*Hoffmanns Erzählungen; The Tales of Hoffmann*], the theater was engulfed by a fire started backstage, killing over 300 people in the audience. This horrific episode provoked a controversy with significance far beyond theater life. Debates raged over responsibility for the lack of safety, hinging on whether the city (including the mayor) or the empire (which oversaw the police) should be held accountable. Imperial and municipal officials bickered over financial responsibility for enforcing the "Regulations on Theater Safety," and the city's mayor was forced to resign as a result of the scandal.[64] This tragedy not only changed official safety requirements for theaters throughout Europe, but lingered in the Viennese collective memory for years to come. As the theater's director, Jauner was held personally responsible for the tragedy, stood trial, and was sentenced to four months in jail. Emperor Franz Joseph granted him amnesty, but his career had reached a temporary impasse.

After the scandal subsided, Jauner was still legally prohibited from theater direction, but he functioned as unofficial director of the Theater an der Wien, where he continued his innovations in stage design and demanded high standards from performers and productions. Some critics felt, however, that he had lost the trust and sympathy of his audience, a loss that would affect not only the theater's business but its integrity as well: "The name of Herr Jauner is associated with dismal memories, and he has no right to invite us to amusement."[65] Audiences forgave him, nonetheless, and attended his state-of-the-art productions in droves. Despite frequent skirmishes with fellow director Alexandrine von Schönerer, Jauner served as artistic director of the Theater an der Wien until 1894, playing a large role in the success of Strauss's *Der Zigeunerbaron* (1885) and other late works. He moved briefly to Hamburg but returned to Vienna in 1895 as director of the Carltheater, where he made extensive renovations and tried repeatedly to lure Girardi away from the Theater an der Wien, finally succeeding in 1896.[66]

At the Carltheater Jauner supported the efforts of the literary circle known as *Jung Wien* [Young Vienna] and was the first to produce works by Hermann Bahr (*Das Tschaperl*, 1897), Felix Dörmann (*Ledige Leute*, 1897), and Arthur Schnitzler (*Freiwild*, 1898); he also produced works by Ibsen and Strindberg, but he won no friends among the Viennese public or critics for these innovations.[67] He suffered a stroke in the winter of 1899 and shot himself in his theater office in February 1900, leaving large debts behind. His death was mourned in all circles of the artistic world.

Alexandrine von Schönerer (1850–1919)

Schönerer bought the Theater an der Wien in 1884 from Franz Steiner (Maximilian Steiner's son) and managed it along with partners Jauner and Camillo Walzel. An innovative businesswoman, she was one of the first Viennese directors to pay royalties regularly to librettists as well as to composers.[68] She dramatically increased the ratio of operetta to spoken works (under her direction plays comprised only 15 percent of the repertoire), making the theater a world leader in operetta performance.[69] She produced the Viennese premieres of Strauss's last operettas, beginning with *Der Zigeunerbaron*, as well as other important Viennese works of the late century, such as Millöcker's *Der arme Jonathan* and Zeller's *Der Vogelhändler*, foreign operettas like Gilbert and Sullivan's *The Mikado* (1888), and operas like Puccini's *La Bohème* (1897). Under her direction in 1893, the Theater an der Wien offered the first German-language performance of Smetana's *Bartered Bride*.[70] As director and owner of Vienna's most prestigious *Vorstadt* theater, Schönerer enjoyed a role in public life shared by few women of her day.

The name "von Schönerer" belonged not only to Alexandrine but also to her brother, the radical right politician and pan-German leader Georg, whose anti-Semitic nationalism inspired Austrian leaders from Karl Lueger to Adolf Hitler. *Der Floh* noted the irony of her family position in a review of her successful production of *Der arme Jonathan* (1890): "Fräulein Schönerer endangered the audience by her striking sets and costumes. They might have had to succumb to a court investigation since in every moment they were close to shouting 'Hail Schönerer!'"[71] The prohibition of such an outcry was due to an event several years earlier: Georg Schönerer had been tried and arrested for assault in March 1888 after storming the offices of the *Neues Wiener Tagblatt*, a newspaper edited by the Jewish Moritz Szeps. Schönerer was imprisoned for four months, lost his noble title, and was forbidden to participate in public politics until 1893.[72] Alexandrine distanced herself as much as possible from her brother's objectionable rantings and once remarked that their only common trait was their right to an inheritance.

The Theater an der Wien experienced difficult times in the 1890s, when the fate of operetta remained hazy. The *Österreichische Musik-und Theaterzeitung* reported in 1891:

> The Theater an der Wien has unpacked the old operetta glitter, and when no more finches want to be taken in by the *Bird Catcher*, *Poor Jonathan* climbs up out of the trap door and Offenbach's *Beautiful Helene* must help the management until something else occurs to them. Horrible sterility of repertoire is characteristic of this stage, but along with that, this theater has great luck, the audience goes in and allows itself to be offered whatever pleases the management.[73]

Business went further downhill after the departures of Jauner and Girardi, and in 1900 Schönerer sold the theater for 1 million fl. to a consortium that included Josef Simon (Johann Strauss's brother-in-law). Such a sum suggests that although the repertoire may have been stale, she must have kept the business at least solvent in order to sell it for almost twice what she paid for it. On her retirement, Emperor Franz Josef honored her with the Golden Service Cross, a medal usually reserved for members of imperial theaters and a singular honor for a woman.[74] She lived in relative seclusion until her death, remembered as a "rarity among theater directors" for her generosity as well as her ambition.[75]

PERFORMERS

In general in Vienna an artist means: actor. The stage work is the center of Viennese life.
Heinrich Laube[76]

They say people in Berlin go to the theater because of the work, the Viennese go because of the performer.[77]

Most important of all in Vienna were the actors . . . anyone who wanted any success had to learn from them.[78]

Leading performers enjoyed unparalleled popularity and influence in late nineteenth-century Vienna. Their names and caricatures appeared regularly in newspapers, and their careers served as topics of public interest and speculation. Although many of them toured other European cities as well as America, their reputations were established on the stages of the Viennese *Vorstadt*. Indeed, Marie Geistinger and Alexander Girardi were of undeniable importance in establishing Viennese operetta as an artistically viable and commercially successful genre.

The performers' function in creating operetta in nineteenth-century Vienna is reminiscent of their role in creating opera in seventeenth-century Venice: "An [operetta] did not exist independent of its singers, either at its conception or its performance; they were its spokesmen, its true publicists. The singers mediated between [operetta] and its audience. Transforming a private arrangement into a public spectacle, they transported the operatic product to the consumers."[79] Because Viennese operetta shared the improvisatory tradition upon which so much Viennese *Volk* theater has been based, performers were allowed more autonomy over their roles than would ever have been granted a Court Opera singer or a Burgtheater actor. Along with greater autonomy, however, came greater responsibility for creating roles that would attract audiences night after night. Although Strauss and his colleagues composed according to the strengths and weaknesses of the performers at a particular Viennese theater, they also considered the limitations of provincial theaters if they hoped for their works to gain wider recognition (and continued royalties). Still, these very limitations made their music more accessible and attractive to the public at large.

Marie Geistinger

One of the most popular and highest paid performers in the history of operetta was Marie Geistinger. Just as Hortense Schneider captured Parisian audiences and created many of Offenbach's leading roles, Geistinger defined those same roles for German-speaking audiences and created many of Viennese operetta's most memorable characters. She became a powerful and respected figure not only for her considerable performing capabilities, but – as we have seen – also for her managerial responsibilities at the Theater an der Wien.

Her Viennese career began at the Theater in der Josefstadt, where she starred in *Die falsche Pepita* [The False Pepita, 1852], a parody of the famous Spanish dancer Pepita de Olivas, and in a local comedy, *Die Entführung vom Maskenball* [Abduction from the Masked Ball, 1854], apparently a parody of Mozart's opera. She went next to theaters in Hamburg, Riga, and Berlin, where Friedrich Strampfer, then director of the Theater an der Wien, came to woo her back to Vienna. Her comic ability and clear soprano voice had become well known to German audiences, and Offenbach made it a condition of his contract with Strampfer that Geistinger play the leading roles. A salary offer of 350 fl. per month and 15 fl. per performance persuaded her to return.[80]

Geistinger's career at the Theater an der Wien lasted from the early 1860s to 1875, during which time she created some of the best-known roles in Viennese operetta and folk plays. She starred as Anna Birkmeier in Ludwig Anzengruber's controversial *Der Pfarrer von Kirchfeld*, as Fantasca in Strauss's first operetta, *Indigo und die vierzig*

Räuber (1871), and as Rosalinde in *Die Fledermaus* (1874), setting the standard toward which all later Rosalindes strove. She enjoyed playing the breeches roles common to operetta of the 1870s and owned many men's costumes. In fact, when she took over direction of the theater in 1869, a cartoon mocked the unusual situation by sketching her in a man's suit with the caption, "The new theater director at Theater an der Wien: Geistinger in a new breeches role."[81] When she resigned her position at the theater in 1875, she left behind substantial contributions to the development of Viennese operetta, but although she made frequent guest appearances in Vienna and Leipzig and toured America four times before her death in 1903, her active role in promoting and creating new operettas was over.

Alexander Girardi (1850–1918)

When Girardi performs, reality is with him on the stage and illusion is in the audience.[82]

Hermann Bahr

Alexander Girardi exercised an unprecedented hold over the Viennese imagination. His engaging personality and compelling acting talent so enthralled the public that his style of speech and dress permeated all levels of Viennese society. He became "the actor of the epoch and generation of economic, cultural, and political upswing."[83] Throughout the tumultuous *fin de siècle*, Girardi remained a reassuring symbol of Vienna's unique identity and cultural heritage. Arriving at the Theater an der Wien in 1874, Girardi became closely associated with this theater, where he stayed for the next twenty years.

Not only did he lend his acting talent to the roles given him, but he also made suggestions for his own roles as they were written. Lili Dietrich (Strauss's second wife) once wrote to librettist Julius Bauer, "Girardi wants to speak to you, he has a good idea for a Couplet."[84] Another widely repeated story explains Girardi's part in creating the hit song, "Nur für Natur," in Strauss's *Der lustige Krieg* (1881).

Disappointed about the original size of his role, which allowed him not even a couplet of his own, Girardi appealed to Strauss for more music, to which Strauss responded by dashing off a waltz tune that occurred to him on the spot. Recognizing its potential, Girardi took it to the librettist Genée for text, but since Genée was busy at the time, he allowed Girardi to take the music elsewhere. Girardi found poet and composer Franz Wagner, who contributed the text to the most memorable and most popular song of the operetta.[85] *Der Floh* complained of the song's pervasiveness with a few parody verses of its own,[86] while *Kikeriki* commented that the song had become a blessing for organ grinders: first customers gladly paid to hear the new piece, and now everyone is so tired of it that they will gladly pay the organ grinders to go away.[87] A few months later, when "Nur für Natur" was all the rage in Berlin, *Kikeriki* darkly suggested that it made the perfect revenge for Königgrätz (the Austrians' military loss to the Prussians in 1866).[88]

Occasionally librettists regretted Girardi's power and eager participation, as Genée grumbled to Millöcker in 1886:

> That Girardi is and will remain an unreachable point, I know exactly and *silently* sigh to some what had to be left out. (For example, I already hear about new texts, strophes written by others at his request, a situation that has already caused us, especially me, much annoyance.)
> Nevertheless, G. still remains for me the unequalled artist who shines through everything with his *golden humor*, NB – when nothing from his party or his environment ruins his mood![89]

By the mid-1880s Girardi could name his price at any theater and commanded not only money but rapt attention from his Viennese public, both inside and outside the theater. Even the Viennese police acknowledged the role Girardi played in the Theater an der Wien's survival. When the theater experienced hard times in 1899, the police administration explained that Alexandrine von Schönerer's recent financial difficulties may have been due "in part to Girardi's exit from the ensemble and the lack of a replacement for him."[90]

Strauss held Girardi in high regard and often attributed the success or failure of his works to Girardi's enthusiasm, or lack thereof. He encouraged the performer while they vacationed in September 1894:

> you have brought me great joy, since all that I strive for is to know that you are more or less content. On your shoulders rests not only every work, but also the existence of the Theater an der Wien. You can understand that all authors who write for this theater cling to you as tightly as possible – hold you by head and foot – never let you go – because you alone have the greatest power to decide *"to be or not to be."*[91]

Strauss wrote to him again after the premiere of *Jabuka* a few weeks later, during which time they had progressed from the formal "Sie" to the familiar "Du" form of address. Strauss congratulated him on a fine performance: "In every operetta the Girardi-role makes the difference . . . In regard to the fate of *Jabuka*, we authors lie in God's – truthfully said, in Girardi's hands."[92]

The following summer Strauss wrote to his life-long friend and business partner Gustav Lewy regarding the upcoming production of *Waldmeister*:

> Girardi *knows* the book, *his* role, and is as you will hear from his own mouth, fired up *about both*. If one were not pessimistic, one would believe what *he* promises about its success . . . Of course one is reassured when Girardi is so satisfied with his role and predicts *his* success with such certainty. In [*Fürstin*] *Ninetta he* was the one who kept it in Vienna.[93]

Strauss did not overestimate Girardi's ability to predict the success of a work based on his performance, for it is evident from Millöcker's account book that if Girardi or Geistinger became ill or took a vacation, the show did not go on without them.[94] Author Müller-Guttenbrunn also acknowledged, "The Theater an der Wien depends on the two eyes of its leading comedian. Should this man become sick – the theater must be closed!"[95] Financial records and contemporary opinion suggest that the Viennese indeed attended the theater primarily to see the performer rather than the work.

Girardi, like Strauss, gradually attained the stature of a national icon, and although he was born at mid-century, his style captured the nostalgic flavor of *Vormärz* Vienna. When he premiered the

Coachman's Song (*Fiakerlied*) at the celebration of the centennial anniversary of Viennese fiakers (24 May 1885), it created a sensation of sentiment and reminiscence: "It became the ballade of a happy *Alt Wien*, where existence was as light and carefree as a fairy tale and the Viennese were 'as light and breezy as the wind.' For the Viennese, the fiaker coachman became the symbolic figure of the golden age."[96] During the 1880s, German nationalist sentiment became stronger in Vienna and figured more prominently in the stage works of that decade. At a time when Vienna's identity was being steadily challenged by workers and their families streaming to the capital from the crown lands, Girardi symbolized the German culture with which many native Viennese aligned themselves. He starred as Augustin in the operetta *Der liebe Augustin* (Theater an der Wien, January 1887), and in the song dedicated to the steeple of St. Stephen's he exclaimed: "Receive today the greetings of your children / a Hooray to the watchman over our German Vienna."[97] Girardi's presence served as a lightning rod for the cultural values of an earlier, more insular time in Vienna's history.

Despite his role as a popular performer, Girardi became close friends with the leading cultural figures of his time. He vacationed in the mountain resort of Bad Ischl along with Brahms, Ludwig Bösendorfer, Johann Strauss, Burgtheater actress Katharine Schratt, and members of the royal family; indeed, he married Bösendorfer's step-daughter Leonie in October 1898 in Ischl.[98] Like many of his colleagues in the *Vorstadt* theaters, Girardi hoped one day to perform on the Burgtheater stage, a goal he achieved in February 1918, only three months before his death, when he appeared before an overflowing house in a performance of Raimund's *Bauer als Millionär* [Farmer as Millionaire].

His death, during the waning days of the Habsburg empire, was mourned by all Vienna. Alexander von Weilen eulogized him as a "bridge from *Alt Wien* to the Vienna of the twentieth century . . . It is truly as if one lost a piece of oneself, insofar as it was connected to the home city [*Vaterstadt*], as if a large piece of our own youth, our own being, has been irrevocably lost." Weilen acknowledged that "what he gave us was that Vienna out of which we've grown, one matured by experience and fate, but that we still carry deeply and passionately in our hearts."[99] Austrians facing loss of empire felt further bereft by the loss of a popular figure who had embodied and shaped their collective identity for decades.

Girardi's power to evoke nostalgia extended into the post-war era; as war-torn Austria struggled to rebuild and repair itself, he remained a happy reminder of what Vienna had once been. The tenth and fifteenth anniversaries of his death were celebrated by the newly established Austrian radio station with programs that included gramophone recordings of Girardi himself.[100] The unveiling of a monument to him in 1929 was accompanied by Strauss waltzes, conducted by Franz Schalk, and speeches by the mayor, Karl Seitz, and the director of the Theater an der Wien, Hubert Marischka. The twentieth anniversary of his death fell shortly after the Nazis had overtaken Vienna, and a poignant tribute to him in the *Neue Freie Presse* concluded, "Alexander Girardi, the actor and the man, belongs really and truly to the Vienna of a time now more distant and dim than ever."[101]

CONCLUSION

The end of Viennese operetta's "Golden Age" coincided not only with Strauss's death, but also with the demise or career changes of many of his colleagues discussed in this chapter. The last five years of the century saw the deaths of Suppé (1895), Zeller (1898), Millöcker (1899), and Strauss (1899), the two major librettists, Zell (1895) and Genée (1895), and the most important theater director, Jauner (1900).[102] Girardi left the Theater an der Wien in 1896, and Alexandrine von Schönerer, who had run the theater for fifteen years, sold it in 1900.

Although composers picked up the thread of operetta once again in the twentieth century, no continuous tradition linked the works of one generation to the next. Operetta composers of the "Silver Age" had backgrounds as conductors of military orchestras (e.g., Franz Lehár and Leo Fall) or music critics (e.g., Richard Heuberger and

Emmerich Kálmán) rather than as theater musicians, and none of these careers spanned the two centuries. In 1900 few of the men who would become leading composers of Viennese operetta were resident in Vienna; Fall worked as a Kapellmeister in Berlin, and Oscar Straus worked (along with Arnold Schoenberg) at Ernst von Wolzogen's cabaret, also in Berlin. Indeed, the growing popularity of the cabaret in Vienna and Berlin may have contributed to the gap in operetta's development. In this smaller, more intimate setting, the improvisatory tradition could continue with less fear of retribution from the censors and less financial risk to directors and owners.

Both leading operetta stages, the Carltheater and the Theater an der Wien, experienced financial crises at the turn of the century; the Carltheater only gradually overcame the debts Jauner left behind at his death, and Schönerer's followers at the Theater an der Wien had no better luck making ends meet. In fact, both buildings were in danger of being torn down when they did not meet contemporary fire safety codes, and with the Ringtheater disaster still in recent memory, the Municipal Theater Commission voted in June 1900 to close both houses. Only a public outcry that summer caused the committee to change its mind and investigate possible renovations.[103] The theaters eventually reopened their doors and contributed to Viennese cultural life once again in this century, but for the operetta world, the close of the nineteenth century marked the end of an era.

3 | "Austria personified": Strauss and the search for Viennese identity

> Johann Strauss is Austria personified.
> All of Austria is in his camp.
>
> *Der Humorist*[1]

> Johann Strauss, he is Vienna's musical genius; if he is silent, then Vienna is dead.   *Friedrich Uhl*[2]

The last third of the nineteenth century saw new inhabitants arriving daily from all over central Europe, each group bringing its own dialect, fashion sense, culinary tradition, and musical taste. For some residents, this influx of immigrants ushered in a period of "de-Viennization," when the town of their parents and grandparents was gradually supplanted by a modern, industrial, cosmopolitan city. Faced with these drastic changes, they found in Strauss a comforting reminder of *Alt Wien*. For others, especially those newly arrived in the city, enthusiasm for Strauss proved to be a means of assimilation as well as a momentary escape from the challenges of urban life. In both cases, Strauss became a focal point for demonstrations of pro-Viennese sentiment. Although the various urban subcultures remained divided by economics, politics, and ethnicity, they shared an allegiance to Strauss and his music, finding in him a means of representing Vienna to the world and to themselves. Contemporary documents testify to the fervor with which Viennese of all ages and backgrounds celebrated their local favorite.

With the exception of the graying Emperor, Strauss was the best-known, most discussed figure in Viennese public life. Unlike other artists in Vienna who were "reviled during their lifetime and beloved after their death," he enjoyed continuous popular support throughout his long career. He, like any public figure, suffered his share of media scrutiny, but there was never any doubt that Vienna wanted to claim him as its own. Over the course of an active compositional life spanning more than fifty years and almost 500 opus numbers, he produced several works with which Austrians identify to this day.

THE STRAUSS FAMILY

Yes, indivisible are the concepts Vienna and Strauss![3]

Vienna already began to associate the Strauss name with dance music in the first half of the century through the career of Johann Strauss, Sr. (1804–49). A violinist by training, he composed and conducted his orchestra in Metternich's Vienna and throughout Europe. When he acquired the title Imperial Ball Music Director, he became the first popular musician to gain official approbation from the Habsburg court. Strauss, Sr. discouraged his son's early musical career, however, and they competed for public attention from the time of his son's debut in 1844 until his own death five years later, when Strauss, Jr. took over many of his father's contracts, a few of his musicians, and much of his repertoire.

Although Strauss inherited his father's music and musicians, he struggled for years to gain recognition from the imperial court. He dedicated many early works to the Emperor and other members of the royal family, hoping to win their approval; but although his orchestra was finally hired to perform at an imperial ball in February 1852, the official title still eluded him.[4] One reason was his participation in the 1848 revolutionary uprisings. While his father remained staunchly loyalist and began each of his concerts with the Radetzky March, the younger Strauss joined the revolutionaries and played the Marseillaise and other forbidden pieces for students at the barricades.[5] Such behavior was not soon forgotten by those with whom he later curried favor.

In the meantime, Strauss established himself as a conductor at local restaurants and beer gardens, and soon he and his musicians became sought-after performers for private gatherings. Like many Viennese musicians, he first made a reputation in foreign countries before finding acceptance at home. His experience performing at private balls began outside Vienna; in fact, it was in Warsaw in 1850 that Franz Joseph heard him play for the first time. Strauss gained the favor of aristocratic Viennese circles by carnival of 1851, when they began to hire him to entertain in their homes. The demand for his music soon exceeded what he could manage on his own – he was known to attend three or four events each night in order to make the promised personal appearance – and he enlisted the aid of his brothers Josef in 1853, and Eduard in 1861. Because of the prominence they held in Viennese ballroom music, the family became known colloquially as the Strauss Firm.

After performing at court for eleven years, touring Europe and Russia, and publishing over 200 works, Strauss finally received the title Imperial and Royal Court-Ball Music Director in 1863. Since his petitions had previously been refused owing to his "immoral" lifestyle, his case had been strengthened by his marriage the previous year.[6] In his petition, he promised to perform only at royal balls and in *Volksgarten* concerts from then on, relinquishing performances at the more questionable taverns and casinos.[7] Although the title explicitly limited his performances to official functions, his health would not permit the grueling schedule of a few years earlier. Strauss handed over many local conducting engagements to his brothers, while continuing to compose dance music for their orchestras, completing commissions from various social and professional groups.

For some, Strauss, Sr. remained the more authentic Viennese musician. *Kikeriki* unfavorably juxtaposed Strauss's career with that of his father decades after his father's death: one page featured Strauss, Sr. leading a rustic ensemble with his violin in hand and dancers twirling in the background, while the opposing page showed Strauss, Jr. conducting bored orchestral musicians and singers gesturing grandly on stage. The caption explained, "While Strauss, Sr. found the greatest happiness stirring enthusiasm in the Viennese through his native sounds, his genial son Johann Strauss lets himself be convinced he must betray the Viennese idiom and, seeking nobility, write an operetta that recalls everything but his home – Vienna."[8] For Viennese experiencing the political turbulence of the latter third

of the nineteenth century, the elder Strauss evoked memories of the
Vormärz, which many recalled as a simpler, more peaceful time.

The family's celebrity continued throughout the *fin de siècle*.
Indeed, *Kikeriki* devoted space to their personal and professional lives
so frequently that the editor suggested they establish a regular
"Strauss column."[9] Johann's brothers also enjoyed their share of the
popular press. Eduard (1835–1916), "der schöne Edi," was frequently
derided for his dandyish style and self-absorbed attitude. One newspaper chided him for proudly sporting medals of all sorts: "In the
ballet *Fantasca* and with Eduard Strauss, the decorations please me
the most."[10] Edi bore the brunt of mockery again a few years later
when *Kikeriki* portrayed him walking down the street followed,
unbeknownst to him, by Richard Wagner. As the crowd gathers,
tipping their hats, Edi remarks: "Strange how these Viennese
worship me!" (see Illustration 3.1).[11]

Although Johann was known to introduce himself as "the brother
of Eduard Strauss," Eduard felt inferior to his older brother all his
life. They disagreed frequently about personal issues and did not
socialize together, yet they begrudgingly acknowledged their mutual
professional indebtedness: Johann needed Eduard to publicize and
perform his works,[12] while Edi needed the performing rights to those
works to ensure his orchestra's financial success.[13] By the time of
Strauss's death in 1899 the brothers were estranged. Eduard did not
attend the funeral, and Johann left nothing of his sizable estate to his
brother. Edi had the last word: in 1907 he incinerated three truckloads
of autograph scores and parts penned by all three brothers.[14] At one
point they had agreed that the last survivor should destroy their
orchestral music in order to keep their arrangements from falling
into the hands of a competing Kapellmeister. In his bitter and impov-
erished old age, this agreement justified to Eduard his wholesale
destruction of irreplaceable autograph manuscripts.[15]

Johann's brother Josef (1827–70) also enjoyed a high profile in
Vienna as composer and conductor.[16] Citizens of the monarchy rallied
around him most fervently, however, after his death. Frequently
in poor health, he collapsed one evening (1 June 1870) during a

Leichtmöglicher Irrthum

(wenn demnächst Richard Wagner nach Wien kömmt).

Eduard Strauß (nicht ahnend, daß Wagner hinter ihm geht). Merkwürdig wie mich diese Wiener anbeten!

3.1 Eduard Strauss and Richard Wagner (*Kikeriki*, 7 February 1875)

performance in Warsaw and died soon after. (High-strung and nervous all his life, Josef smoked, by his brother Eduard's estimation, seventeen to nineteen cigars *daily*.[17]) Local newspapers were filled with rumors that he had been struck down by a drunken Russian soldier. Austro-Russian relations were frequently tense, and the summer of 1870 was a particularly delicate moment with regard to Poland. The Russians resented the relative autonomy the Poles enjoyed under Habsburg rule compared with that under Prussian or Russian rule; since April 1870, Austria even had a Polish minister-president in Count Alfred Potocki.[18] The Poles, in an attempt to prove Austria's sympathy with them against the Russians, used the Strauss family name to provoke anti-Russian sentiment: many Austrian newspapers advised the imperial government to send troops into Russia immediately to avenge Josef's death!

Johann Strauss, Jr. exhibited a lifelong allegiance to the family tradition. As he advised his brother Eduard, a "Strauss concert" meant liveliness, happiness, and merriment: "A Strauss Concert should have a gay character about it; the public believes in the fact that a Strauss concert remains true to its traditional fame." Never underestimating the necessity of local support, he cautioned, "The people in your loge or in other loges do not judge you, since they're for the most part already well disposed toward you, but the public in the orchestra and balcony, in a word, the larger public, judges what it's offered. Vox populi vox Dei!" Unlike those art-music composers who could afford to appeal only to a well-educated elite, Strauss strove to gain the full support of his broad audience, whatever the venue. He concluded his advice with his professional credo: "Just like in the theater, people want to be entertained."[19] Listeners of all ranks repaid his consideration with boundless devotion.

STRAUSS AS LOCAL HERO AND NATIONAL ICON

His popularity is virtually immeasurable: in all parts of the world Strauss melodies resound, and in our part of the world they come from almost every house.   *Eduard Hanslick*[20]

Strauss and his music drew support from the entire Austrian half of the empire, but his career was most closely associated with Vienna. On the occasion of his 1884 Jubilee (the fortieth anniversary of his performing debut) one journalist commented that "a small chronicle of Vienna could be gathered from the titles of his waltzes, polkas, quadrilles and marches."[21] Works alluding to Vienna's environs

("Heiligenstadt Rendezvous," "Leopoldstädter Polka"), leading pro-fessions ("Five Paragraphs from the Waltz Codex," "Morning Edition"), and local events ("Archduke Wilhelm's Recovery March," when the Archduke recuperated from blood poisoning in 1854; the "Demolition Polka," celebrating the destruction of the city wall in 1857; and "In's Centrum Waltz," in honor of a sharp-shooting contest in 1880) exemplify only a few of his colorful commemorations of Vienna's history.

In addition to his music, the composer himself was recognized as one of Vienna's cultural assets. An article of 1891 acknowl-edged, "Strauss belongs to the institutions of our city, and visitors, who admire our monumental palaces, would give anything if they were allowed to visit the delicately built Johann Strauss as a Viennese attraction, open to the public on certain days of the week."[22] A similar sense of monumentality was invoked to describe the composer a few years later at his fiftieth Jubilee: "[people] celebrate the inseparable solidarity of the trio Strauss, 'old [St.] Stephen' and the 'Vienna Prater.'"[23] All three had become established emblems of Austria; placing Strauss in the company of two physical landmarks suggests his permanence in the Viennese imagination.

Strauss's stature as an internationally recognized symbol of Austria began in 1867 with the composition of the "Blue Danube Waltz" and its success at the World Exhibition in Paris that year. With this work his Viennese public felt they showed France that Austria, though no longer a military power, was still a significant cultural and musical force. Their self-consciousness about military might resulted from a difficult loss the previous year to the Prussians at Königgrätz. Austria and Prussia had long battled for supremacy in the German confederation, and events of the 1860s came to a head when they went to war over Silesia. The battle resulted not only in the loss of this province but of Venetia as well. Faced with the necessity of com-promise on many political fronts, it was a welcome relief for the Austrians to support Strauss and his music unequivocally. When he performed the "Blue Danube" at Princess Pauline Metternich's prestigious ball in Paris, newspapers were filled with the language of military victory. As Strauss's wife boasted, "Napoleon [III] had to dance to Johann's fiddle."[24]

A Hungarian journalist linked Strauss's career to current political events more explicitly after the premiere of *Eine Nacht in Venedig* (1883), comparing him to the Hungarian Minister for Foreign Affairs, Gyula Andrássy (1871–79): "[For the Viennese, Strauss is] the Andrássy of music, one who occupies entire societies with his notes, the Napoleon among composers, who conquers wherever his tones reach, who, if Andrássy could have convinced him, could have conquered Bosnia just by leading his orchestra, without drawing a sword."[25] The Austrian occupation of Bosnia in 1878, which attempted to fortify the Balkans against possible attack from Russians or Turks, was largely Andrássy's plan. As a Hungarian, he was imminently aware of potential threats from the east and worked diligently to protect the empire against Russian aggression. The occupation (and subsequent annexation in 1908) was viewed skeptically by most in the monarchy, however, for they feared any disruption of the delicate Austro-Hungarian dualist balance established in 1867. The utopian image of Strauss uniting disparate populations with his music recurred frequently in the press during these unsettling times.

His first two stage works, *Indigo* and *Carneval in Rom*, were written by Viennese librettists and expressly thematized Vienna. When journalists heard that Strauss was working for the first time on a libretto based on a French original (*Die Fledermaus*), they took it as just short of treason that he should "turn his back on the *Vaterstadt*."[26] Once the work was performed, however, it met enthusiastic support at home and abroad. Yet a skeptical reviewer questioned: "It remains to be more thoroughly discussed how much of [the work's success] is attributable to the good things about the operetta and how much to the popularity of the composer, as well as to the strongly expressed local patriotism aroused by a Viennese product."[27]

When *Prinz Methusalem* premiered at the Carltheater in 1877, *Kikeriki* similarly took issue with its compositional style:

Die neue Operette von Johann Strauss
Ist pikant,
Ist melodiös,
Ist voll Chic,
Ist ganz Offenbach und Lecocq,
Ist voll französischer Verve;
Sie ist aber nicht:
National,
Sie entbehrt: das heimatlich Gepräge,
Sie ist nicht: österreichisch
Und will uns eines hinwegdisputiren: den Johann Strauss.

[The new operetta from Johann Strauss
is piquant
is melodious
is very chic
is entirely Offenbach and Lecocq
is full of French verve;
however, it is not: national
it lacks: features of home
it is not: Austrian
and not, some might argue: Johann Strauss.][28]

The operetta included more parody than previous works, an element that *Kikeriki* felt was, or should be, foreign to an Austrian national style. It was also the only one of his works premiered at the Carltheater, which attracted a larger Jewish audience than other *Vorstadt* theaters. The anti-Semitic *Kikeriki* could hardly have approved of a work composed for that theater, even one by Strauss.

Later that year *Kikeriki* returned to the topic of nationality as expressed in operetta. In an article entitled "Viennese Authors as Copiers of the French," *Kikeriki* faults the Viennese for imitating their arch-rivals:

Why then does Strauss betray his idiom with such relish? Is our Austria so poor in historical figures that authors are forced to study the police reports of Paris precincts about French mistresses in order to come up with an interesting plot? . . . Celebrate our own country already – our own customs! . . . Why not? Because we are now in the often-discussed period of De-Viennization. We are, unfortunately, often ashamed of our homeland, instead of laudatory. We have been trained to deny ourselves our special characteristics. They want to teach us to be imitators of the French, fans of the Prussians – to break us of the habit of being Viennese![29]

The urban rivalry between Paris and Vienna, and international tensions between Prussians and Austrians, found a natural playing field on the operetta stage.

German critics, on the other hand, eagerly associated Strauss with their own cultural traditions. Paul Lindau, for example, claimed that "the art of Johann Strauss is as truly German as that of Schumann, and at the same time entirely unfeigned Austrian." Despite the concession to Strauss's Austrian heritage, Lindau concluded, "Strauss's music is for all Germans, wherever they may be, a true shibboleth abroad."[30] Austrian audiences, of course, would not have been so quick to ally Strauss's music with the Germans, as the reception of *Eine Nacht in Venedig* reveals. When Berlin rather than Vienna was favored with the work's premiere, a reporter surmised that "to renounce the upper hand in theatrical matters pains the Viennese more than the loss of hegemony in Germany."[31] Of the work's cool welcome in Berlin, a German journalist reported from Vienna: "As the first reports of the fate of Strauss's operetta in Berlin reached here last night, I wanted to telegraph immediately that the Austro-German alliance is seriously endangered, but my message was refused at the telegraph office for being too alarming. Still, I believe I did not exaggerate."[32] After the reception in Berlin, the Viennese felt compelled to demonstrate how much more they appreciated "their" Strauss. At the thundering ovation he received at the Viennese premiere a week later, *Die Presse* reported: "It was a moment of great historical character. A poor Berliner, who had begged a 30 fl. seat from a scalper in order to report to his countrymen the news of the battle's result, hid himself shamefully behind a stout patron and sobbed sorrowfully: 'We've been conquered!'"[33] Strauss and his work became a symbol of power and prestige equally as important in the popular imagination as territorial control or political alliances.

Some Austrians felt that the work's warm reception in Vienna, following its meager success in Berlin, compensated in some way for Austria's crushing loss to Germany in 1866. Several newspapers made this surprising comparison, including *Figaro*, which reported the comments of this Viennese spectator: "Seventeen years I've waited to take revenge for the defeat at Königgrätz! Seventeen full years it's lasted, but I haven't waited in vain . . . Sure, the text of the operetta seems a little messy, but that doesn't matter. I still didn't stop clapping and shouting Bravo! – because it had to do with our honor, the honor of Vienna and all Austria."[34] The show of national spirit and pride now reserved for sporting events once belonged to the realm of operetta.

As much enthusiasm as Strauss's local audience showed for his works, they demonstrated an equal degree of horror at rumors that he might abandon them. In order to marry his third wife, he had to relinquish his Austrian citizenship, and the Viennese were aghast at the thought that *their* Strauss could be anything but Austrian. (Since Adele was Jewish and he was a married Catholic, he was required to divorce – legally impossible in Austria at the time – and both had to convert to Protestantism for their marriage to be recognized.) Newspapers frequently speculated about the reasons behind their various trips to Hungary in 1884–85. As one reported under the title "Strucz Janos": "Johnny – that true 'Viennese child', Maestro Strauss, who is rooted with every fiber in Vienna and whose blood flows from a warm Viennese heart – is becoming a Magyar and has sought Hungarian citizenship. Johann Strauss, only 30 percent Austrian – it sounds almost unbelievable, yet it may be so."[35] In fact, Strauss accomplished his goal by gaining German citizenship in 1888, which, curiously, did not seem to irritate the Viennese as much as if he had merely crossed the Leitha to the other side of the empire. They accepted his nationality along the lines of German cultural heritage more easily than surrendering him to the politically and economically threatening Hungarians.

Years later, Strauss was compared to another "Viennese child," Mayor Karl Lueger.[36] This unlikely comparison should be quoted at length, for it represents the equal status that Viennese granted their cultural and political leaders:

> Strauss and Lueger. These two names are probably surprised to find themselves together, spoken in one breath . . . [they] embody the light and shadow of the Viennese *Volk* character. At one and the same time it will be fifty years since Strauss's first song and since Lueger's first cry were heard. On the same day will be the great premiere of *Jabuka* [Strauss's operetta of 1894] and the publication of the anti-Semitic festival program.
>
> . . . Of course, besides the anniversary, they have little in common. Both are certainly rulers of the masses; the one like the other inspires and causes movement: one movement is the graceful dance, the other the movement of anti-Semitism; they also have in common the ingratiating manner of the Viennese. Yet besides their external commonalities, only opposites emerge in their anniversaries. . . . Strauss is the Viennese genius of harmony, Lueger the Viennese demon of disharmony.
>
> . . . The differences, like the similarities, have their roots in one soil. They are two sides of the same coin. The kindness of a Strauss, the unkindness of a Lueger lie folded together in the Viennese manner. We can see united here the winning fun and the mean bitterness of Viennese children.[37]

Despite their apparent differences, Strauss and Lueger were united in their devotion to – and evocation of – Vienna.

Two words often used to describe Lueger, as well as Strauss and his music, are "natural" and "true" (*echt*), adjectives that reveal undercurrents of nationalism when compared to those like "artificial," frequently used for French operetta composers. In a full-page notice for Strauss's unsuccessful *Blindekuh* (1878), *Der Floh* noted: "Strauss is to most French composers as a truly loving girl is to a coquette. What is art for the others is for him nature, true unadulterated nature."[38] Hanslick used both adjectives in his review of *Der Zigeunerbaron*: "Everything is authentically [*echt*] and naturally felt, the sentiments conveyed by simple means, and the characterizations are never contorted into the bizarre or ugly."[39] *Der Floh* again characterized Strauss's music as "natural" after his foray into the Court Opera, reclaiming Strauss for the *Vorstadt* theaters: "He is a king rooted in the *Volk*, a completely natural artist. The atmosphere of a court opera dampens his mood, constrains his verve, cramps his unrestrained naturalness."[40] As the *Wiener Tagblatt* attested in dialect: "His waltzes are the surest, most unselfish, and most tactful matchmaker, and the folks in the crown lands understand his language just as well as the Beduins do."[41]

The adjectives "cosmopolitan" and "artificial" were regularly applied to the Jewish population as well as the French. These two categories overlap, of course, in Offenbach, to whom Strauss was often compared. Not only did music critics like Hanslick, Ludwig Speidel, and – later – Theodor Adorno evaluate the two composers' works but the general press also weighed their merits and deficiencies, often with an explicitly anti-Semitic bias. A cartoon published soon after the premiere of Strauss's first operetta shows a hanging scale weighing Strauss and Offenbach against each other. One end of the scale drags the ground with Strauss holding his violin and the score to *Indigo*, while Offenbach dangles from the other side of the scale even though he holds his baton and scores to several operettas, while three Jews try to weigh him down by his feet and coat-tails.[42]

As active as the Jewish population was in business, music, and theater, Vienna's general population remained almost 90 percent Catholic throughout the nineteenth century. The "interpenetration of religion with worldliness" that typified many Austrian intellectual achievements could also be found in operetta, not only in the works themselves but in the esteem in which Strauss was held by the public at large.[43] Emphasizing their regard for the composer, several authors described him in religious terms, including his one-time librettist, Victor Léon: "Even more than for most people in Vienna, Johann Strauss was for us young people in the profession something like the Pope . . . This genius enthroned at the peaks was for us – I'm really not exaggerating – almost a divinity."[44] On the centennial of Strauss's birth in 1925, another journal reported: "The Viennese celebrate their Johann Strauss as one of their great men, but that is too limited; Johann Strauss was more than a great artist, more than a genial Waltz King, he was a Viennese Messiah, one blessed by God, who expressed Viennese-ness [*Wienertum*] in music, made it wonderful and immortal."[45] In a literal sense, Strauss was idolized by his Viennese public, during his life and long after his death.

Religious metaphors also arise regularly in connection with his works. Alexander Dumas, *fils* recalled that

> in my youth I passionately loved the dance and particularly the waltz. I have, therefore, swung others and myself around quite a bit, under the enchanting magic of the music by Johann Strauss. But very often it happened that my partner and I would pause in order to listen to this music and follow the eternity of dreams that it aroused in us. It seemed to us almost a desecration to allow such melodies to be used for physical pleasure.[46]

Max Kalbeck wrote an extended analogy of the creation in Genesis to parallel the genesis of *Der Zigeunerbaron*,[47] and at the Berlin premiere of *Eine Nacht in Venedig*, a Viennese reporter observed, "For the Berliners [Strauss] is a famous, a world-famous man, but not flesh of their flesh, not blood of their blood."[48] Both religion and operetta were a matter of ritual and self-identity to the Viennese; little wonder, then, that they could be juxtaposed in the popular imagination.

ANTI-SEMITISM AND JEWISH IDENTITY

Vienna's precarious relationship with its Jewish population dates back to the Middle Ages and became increasingly problematic during the last thirty years of the nineteenth century, when political parties began to organize themselves around issues of German nationalism and anti-Semitism. Scholarship on the subject is large and growing, yet few studies have examined representations of Jews on the popular stage or Jewish participation in the production of operetta.[49] Primary sources, however, offer plentiful evidence of the connection between popular theater and the Jewish population; the weekly newspapers *Kikeriki* and *Der Floh*, for example, both exhibit blatantly anti-Semitic agendas with frequent caricatures of theater audiences full of businessmen with crooked noses, small eyeglasses, and balding foreheads. *Der Floh* even featured a regular column of "German-Jewish Theater Letters" (*deutsch-jüdische Theaterbriefe*), fictional letters to the editor regarding theater finances or visiting Jewish performers like Sarah Bernhardt, along with satirical, anti-Semitic columns by Ludwig Bösendorfer. These sources reflected, but also created and reinforced, the link between operetta and the Jews.

Jews indeed comprised a large percentage of operetta audiences and funded, often speculatively, many theaters and productions. Like the Secession artists, whose style was known as *le goût juif* not because of the artists but because of their patrons,[50] leading nineteenth-century Viennese operetta composers and librettists were not Jewish, yet operetta gradually gained a reputation as a Jewish business. After the turn of the century, operetta became more closely associated with Jewish composers: Leo Fall, Edmund Eysler, Oscar Straus, and Emmerich Kálmán were all of Jewish descent.[51] But these representatives of the "Silver Age" of Viennese operetta differ from their predecessors in this respect.

Jewish stereotypes could readily be found on the Viennese suburban stage, where actors, such as Martin Kräuser at the Theater in der Josefstadt, specialized in performing and extemporizing such roles.[52] Suppé's *Schöne Galathee* includes an art enthusiast by the name of Mydas, portrayed by Karl Treumann as a caricature of a *jüdelnde* Viennese banker.[53] Josephine Gallmeyer's parody *Sarah und Bernhardt* includes patently Jewish characters like Sarah, Aron, and the old Kohn, but Gallmeyer instructed that the performers were not to exaggerate their Jewishness (*nicht judeln*).[54] This comment does not indicate, however, that their Jewish characterization would have eluded a contemporary audience. On the contrary, her instruction closely echoes that of Wagner, who stated "that 'there must be *nothing approaching caricature*' in Mime's appearance"[55] [Wagner's emphasis], though Mime was widely recognized as an anti-Semitic parody. These stage directions, which contradict the actual characterizations, demonstrate "the psychological function of the aesthetic representation of the Jew" for Austro-German audiences, "because in formulating such a wish, [Wagner and Gallmeyer] sought to efface the image of the Jew as a cultural construct, insisting instead that it was true to life and 'real.'"[56]

Strauss never created the extended caricatures of Wagner and Gallmeyer, but such figures function as minor characters in several of his works. In the Act III opening chorus of *Indigo*, various professions are represented in a market scene: fishwife, slave dealer, barber, basketweaver. Among these professions is a clothing salesman and tailor, labeled a *Kleiderjude*, who sells the most fashionable European clothes and top hats; the chorus exclaims, "See his hat, it suits him well! The tailor is a Jew!" [Seht den Hut – der steht ihm gut! Der Schneider ist ein Jud'!]. Jewish characters also appear in *Die Fledermaus* and *Der Zigeunerbaron*, as we will see in following chapters.

Authorities occasionally advised composers to tone down explicit Jewish parody. Strauss modified *Simplicius* at the censor's demand, changing a "Judenszene" to involve "Slovakian farmers" instead of Jews. Millöcker also, on Director Jauner's advice, changed his "Juden-Polka" to the "Bettelstudenten-Polka" at the last minute.[57] A review of Strauss's second operetta, *Carneval in Rom*, commended it for "only sparingly and seldom offend[ing] people with a Greek view of life"[58] – a euphemism derived from a general association with the east and the superficial similarity between a rabbi's traditional robes and the flowing Greek dress.

The only Strauss work whose title suggests a Jewish topic, *Prinz Methusalem*, was also the only one to be premiered at the Carltheater.[59] The theater was located in the Leopoldstadt, the district with the highest concentration of Jewish residents in Vienna; in fact, the district's Jewish population increased at the end of the century from 29.6 percent in 1880 to 36.4 percent by 1900.[60] French operetta, a staple of the theater's repertoire, was closely associated with Judaism in the Viennese imagination, not because of Jewish characters (which rarely appear in French operetta) but because of Offenbach, who is invariably portrayed in Viennese caricatures with a conspicuously crooked nose and small eyeglasses. The popularity and frequent guest appearances of Sarah Bernhardt in Vienna also reinforced the connection between Jewish entertainers and France. Cultural chauvinism and nationalism led to the general association of Judaism with things French (frequently described as artificial, cosmopolitan, and derivative) as opposed to Austrian (natural, *völkisch*, and true).

Although his Jewish characterizations are generally subtle, Strauss brought anti-Semitism to his music more overtly at least once when he sketched a "satiric waltz song" (designated as such in the Vienna City library catalogue) with an anti-Semitic text.[61] The song mentions Vöslau, a fashionable Jewish spa near Baden, and Strauss's summer home in Schönau. He may have written the text himself, for it is in his hand and no author's name accompanies it. No date appears on the sketch, but based on his residence at Schönau, which he bought in 1880,[62] it probably dates from that decade or later. The piece is ternary, and text to the A sections reads:

> Weitsichtig sein im Vöslauer Wald
> Wo Alles von Jargon wiederhallt
> Wo die Frauen sind von einer Klasse
> Die man nennt die schöne Rasse.
> D'rum vorsichtig sei im Vöslauer Wald
> Wo Alles von gebog'nen Nasen wiederstrahlt
> Vorsichtig sei im Vöslauer Wald
> Wo Alles von gebog'nen Nasen wiederstrahlt.

> [Look around you in the Vöslau Woods
> Where everything rings with jargon,
> Where the women are from a class
> That one calls the beautiful race.
> Therefore, be careful in the Vöslau Woods
> Where everything beams with crooked noses . . .]

The C major waltz is simple, regular, and similar to any Strauss melody before its development and orchestration. It is unclear if this song was ever finished or performed; however, the B section is marked "unused," indicating that perhaps the A section was indeed performed on some occasion.

Strauss's personal relationship to Judaism was a complicated one. His third wife, Adele Strauss (1856–1930), was a young Jewish widow (her first husband's name was also Strauss, no relation to the composer). She had been a family friend and was quick to offer emotional support after Strauss's second wife left him; the pair was inseparable from the fall of 1882 until the end of his life. She became a financial and artistic advisor, much as his first wife had been, although she could not offer the first-hand musical experience of her predecessor. For various reasons, Adele was not well liked by the Viennese public. It was for her that Strauss abandoned his two most overt links to Vienna: his Austrian citizenship and his Catholicism. The Viennese feared, not unreasonably, that Strauss would leave Vienna altogether on her account. Adele was fiercely protective of his interests and guarded his legacy with a careful editorial eye. The following newspaper criticism is representative of the public attitude toward her:

> It must deeply hurt the Master's truest friends and admirers to have to stand by while the genial man is genuinely whipped on [*hineingepeitscht*] to an activity for which he has no personal motivation, by a female ambition whose goals are more social than artistic. Granted, female ambition that spurs an artist to create is a powerful and undeniable factor – but, as has already been mentioned, this must be an understanding, really artistic ambition, as he was blessed with in the unforgettable Henrietta *Treffz*, – the excellent Lieder singer, who had such a true and strong musical nature at her disposal – who stood at her genial husband's side as a true lifelong artistic partner. As generous and inspiring as such an artistic and understanding female ambition is, just as damaging and dangerous is the female ambition that goads one at any cost to unnatural and feverish production, and under whose drive works like *Ritter Pásmán* and [*Fürstin*] *Ninetta* are forced into a pathetic stage life.[63]

Typical anti-Semitic slurs emerge in the comparison of the greedy, ambitious Adele with the "natural" and "true" (*echt*) Henrietta.

Strauss himself was of Jewish origin: his father's grandfather was Jewish, making Strauss, Sr. one-fourth and Strauss, Jr. one-eighth Jewish. Contemporaries may have been unaware of his ancestry, but when genealogical researchers discovered it after the *Anschluß*, an alarm sounded through the ranks of the Nazi hierarchy. Under racial laws, his music would not have been banned, but his father's would. Goebbels authorized the birth records to be falsified, and after they had been sent to Berlin, doctored photocopies were returned to the archives at St. Stephen's. Only years after the end of the war did the truth come to light.[64] Baptized and twice-married in the Catholic church, Strauss was unobservant of and unconcerned with his Jewish heritage.

In the late 1880s, after he and Adele had both converted to Protestantism, Strauss wrote his (Jewish) friend Josef Simon a curious letter in which he rehearses various religious stereotypes. Following disagreements with Adele he complained:

> To give an eye for an eye is forbidden to me by a Christian – (or, I don't know at all anymore which religion I belong to) feeling, although in my heart I've become more Jewish than Protestant – while Adele finds them both too nice to reconcile. When it comes to giving out money, she honors the Mosaic traditions – in everything else she agrees more with *Protest*antism. You will understand how I, as a good-hearted Jew, always get the short end of the stick under these conditions.[65]

In another letter to Simon, who lived in Prague, Strauss joked about the prominent Jewish population of that city: "As long as you all don't have a St. Stephen's spire, Prague is worth nothing. What would a Stephen's spire be in Prague? If you built a Samuel's spire, then Prague would be famous . . . Nothing is as good as the women of Prague. They understand immediately!! Such a Prague Jewess! The best!!!"[66] In both of these examples Strauss alludes, with little sense of irony, to prevailing cultural stereotypes. Despite differences in his and Adele's religious backgrounds, and despite the lengths to which both went to alter their faiths, nowhere does he reflect seriously on religion or his own spirituality.

STRAUSS IN THE TWENTIETH CENTURY

All Vienna once sang and danced to Strauss's waltzes, in Strauss's music the old Austria can be found . . .   *Karl Kobald* (1925)

Johann Strauss stands among us. He belongs to us because he is a part of all of us, because he embodies a piece of the German spirit.

Kurt Arnold Findeisen (1941)

Strauss's music and personality have retained their significance for Austrians throughout the twentieth century. Especially during the economically depressed period after World War I, the Viennese clung to Strauss as a source of identity and reassurance. The gilded monument to him in the City Park, erected in 1921, inspired these thoughts from the *Neue Freie Presse*:

> Johann Strauss is also a political figure . . . Through Johann Strauss, more than any other figure, Vienna has become known and loved throughout the world, and in his empire reigns truly eternal peace, a people moving happily to the heart-warming, all-conquering, irresistible harmony . . . Even if the enemy takes everything from us, they must leave us Johann Strauss and his waltzes. That is our political statement for the day.[67]

Although Austria had recently lost her empire, the figure of this musician evoked the feeling of peaceful rule over a happy, unified population, a utopia he created repeatedly through his dance music and, more explicitly, through his stage works.

Strauss's music continued to play a leading role during the interwar period as Austria suffered economic hardships and political instability. One unifying element was the newly invented radio. The Austrian radio station, RAVAG, began broadcasting in October 1926, and a large percentage of its programming was devoted to "light" music. Not only were Strauss concerts and stage works broadcast live from the State Opera and other venues, but the radio sponsored studio productions of Strauss operettas infrequently seen on stage. The program guide, *Radio Wien*, included articles about a variety of musical figures, including Strauss and his works. At the conclusion of one such article, biographer Siegfried Loewy reminded his readers, "Johann Strauss has now rested in the heavens for thirty years – his memory is unscathed, his name shines like a powerful ruby in glowing sunlight and the Viennese are proud to be able to say: He not only *was* ours – he *is* ours!"[68]

In the 1933/34 season, RAVAG planned celebrations of both Richard and Johann Strauss; Richard Strauss's seventieth birthday was marked with broadcasts of all his orchestral music, while the sixtieth anniversary of *Die Fledermaus* was recognized with a two-year cycle of all Strauss's operettas, many of which had not been performed since the nineteenth century.[69] The technological advances of the radio provided a new means of uniting the population in a celebration of its collective musical heritage.

Strauss's works also proved to be astonishingly durable in the newly installed Nazi regime. Immediately following the *Anschluß* of 12 March 1938, the press urged the public to continue attending the theater: "It is the duty of every German comrade to participate actively in this significant cultural event by frequent theater attendance."[70] Strauss's stage works were among those officially supported by the new regime; during the Reich Theater Festival Week of 1938, *Der Zigeunerbaron* joined *Der Rosenkavalier*, *The Marriage of Figaro*, and *Lohengrin* on the official program. Wagner and both Strausses remained constant figures in the following year's Festival, which included performances of *Eine Nacht in Venedig*, *Friedenstag*, *Tannhäuser*, and Handel's *Julius Caesar*.[71] The general public had no access to these festival performances, however; tickets were reserved for dignitaries, government officials, and representatives of the press at home and abroad. Nonetheless, Strauss's operettas took their place alongside highly regarded works of "high art" as representative of the new German cultural ideal.

Biographies of Strauss published during the Nazi period reflect the reigning anti-Semitic ideology. In the index of Erich Schenk's *Johann Strauß* (1940), those figures "of Jewish heritage" are indicated by an asterisk. When reviewing the contributions of previous biographers, Schenk acknowledged the work of "the Jew [Ernst] Decsey."[72] Another biographer cited Strauss and *Die Fledermaus* as evidence of the victorious struggle against Jewish excesses:

> That Strauss, with his *Fledermaus*, also accomplished two lasting cultural-political achievements, should at least be explained here in brief: with his healthy, native music grown from the depth of the *Volk* he eliminated from the field the sultry, thoroughly morally depraved operetta magic with which the Jew Jean Jacques [*sic*] Offenbach of Paris amazed the West. He belongs, then, to the fighters who have helped conquer the racially foreign and destructive elements in music.[73]

The Nazi administration that expediently annexed Bruckner symphonies and Schubert Lieder found Strauss's works equally useful in representing a "healthy" native German ideology.[74]

Just as Strauss was regarded as a unifying figure during his own lifetime, he was again used in this capacity by the National Socialists to smooth the unification between Austria and the German Reich:

> We live today in harder, more virile times than those when Johann Strauss, the waltz king, wandered among mortals. Austria has, in the meantime, returned to the Reich. Austria, its shimmering homeland [*Mutterland*], that it loves from all four chambers of its heart like a beautiful woman, and over whose coming fate it has great worries . . . Johann Strauss stands among us. He belongs to us because he is a part of us all, because he embodies a piece of the German spirit.[75]

This author personifies Germany as masculine, Austria as feminine, and Strauss as a means of reconciling the two.

Strauss's music, like Austria itself, survived the Third Reich and continues to be performed regularly in Vienna. The annual New Year's Eve performances of *Die Fledermaus* at the State Opera began in the 1930s and continue to this day. The Strauss concert heard in the Musikverein on New Year's Day is also a tradition dating back to the beginning of World War II. Clemens Krauss conducted an all-Strauss concert on 31 December 1939, and in the years following the war the concert was set on the following day. Today this event reaches millions of television viewers around the world. Strauss's gilded statue still welcomes visitors to the City Park, and his childhood home in the Leopoldstadt, renovated in 1995, is now open to the public as a museum. Finally, 1999 brought special performances and recordings, museum exhibitions, and publications celebrating the 150th anniversary of Strauss, Sr.'s death and the centennial of Strauss, Jr.'s death.[76] Few popular composers can claim such a long heritage of devoted listeners as Johann Strauss, but what has made his music appeal to generation after generation? The following chapters will seek to answer that question.

4 | From ballroom to theater: musical style and *Indigo und die vierzig Räuber*

We ourselves are these melodies; what we laugh and cry, what we feel and dream, that is hidden in Strauss's music.[1]

During the first twenty-five years of his career as a dance musician, Strauss developed a distinctive compositional voice, and although the requirements of dance music and stage music differ considerably, many characteristics of Strauss's style moved from ballroom to theater unchanged. None of the elements that contribute to the "Strauss sound" – prevalent diatonicism, conventional phrase rhythm, and standard dance forms – is particularly notable, yet his music is eminently engaging and unmistakably his own. The following discussion explores the combination of rhythmic, melodic, instrumental, and structural traits that he synthesized into a unique personal style.

In Strauss's operettas, the most salient vestige of his family background and earlier career is his preference for dance forms, especially the waltz. This dance had come to be associated with Vienna as early as the Congress of Vienna in 1815, and before the century was out, the Strauss name became as inextricably tied to the genre as it was to the city. Like his father, Strauss conducted hundreds of balls at court and in the homes of the Viennese aristocracy, as well as dances in *Heuriger* and other entertainment establishments. Through personal experience he was familiar with Viennese behavior in such situations and replicated that atmosphere in his operettas, where his fidelity to Viennese social and musical customs allowed local audiences to recognize themselves on stage.

Dance forms require regularity, and most of Strauss's music appears simple in construction, an impression that is achieved, however, only through considerable skill and experience. In addition to his music's practical function, in theater and ballroom, it had the ideological function of conveying a feeling of (temporary) social unification. As Robert Walser has written about more recent popular music, "the musical construction of simplicity plays an important part in many kinds of ideological representations, from the depiction of pastoral refuges from modernity to constructions of race and gender."[2] Strauss's simplicity represented a unified, happy population, all whirling in time with one another. A waltz, for example, evoked different associations for each social class (from a private formal ball to a public beer garden), but it evoked some association for everyone, an effect that would not hold true for most genres of concert music. Thus, a waltz like "Trinke, Liebchen" (*Die Fledermaus*, Act I) could effectively appeal to a range of ages and social strata, all united for the moment simply by virtue of their common Austrian (or Viennese) heritage. Strauss's music became popular at precisely the time the empire was experiencing great internal stress. Since the spinning step of the waltz creates a centrifugal force between the two partners, it requires that they cling to each other with equal or greater force if they are not to be flung apart – an apt analogy for the social and political changes the empire experienced at the end of the nineteenth century.

One of the ways Strauss created the impression of simplicity was through predictable phrasing, rarely abandoning a regular phrase structure in any of his music (see chapter 7 for exceptions). Unlike his colleague Offenbach, who never composed exclusively for the ballroom, Strauss created music that is almost invariably balanced in 16- or 32-measure sections made up of 8-bar phrases. An introduction or coda might vary from this model, but dancers and audiences could rely on a 4-plus-4 phrase rhythm. In his stage music, phrases may be repeated, but usually the repetition differs from the original statement in some respect, either in accompanimental pattern or instrumentation.

He also achieved simplicity by consistently using a single form for his ballroom waltzes, modified for use on stage. A short introduction, sometimes in duple meter, either establishes the key of the first waltz or, more often, leads to the dominant of the first waltz's tonic key. Any allusion to the dance's title is frequently found only in the introduction. For example, the zither plays in the introduction and coda to "Geschichten aus dem Wienerwald" ["Tales from the Vienna Woods"], not in the body of the dance; the introduction to the "Kaiserwalzer" ["Emperor Waltz"] is a march; and "Rosen aus dem Süden" ["Roses from the South"] begins in the 6/8 meter common to Italian gondolier songs. The body of the piece comprises a series of four or five waltzes, each with two sections (performed either AB or ABA). The waltzes follow one another in closely related keys with a brief interlude occasionally effecting a modulation from one waltz to the next. Strauss was sophisticated among his colleagues for including harmonic transitions of any kind; overtures and dances by Millöcker or Carl Michael Ziehrer, for example, are highly sectional and rarely have transitional material. The first waltz (and sometimes each subsequent waltz as well) often begins with one bar marked *poco ritardando*, played by the violins alone or in unison with other instruments. The set of waltzes always concludes with a coda in which two or more of the waltz melodies are recapitulated, usually in their original keys. If the number of melodies per waltz (usually ten) is multiplied by the number of waltzes (around 200) that Strauss composed prior to 1871, the evidence of his melodic invention, even before he reached the theater, is overwhelming.

Strauss preferred conducting waltzes for his stage orchestra just as he did his dance orchestras, with violin in hand. Late in life he lamented: "If only I could still play the violin, then at least I could show what a waltz ought to be! But to conduct a waltz with the baton in hand is too dumb!"[3] Subtle agogic rhythms, as well as the dance's overall character, could be better conveyed to the orchestra and co-ordinated through Strauss's body language while holding a violin than a baton. Critics often praised the dances in production numbers as Strauss's most successful writing for the stage; even Hanslick admonished Strauss's librettists for not creating more opportunities for his dance music to shine. He felt that too many of his operettas indulged in the fashion for exoticism; instead of scenes requiring Viennese dance music, characters found themselves in Spain (*Das*

Spitzentuch der Königin), Italy (*Carneval in Rom, Eine Nacht in Venedig*), or Hungary (*Der Zigeunerbaron*) where the waltz was out of place.

Strauss's overtures and entr'actes resemble his waltz codas and introductions in that they offer a potpourri of melodies from the larger work. Like most overtures, his were composed after the bulk of the composition was finished and were closely linked to the larger work.[4] As his career progressed, his waltz introductions became longer and his overtures shorter until, after the mid-1880s, his overtures had the character of a brief introduction rather than an extended preview of the work. His most finely crafted and frequently performed overture is that from *Die Fledermaus*. Although superior to most in invention and construction, it is instructive for its use of several techniques that recur throughout his career.

The *Fledermaus* overture includes six melodies, each reflecting a sentiment that will be more explicitly associated with it later in the operetta (melancholy, frivolity, flirtation, etc.). It offers a variety of textures and dance genres, from waltz to can-can, but all sections are joined by some kind of harmonic modulation, if only a common tone. Strauss makes an obviously programmatic gesture soon after the overture's introduction, as bells interrupt the galloping texture with six slow strokes, a preview of the Act II conclusion when various party guests must leave at the clock's stroke of 6 a.m. Although later overtures follow a similar pattern, few are as tightly constructed or as well integrated with the rest of the operetta.

Strauss's melodic style in the *Fledermaus* overture and elsewhere features several distinguishing traits. Unlike Offenbach's predominantly scalar style, most of Strauss's melodies include leaps of some kind that are often quite wide. Indeed, many of his melodies seem better suited to the violin than to the voice. The defining melodic characteristic of his music is the emphasis on the sixth scale degree (*la*), especially when supported by the tonic triad. The use of the sixth scale degree as the most prominent melodic note has precedents in Austrian folksong and Schubert's piano music, but Strauss makes it an indispensable feature of his melodic writing. Although scale degree 6 is emphasized in folk music, it is rarely harmonized with the tonic triad, a device that lends his music its yearning, slightly melancholy quality, since the anticipated resolution occurs only briefly, if at all. One well-known example comes from the "Blue Danube Waltz" (see the last measures of Example 4.1), but further examples may be found in almost any of Strauss's music.

Die Fledermaus contains some of his most easily grasped melodies, a characteristic for which he continually strove. The most famous melodies rarely span more than an octave, frequently repeat material, and are based on the dominant-tonic harmonic axis. These qualities also characterize the yodeling-style refrains of Viennese folksongs, and Strauss imitates this style in several popular works ("Brüderlein" from *Die Fledermaus* or Barinkay's entrance song in *Der Zigeunerbaron*). Ascending leaps of sixths, easily executed on the violin, are typical of his style and of traditional Austrian folk music. In this idiom the melody does not usually move in one direction (ascending or descending a triad) but reverses itself. Even when Strauss borrows the rustic yodel for nostalgic effect, however, it is relatively urbane and stylized in comparison to similar passages by his contemporaries Millöcker or Carl Zeller.

While honing his gift for melody, the young Strauss also received solid training in harmony, counterpoint, and figured bass from Josef Drechsler, Music Director at St. Stephen's Cathedral. (Suppé, who studied theory and composition with Simon Sechter, was probably the only one of his colleagues to have received comparable contrapuntal training.) Strauss's extant exercises demonstrate a thorough grasp of the rudiments of chord progressions and resolutions, along with correct voice leading, fundamental training that served him well throughout his career.[5] Although his music is unquestionably melodically driven, supporting material was conceived not just as harmonic filler but as independent contrapuntal lines. The best example of his contrapuntal thinking, as well as his adherence to a traditional style, is the canon in Act II of *Die Fledermaus*, when the party guests sing the eight-bar opening of "Brüderlein" in a four-part round. By the 1890s he had somewhat relaxed his contrapuntal standards. To his brother Eduard he reasoned: "No one cares anymore

Example 4.1 "An der schönen blauen Donau" (1867)

today about parallel 5ths – they're also impossible to discover – because in a large ensemble no musical ear is in a position to pick them out – they can at most be found on paper. Tempi passati! A vocal piece is the only exception."[6]

In addition to Strauss's ear for counterpoint, his sure sense of instrumentation contributes to his distinctive sound. Most strikingly, the first violins play the melody more often than any other instrument, an orchestrational choice reflecting Strauss's habit of leading the ensemble with his own instrument. Had he relegated the first violins to an accompanimental figure, he would have been less successful at imparting the appropriate tempo and tone of the work. Other instruments (cello, flute, or clarinet) may join the violins to lend various colors, but almost every melody seems to have been conceived for the violin.[7] He rarely doubles the entire violin melody with another instrument throughout. Instead, he highlights individual phrases with various instruments, or two instruments (clarinet and oboe, for example) alternate in doubling the melody.[8] The writing for violin is highly idiomatic; he had a secure grasp of the range of his instrument and created runs and double- or triple-stops that sounded more impressive than they were difficult. He also used pizzicato and *col legno* playing for special effects. The opening scene of *Die Fledermaus*, for example, when Alfred serenades Rosalinde from the street outside her window, simulates the sound of a guitar through pizzicato strings and harp accompaniment.

His fine sense of instrumentation was praised by critics, composers, and performers alike. On the occasion of *Der Zigeunerbaron*'s premiere, Max Kalbeck, theater critic and *Jabuka* librettist, commented: "Strauss handles the orchestra with the modesty that characterizes a distinguished musician; he values the meaning and character of the instruments too highly to single out an obvious one or to exploit it in the sense of a pedestrian effect against its nature. All things considered, though, he values nothing more than the human voice, which he always shows the greatest respect."[9] Singers may disagree with Kalbeck's assessment, but he was here not so much referring to Strauss's melodic style as subtly juxtaposing his vocal music to that of the Wagnerians, most of whom required singers to contend with a full orchestra. Strauss's orchestrational style, on the other hand, was more akin to that of Mozart, as Brahms once observed.[10]

Although many dance and operetta composers allowed their works to be orchestrated by others, Strauss opposed this practice for his own works, noting to his publisher Simrock that he had never allowed anyone else to orchestrate his dances. He further insisted, if any dance music from his operettas were extracted, arranged, and published, that the name of the arranger and orchestrator appear prominently on the title page, claiming that "it cannot be assumed that anyone else understands better than I how to handle a dance effectively for orchestra, much less choose more suitable themes and their order of appearance."[11] For Strauss, instrumentation was a compositional choice equal in importance to melody or harmony.

One aspect of operetta composition to which he had rarely been exposed during his career as a dance musician was working with text. Some of his waltzes, including the "Blue Danube," originally included chorus, but Strauss never composed Lieder and only rarely composed choral pieces prior to his operetta career. In fact, he composed some of his most successful operetta numbers before having seen the libretto. Although such a practice seems unlikely to yield acceptable results, his regular phraseology easily lends itself to verse, and many of his rhythms naturally fit the Viennese speech pattern. In some cases, however, the text setting is awkward despite a coherent musical thought, suggesting a librettist's struggle to accommodate his text to preexisting music.

Despite a proven compositional facility, Strauss was well aware that additional skills were necessary to compose successfully for the theater. His musical style remained unchanged at first, for which audiences were grateful, but the process of accommodating narrative, actors, and *mise en scène* was entirely new to him. His dedication and hard work were amply rewarded, however, when his first efforts brought him far more than an *Achtungserfolg* (a polite success). Strauss had always been a quick study, and he benefited from experienced professionals who smoothed his path from the ballroom to the theater.

TRANSITION TO THE THEATER

Here we dance and make music, go to the theater and hear Strauss, and, with him, stick our heads in the sands of coziness.[12]   *Theodor Billroth*

From his very first operetta, Strauss encountered an audience intimately familiar with his work. They adored his dance music, and his career as a ballroom musician shaped many of their expectations and reactions to his work as a stage composer. These expectations were both helpful and limiting, for just as listeners enthusiastically greeted any hint of a dance, they easily grew impatient and were reluctant at times to accept anything else. Some loyal fans insisted on viewing him through the familiar lens of local folk tradition; *Die Presse* reported, for example: "The romantic names [in *Indigo und die vierzig Räuber*] should not alienate us, they are only carnival masks behind which perhaps a Pepi and a Sepperl hide, and neither one has the urge to betray Schwender's *Lokal*, although they also flirt with the grand opera."[13] The Viennese required time to adjust to the idea of Strauss in the theater, where they could not dance spontaneously as they could at balls, in restaurants, or in *Volksgarten* concerts, the venues where he established his career. Hanslick reported of Strauss's first theater performance: "In the middle of the overture when a Pied-Piper-ish polka theme appeared, the unheard-of occurred when the balcony immediately broke out into jubilant applause: apparently people dreamed they were in the *Volksgarten*."[14] These representative comments suggest the liminal space his operettas occupied between the theater stage and musical life at large, a boundary that remained more permeable for him than for any of his contemporaries.

Strauss owed much of his initiative to strike out on a new compositional path to his first wife, Henrietta "Jetty" Treffz, an accomplished professional singer in her own right. She suggested that Strauss begin composing for the stage for two reasons. First, his health could not bear the demanding schedule of a professional performer. The late hours and constant travel, in addition to the stress of fulfilling commissions, had stretched his endurance to the limit. Second, the system of compensation was far less favorable for dance music than for stage works. While publishers bought each dance for a one-time fee, theaters paid composers royalties for each performance, including those in foreign countries. Millöcker's financial records, for example, show that he profited significantly from worldwide performances of his most successful operettas.[15] In addition to this regular income, composers negotiated for a percentage of the profits from certain benefit performances, usually anniversaries of the work's premiere (twenty-fifth performance, fiftieth performance, etc.).

Composers also profited from the fact that dance music composed for the stage could also be sold to publishers for the usual fees. From his first operetta, Strauss culled nine individual pieces for dance and concert use: he made 16,000 fl. for the stage work and an additional 10,000 fl. selling the dances to his publisher, Spina,[16] thereby increasing the profits generated from the stage work by more than half. (Only three years earlier Strauss had sold the "Blue Danube Waltz" for only 250 fl., a sum the publisher immediately recouped many times over.[17]) An operetta composer was obligated, however, to withhold individual pieces from general performance by dance orchestras until after the stage work's premiere. In the 1890s Strauss warned his brother Eduard that he must be sure to bring the parts to a new entr'acte home with him from St. Petersburg since Strauss would have trouble with his publisher and the theater director if the music became more widely available before the work's premiere.[18]

Despite the obvious financial advantages, Strauss was not immediately persuaded that his compositional talents were suitable for the stage. Jetty secretly took some of his dances to Theater an der Wien director Maximilian Steiner, who put text to them, convincing Strauss with the final product. Steiner secured a libretto for him, and soon thereafter Strauss began work on Josef Braun's *Die lustige Weiber von Wien* [The Merry Wives of Vienna] but never completed the operetta.[19] Apparently, Strauss had hoped Josephine Gallmeyer would assume the main female role, but she was not a regular member of the Theater an der Wien; in fact, her arch-rival, Marie Geistinger, was co-director of the theater. When Gallmeyer declined the role, Strauss refused to give it to anyone else and withdrew the work. No score to *Die lustige Weiber* survives, although he undoubtedly reused its music for other purposes.

Nonetheless, Geistinger and Steiner signed a two-year contract with Strauss on 26 May 1870. It granted the theater exclusive rights to all his stage works written during that period, including the operetta on which he was already at work, *Ali Baba (Indigo)*. For each evening performance of a full-length work, Strauss would receive 10 percent of the gross profits, and every twentieth performance would be a benefit from which he would receive half the net profits. Both parties were bound to the contract by a 10,000 fl. penalty, and subsequent contracts with the theater set similar terms. Rumors began circulating immediately, for all Vienna eagerly awaited the first fruits of his efforts for the stage. The *Fremdenblatt* reported prematurely: "In September or October, the sea monster of Viennese theater notices, the opera by Johann Strauss, should become reality."[20] The premiere, originally scheduled for November, sold out immediately: "from the first news of a performance of this opera, orders for loges and seats have been coming in over the telegraph from the most distant summer resorts and spas."[21] The city could hardly wait to see its favorite ballroom musician conquer the theater at last.

After long delays, *Indigo* premiered 10 February 1871, attended by many luminaries of the Viennese musical world; Johann Herbeck, director of the Court Opera, arrived late and was forced to sit in the orchestra pit, the only open seat in the theater.[22] Audience response was overwhelmingly enthusiastic; those who had been accustomed to enjoying Strauss's performances in other venues transferred their expectations to the theater. According to one critic, "at the centerpiece of the evening, the waltz-song 'Ja, so singt man, ja so singt man in der Stadt, wo ich geboren,' the whole house broke out into a cry . . . one believed that now Strauss must rip the violin out of the hand of the closest violinist, swing it to his chin, and as at Sperl, at Zeisig, at Dommayer, Unger, and Schwender, strike up the dance."[23] Although critics complained about the poor quality of the libretto, *Indigo* received widespread public acclaim, premiering with similar success later that year in Graz and Berlin. With this work Strauss launched not only a stage career but a new and lasting genre, the Viennese operetta.

INDIGO UND DIE VIERZIG RÄUBER

The entire Ringstrasse affected me like a fairy tale out of the *Arabian Nights*.
Adolf Hitler[24]

Indigo sits Janus-faced on the last three decades of the nineteenth century.[25] It relies on familiar musical and narrative precedents, while pointing the way toward a new, specifically Viennese genre. A consistent feature of Viennese operetta is its overt and specific reference to regions of the Habsburg monarchy in general and to Vienna in particular. This subjectified Vienna is often established in opposition to some Other: a fictional tropical island in *Indigo*, Hungary in *Der Zigeunerbaron*, or Germany in *Simplicius*. Strauss was the ideal composer to shape the new genre, for who else could claim familiarity with the standard orchestral repertoire as well as an innate sense for Viennese popular music? Although his musical expression occasionally flagged under inadequate texts, his operettas both reflected and generated a musical identity for his city and his age. For his operetta debut, Strauss relied on three key elements for success with the audience he had come to know well: (1) use of the Turkish idiom, long popular in Vienna; (2) inclusion of contemporary political satire, typical of Offenbach's style; (3) allusion to Vienna's musical heritage, including traditions of carnival. Although Strauss soon abandoned the Turkish references and satirical style, allusions to Vienna and carnival remained hallmarks of his most popular works.

Operetta *alla turca*

The Ottoman empire posed a long-standing threat to the security of western European countries, particularly the Habsburg empire. Western authors engaged and tamed fear of the "heathens" by making them either unbelievably barbarous or ridiculously comic, while composers exploited the subject matter for exotic orchestral effects. Turkish music and its military equivalent, Janissary music, had been imitated by Viennese composers in a variety of contexts since the seventeenth century.[26] Typical traits of this style – including duple meter, prominent use of triangle, cymbals, and bass drum, and the harmonic minor scale – appear in two Strauss marches composed shortly before *Indigo*: the Persian March, op. 289, and the Egyptian March, op. 335. When given the opportunity to expand upon this topos, he eagerly complied.

Steiner based the patchwork libretto to *Indigo* on the Arabian stories of *1001 Nights*, a collection that inspired countless other operas. *1001 Nights* had long been popular as bedtime stories and thus were perfectly suited for Strauss's stage debut,[27] for they combine the popular Orientalism and fashion for the exotic with the nostalgia for childhood, offering the audience a familiar grasp within the new genre. Preparations for the work also coincided with the opening of the Suez Canal in November 1869, an event that Franz Joseph attended personally, taking a three-month journey from Constantinople through the Arab lands to Jerusalem and Egypt, during which the popular press was filled with tales from the Middle East.[28] When *Indigo* premiered early in 1871, his public would have associated the fictional scene with recent events.

The title of the operetta, along with its cast of characters, suggests the Eastern setting. Indigo reigns over the island of Makassar, aided by his high priest Romadur and "cheerful advisor" Janio. Other characters include Ali Baba the mule shepherd and his wife Toffana; the government minister Corruptio; members of Indigo's harem, Tulipa, Lili, Cigara, Valida, and Dodo; and the eunuchs who guard them, Falsetto and Soprano. These names make obvious associations between the characters and qualities associated with them, but a more subtle association is in Toffana's name: 'Tophana' was the name of the arsenal in Constantinople where cannons and artillery were kept – the name reveals the character's explosive temper before she arrives on-stage.[29] These characters recall similarly descriptive names in Offenbach operettas, but traditional Viennese folk plays also alluded to personality traits through a character's name. In Nestroy's *Die verhängnisvolle Faschingsnacht* [The Fateful Fasching Night, 1839] the dandyish playboy is Herr von Geck; Dusterer is the dry-humored peasant dressed in black in Anzengruber's *Der G'wissenswurm* (1874). Janio's name, too, suggests (auto)biographical significance; Romadur occasionally refers to his cheerful Viennese sidekick as "Schani," a nickname shared by Johann Strauss himself.

The music associated with these characters also defines their personalities. Strauss uses the *alla turca* style – often in deliberate juxtaposition with a Viennese style – to indicate the characters' origins. The overture introduces this idea by including several typically Turkish gestures: duple meter with emphasis on the first beat, static harmonies and frequent unisons, repeated-note patterns, and phrase rhythms that sound deliberately "wrong" (8-bar phrases divided into 3 plus 5).[30] Although the overture is longer than most of Strauss's later overtures, it comprises only a few melodies, not including the waltz that would become the work's signature piece ("Ja, so singt man"). Unlike the overture to *Die Fledermaus* three years later, the tunes in *Indigo*'s overture are merely presented, linked together with necessary modulatory material, but left undeveloped and hardly varied in their appearance.

The operetta opens with a chorus of harem women, but although they inhabit a distant, exotic island, the music suggests that they are more Western than Oriental: their melody is in a gentle 9/8 meter and carries the unmistakable Strauss stamp of a prominent, recurring sixth scale degree over tonic harmony. As is typical of seraglio works, the origin of the harem women is more ambiguous than that of other characters, and their music features fewer blatantly exotic markers. They remain more closely allied to the audience's expressive world, "and thus call on a range of depth of associations unavailable for the Turks."[31] The women eagerly greet Fantasca, hailing her as their leader and pledging their loyalty. (As is often the case in operetta, this scene operates at two levels: it follows the fictional plot, but since Fantasca was played by theater director Marie Geistinger, the chorus indeed greets her as their true leader.) Fantasca introduces herself with an off-stage coloratura cadenza and in her recitative claims that although she comes from a foreign land, she will soon reign on the island because the ruler is in her sway. She sings a short strophic couplet in polka rhythm and indicates her solidarity with the harem by returning to the key of their chorus, E major. This opening scenic complex resembles the *Introduzione* of early nineteenth-century Italian opera (chorus, *cantabile* for one or two characters, cabaletta), while also drawing on a trope common to Mozart's *Die Entführung aus dem Serail* and other seraglio works, setting the opening scene in the ruler's garden.[32] In his pioneering effort in Viennese operetta, Strauss relied on conventions both of Italian opera and the Viennese *Singspiel*, genres liberally included in the Theater an der Wien's repertoire.

In seraglio operas, "the most flamboyant and pervasive uses of the [*alla turca*] topos occur in connection with the low-Turk characters,"[33] a statement also applicable to Ali Baba, the mule driver, whose entrance couplet typifies strategies of Turkish characterization: duple meter, open fifths in accompaniment, slow harmonic motion, and a prevailing anapest rhythm (see Example 4.2). Ali Baba introduces himself as the mule trader who sells flowers and fruit, and syllables such as *ho* and *hü* pepper his song in imitation of Turkish speech. When Janio disguises himself as Ali Baba in Act II, he uses the *alla turca* music from Ali Baba's entrance song as part of his disguise. The harem women have captured Janio, believing he is a spy, but the orchestra supports his deception by playing Ali Baba's music while he begs for mercy.

In a choral march later in the act, the islanders praise their powerful ruler, singing in open parallel fifths and octaves in a minor key.

Example 4.2 *Indigo und die vierzig Räuber*, Act I, No. 2

Strauss rarely used the minor mode except to evoke a non-Viennese atmosphere, and, given his training in harmony and counterpoint, the forbidden parallelisms were undoubtedly intentional, meant to evoke a "primitive" state. The accompaniment is entirely homophonic, sometimes involving a single unison melody, also a trait of Turkish music.[34] Additional exoticisms include the melodic augmented second, lower-neighbor grace notes, and slides ascending to notes both in the melody and in the bass.

The operetta's conclusion alludes to another seraglio work then popular in Vienna, Rossini's *L'Italiana in Algieri* [*The Italian Girl in Algiers*].[35] As the crowd gathers before Indigo, shocked by the news that "their" women might be armed robbers, they see a ship in the harbor and hear sailors singing the waltz associated since Act I with Vienna. Similar to Rossini's opera, where Isabella, Lindoro, and Taddeo escape by ship from the Bey Mustafà, Fantasca and the harem, Janio, Ali Baba, and Romadur board the ship and set sail for home, leaving Indigo on his island with Toffana, Ali Baba's angry wife, as revenge. Just as the opening scene replicated familiar operatic models, Strauss's conclusion borrowed from an established precedent. But using the *alla turca* style was only one way of assuring success for his stage debut. He also relied upon another tradition with proven success in Vienna: the operettas of his French colleague, Jacques Offenbach.

Links to Offenbach

Strauss's early stage works inevitably drew comparisons to Offenbach, whose style of political satire is indeed apparent in *Indigo*. Jokes narrowly escaped the censors on a variety of issues, including taxes, the military and police, the "king," and marital infidelity. At the end of Act I, for example, Janio addresses the crowd in a burlesque of contemporary political speeches and governmental policy. Omitting any sign of exoticism in this song and chorus, Strauss rather emphasizes the reference to Vienna by beginning in a waltz meter and tempo. The waltz simply draws the crowd's attention, however, for when Janio begins his speech, the meter changes from triple to duple. His ideas for filling the monarchy's tills include a beauty tax (since few consider themselves ugly), an intelligence tax (only the unintelligent are exempt), a marital fidelity tax, and a virtue tax. With these tax laws, proud citizens will gladly contribute, and only thieves, robbers, and bums will be free of responsibility. The crowd approves of Janio's clever plan and urges him to adopt it immediately.

This satire of economic policy-making had as its object many of the bourgeois Liberals sitting in the audience. The late 1860s and early 1870s saw great economic expansion in Vienna. Over 1,000 licenses were issued for joint stock companies between 1867 and 1874, during which period at least twenty-nine railroad companies were formed: fortunes were made practically overnight.[36] Growth of jobs, industry, and personal wealth through speculation in the stock market found a powerful expression in the construction along the Ringstrasse. To offset the exorbitant property prices and stimulate building interest along the Ring, a concession was made to new builders exempting them from taxes for thirty years.[37] When Janio announces that only scoundrels will be exempt from taxes, he chides the very business barons enjoying the performance. Ali Baba's eventual transformation from a poor mule trader to a wealthy man also reflects Vienna's burgeoning prosperity, but Strauss mocks this new-found wealth by giving Ali Baba the same music from the beginning. Although risen in social status, he remains the same rough animal handler.

Offenbach often poked fun at the French military, and Strauss could not resist mocking the Austrian army, an organization recognized more for its looks than its effectiveness. Emperor Franz Joseph had been far better trained in parade maneuvers and organization of army hierarchy than in military strategy;[38] until 1878, the empire had only lost territory under his reign. Strauss's Soldiers' Chorus in Act II, perhaps the first ever marked *pianissimo* throughout, offers all the expected attributes of a military march: duple meter, male singers, drum-like dominant/tonic alternation, and flourishes of quick triplets. But these soldiers take great care not to disturb the enemy, for if they do not call attention to themselves, then battle may be avoided – a scenario that greatly appeals to them. In another military parody (Act III), soldiers sing *sotto voce* a hymn of praise in a minor key. Their battle unfortunately has resembled a fast retreat, owing to poor weather conditions, but they have returned in one piece. These scenes stand in stark contrast to the bellicose attitude presented in *Der Zigeunerbaron* nearly fifteen years later, by which time attitudes toward and representations of the Austrian military had changed significantly.

Despite its initial popularity, *Indigo* did not find lasting success in Vienna. Some critics blamed the Offenbach-style political satire, "a heavy burden that the light Viennese waltz cannot carry. A Strauss waltz should make us forget our political misery, not make fun of it."[39] Although the satirical tone never disappeared entirely from Viennese operetta, the genre began to emphasize the romantic and sentimental vein already present in *Indigo* – Janio and Fantasca, the long-separated couple, are reunited by the final chorus when they set sail for their long-lost homeland, Vienna.

Musical Vienna

Strauss's operettas preserve a distilled vision of Vienna, one free of domestic strife and populated by a happy *Volk* united against common enemies. With his father's music accompanying dim memories of the Viennese *Vormärz*, contemporary audiences recognized Strauss's inheritance from a "better time," a sense of nostalgia that he cultivated and encouraged. In addition to specific references to earlier eras, his music avoids perfect authentic cadences and relies on long, sometimes unresolved appoggiaturas, techniques associated in his music with a sentimental, unrealizable longing. Strauss had already developed this sound in his dance music, but in his operettas the reference to an idealized Vienna becomes explicit.

Indigo's Act I trio involving Janio, Fantasca, and Romadur demonstrates techniques of musical characterization that became a signature of Strauss's writing for the stage. Fantasca would rather be home in her beautiful *Vaterland* on the blue Danube, alluding to the connection between national pride and the Danube river established by Strauss's waltz only a few years before. The men accompanying her quietly sing "Duliä, duliä!", an expression associated with folksongs and the *Heuriger* of the Viennese suburbs.[40] The first few measures of the introduction are in 6/8, but they cannot resist the swinging meter associated with their origins and soon break into 3/4. The text clarifies the musical significance of their waltz: "Yes, that's how they sing in the city where I was born; yes, that's how they sing, only in Vienna" (see Example 4.3).[41] The audience would have recognized several traits in this waltz with which they were already familiar. Tonic harmony does not arrive until the eighth measure and is then accompanied by a 6–5 appoggiatura. This elusive root-position tonic reflects the characters' loss of home; they can imagine it, sing around it in various inversions, but the actual arrival "home" is delayed. The rhythm is especially typical of Strauss, who frequently tied the third beat to the first beat of the following measure. The hesitation on the second beat, specifically notated by the fermata in the opening measure, is another common feature of the Viennese waltz, allowing the spinning couple time to complete a turn within the three beats of the measure.

Similar examples of musical allusion to Vienna abound. Janio's entrance song describes his dislike for his present job, then dreams about his far-off home before returning to the present surroundings. The three sections (ABA) are made distinct by key and meter, with the waltz tempo reserved for the central section, his reminiscence of Vienna. In Act II, Janio and Fantasca again recall Vienna together as they did in Act I. He begins their duet by declaring his love for her (in duple meter); but when he reminds her that they were fond of each other already back in Vienna, the meter changes to 3/4, Viennese dialect appears, and the melody is dotted with the rising melodic sixths typical of Austrian *Ländler* and the sixth scale degree harmonized by the tonic triad (see Example 4.4). When Fantasca fails to respond to his declaration, the meter, key, and language change yet again. Thus, Strauss highlights the textual and musical

Example 4.3 *Indigo und die vierzig Räuber*, Act 1, No. 5

Example 4.4 *Indigo und die vierzig Räuber*, Act II, No. 12

allusion to Vienna by framing the reference with contrasting material.[42]

A Viennese musical and social tradition with which Strauss had long been associated was carnival, the pre-Lenten festive season marked by frequent drinking and dancing at masked balls. *Indigo* was the first of many operettas to invoke the habits of carnival and its associations with both disguise and the waltz. In the second act, the harem welcomes the night for helping to obscure their plans; as long as stars blink in the sky, they are the "masters of creation." This celebration of women's power seems progressive in isolation, but Strauss inflects the text by setting it to the familiar waltz paradigm (in the same E major of their opening chorus), thus leading the listener to apply the situation to her own life. Hearing such a bold assertion within the context of a waltz, the audience would associate the disguised women on stage with guests at a masked ball, a site where women generally had more power to control their environment than they enjoyed by the light of day. At a private ball they might in fact be "masters of creation" – controlling the decorations, the guest list, their costumes and personae – but morning inevitably restored traditional patriarchy. Moreover, the women conclude their chorus with a trumpet-like proclamation that they are free from tyranny since they are no longer weak women but clever robbers. The carnival custom of *Maskenfreiheit* (the right *not* to remove one's mask) was one of the few freedoms women enjoyed in contemporary public life. A costume, especially one that inverted gender, offered temporary freedom from restrictive social obligations and expectations.

While *Indigo* includes some carnivalesque elements, Strauss dealt with them more explicitly in his next two stage works, *Carneval in Rom* and *Die Fledermaus*, and again a few years later in *Eine Nacht in Venedig*. After years of observing Viennese social customs at masked balls, he could now hold a mirror up to his public through his stage works. His dances regularly lent a bacchanalian tone to the carnival season, an atmosphere which his operettas could now replicate throughout the year.

Strauss had become for the Viennese the essence of the carnival spirit, and to attend a ball or any dance entertainment without his melodic magic would be unthinkable anymore.[1]

With these words Strauss's first biographer captured the central role he and his music played in the social and cultural life of Vienna. During the twenty-two years before he began composing operetta, Strauss enlivened carnival celebrations with hundreds of waltzes, polkas, quadrilles, and marches, dances both greater in number and higher in quality than those by any contemporary composer. Whether performed in a ballroom by full orchestra or at home in one of numerous published arrangements, his music heralded a season of indulgence, intrigue, and romance.

His most famous stage work, *Die Fledermaus*, relies on precisely these elements for its immediate appeal; yet its popularity would have lasted only a few seasons had these attributes not been accompanied by music of the highest caliber. This operetta represents the culmination of his experience as orchestrator, melodist, and dramatic composer, and although later works have their highlights, none achieves the overall coherence or the irrepressible Viennese tone of *Die Fledermaus*. Its subject, the antics of the Viennese during a masked ball, augured well for Strauss's success, for who could be more familiar with this scenario? With two moderately successful operettas behind him, he found his stage legs at last, and the libretto, implausible though it may be, freed him to compose in a style with which he felt most comfortable – Viennese dance music.

The Strauss family performed Viennese dance music throughout the year, but at no time was their presence more in demand than during the weeks between Christmas and Lent known as carnival. Strauss's music played a key role in carnival events, which included

vast public balls and elaborate private parties. Aristocrats and
financial barons strove to outdo one another in decorations, music,
and fashionable dress for gatherings in their homes, where masked
balls provided a prime opportunity for casual flirtation as well as
serious matchmaking. The festivities usually began around 8 or 9
o'clock in the evening and lasted well into the morning hours, sometimes as late as 6 or 7 a.m. Although the demanding work of composing every day and conducting every night placed great strain on
Strauss's health, these challenges ultimately facilitated his career as
an operetta composer, smoothing his path from ballroom to theater.

Strauss's most popular operettas capture the feeling of hedonism
and *joie de vivre* of Viennese carnival, replicating on stage many traditions associated with the season. Drinking heavily and exchanging
the intimate "Du" form of address are typical carnival events found
in *Die Fledermaus*. Perhaps the most prominent tradition of carnival is
disguise, and this work, like many Viennese operettas, offers a full
array of disguised characters. The custom of *Maskenfreiheit*, discussed in the previous chapter, granted party guests the liberty to
remain masked throughout the evening, thus leaving their identity
undisclosed. Rosalinde insists on this custom when she carries out
her impersonation of a Hungarian duchess. As characters transform
themselves, some boundary is invariably crossed, either of gender or
social class; yet as in real life the morning must come, so too are traditional hierarchies reestablished by the final curtain. Although most
composers relied solely on costumes and skillful acting for these disguises, Strauss used musical means to aid some characters and betray
others. He composed a dozen stage works after *Die Fledermaus*, but
this work stands alone for its integration of drama and music as well
as its distinctly Viennese flavor.

The operetta has held special significance for the Viennese ever
since its premiere in 1874, when it appealed not only for its elegant
music but also for its attention to contemporary concerns.[2] It has
become the best-known representative of a theatrical trend then
popular, a new *reportage* style that used local current events as
evening entertainment. Although some authors have mistakenly

reported that it found success in Vienna only after being warmly received in Berlin, the work was, in fact, an immediate hit. Because it premiered in April, it could not enjoy a long continuous run, as the Theater an der Wien had already engaged a visiting Italian opera troupe and other summer entertainers. But *Die Fledermaus* soon resumed its prominence on the theater schedule and was greeted by eager audiences in the fall.

Its plot stemmed, as many operetta libretti did, from a French comedy. However, the work's parentage extends beyond its immediate French source (Henri Meilhac and Ludovic Halévy's *Le Reveillon* of 1872) to a German play, *Das Gefängnis* (1851) by Roderich Benedix. The Viennese version, by Richard Genée, was originally entitled *Doktor Fledermaus*,[3] perhaps a comic twist on *Doktor Faustus* or a reference to the once-popular Viennese *Singspiel* by Dittersdorf, *Doktor und Apotheker*.

The public's first introduction to the work came six months before the stage premiere. On 25 October 1873 (the composer's forty-eighth birthday) Strauss conducted a benefit concert in the Musikverein for Hungarians affected by the cholera epidemic. There Marie Geistinger performed the "Csárdás für Gesang" with text by Genée that became Rosalinde's signature csárdás. The piece's success inspired quick work from Strauss, who allegedly finished the operetta in forty-two days and nights. He whetted the public's appetite once again a few months later when he conducted the "Fledermaus Polka" at the Concordia Ball sponsored by the fraternity of journalists and writers. The operetta's technical rehearsal was 1 April, the dress rehearsal for invited critics and actors was 4 April, and the premiere followed the next evening, Easter Sunday.[4]

Die Fledermaus achieved over 300 performances at the Theater an der Wien by the end of the century and was the first of Strauss's operettas to be performed at the Court Opera. It was performed almost 12,000 times on German-speaking stages between 1896 and 1921, a number far greater than for any other operetta.[5] As with any work that finds immediate and lasting resonance, its success derives from reasons both intrinsic to the work and circumstantial to the time of its premiere. In addition to the inherent charm of its music, which has hardly faded in the 126 years since its first performance, its story and musical style suited, indeed shaped, the very climate in which it was written.

ECONOMIC CIRCUMSTANCES

While his first two operettas exhibit the self-assurance of a wealthy, growing city, Strauss's *Fledermaus* is characterized by a nihilistic gaiety reflecting the mood in Vienna following the stock market crash of 9 May 1873. This economic downturn destroyed many family fortunes and political careers, striking a blow to theater business at the same time. A range of social classes had participated in stock market speculation: "Professors, handworkers, teachers, clergy, industrialists, officers, and actors all found themselves among the insolvent as a result of the crisis."[6] These groups also became ardent fans of this timely operetta.

Strauss was the first operetta composer to achieve success after the crash with the *Fledermaus* premiere in spring 1874. The work is unprecedented in setting and tone, and its innovations relate directly to the uncertainty accompanying the financial collapse. By rejecting exotic foreign settings in favor of interior scenes, it reflects a social trend often observed after a national crisis: retreat to home and family. A similar reaction occured during the Viennese *Vormärz*, as well as during the period immediately following the revolution of 1848; the Viennese populace restricted spending, denied themselves luxuries, and concentrated on restoring order to their homes and businesses. Strauss took the opportunity to unite his diverse and dejected audience through their common musical tradition, reassuring them that although they might have lost their financial fortunes, they still enjoyed a musical heritage that bound them with their geographic home and their immediate ancestors.

Another result of the uncertain economic climate is the operetta's constant references to drinking. For the first time, a stage work explicitly suggested alcohol, specifically wine and champagne, as a socially acceptable means of coping with anxieties about the future and regrets about the past, a suggestion echoed in countless later operettas. Many previous stage works – plays and operas alike – had included drinking choruses, but these were traditionally enjoyed in a spirit of celebration and community. The Act II finale of Strauss's *Carneval in Rom* begins with the chorus's praise, "Champagner leiht der Seele Schwingen, er löst der Zunge Band" [Champagne teaches the soul to swing and loosens the tongue].[7] However, *Fledermaus's* Alfred and Rosalinde share a melancholy drinking duet, as Alfred observes: "Flieht auch manche Illusion, die Dir einst Dein Herz erfreut, gibt der Wein Dir Tröstung schon durch Vergessenheit!" [When many illusions that once brought joy to your heart fly away, wine will give you comfort through forgetting].[8] Although the entire company concludes the operetta by hailing champagne as the "King of all wines," their chorus exhibits a distinctly ironic tone in Rosalinde's concluding verse: "Doch gab er mir auch Wahrheit und zeigt in voller Klarheit mir meines Gatten Treue" [(Champagne) also gave me the truth and showed me my husband's fidelity in full clarity].[9] While alcohol offers a means of comfort and amnesia, it also may reveal more than one wants to know.

Die Fledermaus premiered almost a year after the collapse of 1873, and while some businesses and families continued to struggle, many were on their way to recovery. Although they had not yet recouped the financial resources necessary to entertain friends or extravagently feed their families, they were looking ahead to more prosperous times. Strauss's Act II banquet and ball scene offered the voyeuristic enjoyment of pleasures they had once known and hoped to experience again. In its attempt to replicate familiar social situations, however, *Die Fledermaus* diverged in several ways from preceding Viennese stage works. Instead of the fussy adornments of the typical *Kostümoperette*, performers dressed in contemporary public attire. While many operettas opened with a rousing chorus set in a large open space or outside, *Fledermaus's* curtain rose on a bourgeois living room, the second act took place in a ballroom, and the third in a jail, offering the intimacy of private homes and the familiarity of a haphazardly run police station. Posters advertising the work's premiere boasted specifically of the new sets for the first two acts, even naming the stage furniture's previous owner.[10]

These innovations resulted less from a change in taste than from the altered economic situation. The stock market crash left theaters scrambling to stay afloat in any way they could. With so many fortunes ruined overnight, even enthusiastic theater-goers were reluctant to spend money on tickets, much less invest in producing extravagant new works. Theaters were forced to make do with existing sets, and performers, who always provided their own costumes, were more likely to coalesce into a credible ensemble if they could wear contemporary fashions.

Still, the operetta stimulated the memory and imagination of the financially shaken audience. Expectations of dress and public entertainment had diminished in the year after the crash, and *Die Fledermaus* offered a ball scene more elaborate than most audience members had seen that season. Indeed, many of the public had forsaken attending balls altogether. Overall attendance at masked balls fell by almost two-thirds; attendance at Schwender's (one of the main public ballrooms), 8000 on good nights in previous years, reached only 3000 on the best nights that year. Champagne consumption also dropped dramatically; one prominent city restaurant reported that while in December 1872 the average champagne consumption per night was forty bottles, in December 1873 the average was only two.[11] Articulating the fantastic quality of the scene, Strauss's chorus in Act II sings: "Alles was mit Glanz die Räume füllt, erscheint uns wie ein Traumgebild, wie in einen Zauberkreis gebannt ruft Alles: Ha, charmant!" [Everything that sparkles and fills the room appears like a dream; as if enclosed in a magic circle, everyone yells 'How charming!']. When the champagne flowed freely on stage, the audience could immerse itself in the happy mood, if not the actual inebriation, accompanying a well-stocked party.

In the post-crash atmosphere Strauss and his colleagues also took the opportunity to focus a work exclusively on Vienna. Many of the foreign workers who had come to the capital during the *Gründerzeit* now returned to their homes in Bohemia and Italy; in fact, the imperial Security Commission required them to show proof of income or be expelled from the city.[12] Entertainment at all levels, which had previously relied on their patronage, could now afford to exclude such groups. Although they did not influence the theater business directly through their absence, in a time of crisis and recovery local audiences were more likely to favor works that focused attention on their own social and ethnic groups. *Die Fledermaus* thus played a vital role in reinforcing a native Viennese identity during this time of economic insecurity.

Despite the work's modern setting, its music and message reflect a longing for an earlier time. At the center of the work, both figuratively and structurally, lies a profound sense of nostalgia. The work's curious title comes from a joke the main characters had played on each other during a previous carnival season. When Falke and Eisenstein tell the story during the Act II banquet scene, they recall for everyone the carefree antics of bygone years. In their Act I duet, Alfred and Rosalinde proclaim the motto of the post-crash 1870s: "Glücklich ist, wer vergisst, was doch nicht zu ändern ist" [Happy is he who forgets what cannot be changed]. Not only the altered economic circumstances provided cause for nostalgia, but also changes in the physical architecture of Vienna's cityscape. During the 1860s, much of old-world Vienna had disappeared before the inhabitants' eyes as the medieval city wall was torn down, making way for imposing new public buildings along the Ringstrasse. Not everyone greeted these efforts at urban modernization with enthusiasm,[13] and the very act of attending a performance at the Theater an der Wien, an institution untouched by the inner-city construction projects, inspired a sense of nostalgia and reminiscence for a simpler time.

MUSICAL ANALYSIS

Die Fledermaus is today considered a typical Viennese operetta, yet for its time it was strikingly innovative and in many ways more sophisticated than any contemporary stage work. A close collaboration between composer and librettist led to an unusually integrated work, and, presented with situations he knew intimately – a bourgeois household, a ball, the Viennese demimonde – Strauss supplied music full of grace and wit. This work shows vast improvement over his previous two operettas in several areas. He became more skilled at integrating music with text and dramatic action, as well as composing specifically for the voice. Along with improvements in creating a musical personality for each character, Strauss made strides in mastering national musical idioms, while simultaneously strengthening the identity of a Viennese sound. His growing confidence as a stage composer is suggested by his borrowing of musical devices from other composers; he observed the techniques of his colleagues, and, instead of continuing to produce discrete dance numbers, began to compose in terms of specific requirements of the stage. *Die Fledermaus* is Strauss's most tightly knit work, demonstrating a large-scale continuity among the acts that he had not achieved before and would never achieve again. Its internal integrity, perhaps due to the inspiration with which it was composed, suggests that he conceived the whole work at a stroke. An examination of these aspects will suggest why *Die Fledermaus* has remained the representative stage work of Vienna, highly regarded by listeners of all ages and musical backgrounds, for over a century.

Musical characterizations

In *Die Fledermaus* Strauss frequently included melodrama in order to support the characters' actions and dialogue; in Act I the accompanying music rises chromatically when Rosalinde and Alfred hear Frank, the jail director, ascending the stairs outside the apartment, and as he enters the room and introduces himself the orchestra softly foreshadows the tune he will sing several moments later. In a similar instance, Rosalinde sends Alfred out the door calling, "Leben Sie wohl!", but as he leaves, he narrowly escapes crossing paths with her husband and his lawyer. When Eisenstein bitterly blames his lawyer

Example 5.1 *Die Fledermaus*, Act 1, No. 5, Finale

for the extension of his jail term, the horns in the orchestra wittily echo Rosalinde's sentiment with their own "Lebe wohl!" motive. Horns themselves underscore the stage action, for the instrument has long been associated with the "horns" of the cuckolded husband.

Strauss enhanced his musical characterizations not only through instrumentation but also through melodic style. In Act I Rosalinde sings a short strophic couplet in waltz tempo, persuading the prison director Frank that any man dressed in smoking-cap and robe with whom she eats dinner alone must be her husband. Her coquettish charms include a grace-note ascending leap, and she portrays their intimacy with a winding chromatic phrase to the words "so traulich und allein" [so cozy and alone] (see Example 5.1). This moment of text painting reveals a level of interaction between librettist and composer that was unusual for Strauss.

Die Fledermaus demonstrates Strauss's growing confidence in the talents of the singers employed at the Theater an der Wien; whereas in earlier operettas the violin frequently doubled the singer, Strauss now allows the voice its own part. For example, following her virtuosic entrance at the beginning of Act I, Adele continues in counterpoint to the violin melody, while later in the same act, the lawyer Blind similarly sings his patter in contrast to the melody. This may seem a small point, but most performers in *Vorstadt* theaters had little vocal training, could not read music, and learned their pieces by rote memorization;[14] Strauss recognized the unusual musical capability of his leading performers at the Theater an der Wien and took advantage of it. By allowing the voice to function as an independent instrument, he could create a more transparent sound, a texture that contributes to the work's light elegance.

Strauss manipulated standard musical conventions to convey irony in the trio for Rosalinde, Adele, and Eisenstein in Act I. Alternating between high pathos and barely suppressed glee, the trio begins in minor; prominent use of the clarinet and solo oboe supports the melancholy mood, while the violins reinforce the effect with their sighing, descending half-steps, a traditional expression of lament. As the characters realize the possiblities the night could hold, they break into a lively polka, accompanied by full orchestra and tambourine. When Rosalinde abruptly returns to her sad musings, the instrumentation mirrors her shift in mood as solo woodwinds and tremolo strings accompany her growing anxiety. Once again they soon break into a polka rhythm and C major, beginning at a secretive pianissimo but becoming carried away to fortissimo within fourteen bars. The text, appropriate to the more somber attitude ("wie rührt mich dies" [How touching this is]), gains dramatic irony when set to the frolicking polka. They halt suddenly on a dominant seventh when they realize their behavior contradicts what decorum demands.

The music at the beginning of Act II, while typically Austrian in tone, signals a change from the bourgeois salon of Act I. The difference between the urban home of Eisenstein and the country palace of Prince Orlofsky is reflected in a shift in instrumentation from the full orchestra of the Act I finale to a rustic open-fifth drone played by the cellos and double basses. Violins also contribute to the rural Austrian atmosphere with hearty triple stops on open strings, grace notes, and major-sixth leaps. The Entr'acte begins in G major, facilitating the coarse sound of open strings, and its tempo marking of *Allegretto con fuoco* and energetic unison sixteenth notes create excitement and anticipation of the events to come.

Adele's "Laughing Song" that soon follows exemplifies the essence of Viennese carnival: the servant interacting with her employer as a musical, if not social, peer. Although it seems to have been conceived first for violin, this song has become a benchmark of the soubrette repertory. Orlofsky introduces Adele's couplet, expressing disbelief that anyone could be so gauche as to think she was a chamber maid. His short melody in duple meter, doubled by oboes and bassoons, stands in contrast to Adele's strophic couplet with its open strings and swinging 3/8 meter, thus distinguishing the eastern Russian from the local Viennese through both meter and instrumentation. Adele proceeds to enumerate physical features that contradict Eisenstein's assessment: her fine hands, her small and dainty feet, her speech, her waist, her dress. The chorus chimes in with mocking, stylized laughter while Adele sings a coloratura descant above them, a further demonstration of Strauss's confidence in his singer. The couplet ends with an extended cadenza for Adele including sixteenth-note runs, a two-octave leap to a high C, and a two-measure trill, all further proof of Eisenstein's misjudgment.

The laughter expressed in her song and engendered in the chorus is typical of carnival. As Bakhtin observes, "carnival laughter is the laughter of all the people"; directed at everyone, it embraces the whole society from household servant to civil servant. Yet her song also replicates the ambivalent nature of carnival laughter; "it is gay, triumphant, and at the same time mocking, deriding."[15] This dual nature of celebration is especially typical of Vienna, a city whose attitude toward life has been described with oxymorons such as the "gay apocalypse" and "happy nihilism," a city that found apt representatives in both Strauss and Karl Lueger, as we saw in chapter 3. Adele triumphs in the moment, but her laughter also conveys resentment at her ultimately unchanged social position.

Strauss carefully observed all threads of Viennese society, and his musical characterizations embraced not only the exuberance of a disguised chamber maid, but also the anti-Semitic portrayal of Dr. Blind, Eisenstein's lawyer. Blind's professional incompetence is already suggested by his name, but more importantly, his character represents the stereotypical Viennese Jew. Inasmuch as most government positions in the judicial hierarchy were closed to Jews, lawyers who did not convert to Catholicism had little choice but to enter private practice. By 1890, 86 percent of lawyers in Vienna were Jewish, an overwhelming majority.[16] This fact, combined with Blind's musical style, suggests that contemporary audiences would have viewed the role as a Jewish caricature.

The Act I trio for Eisenstein, Rosalinde, and Blind begins with the men rushing home after Eisenstein's court appearance, each accusing the other of having caused the increased jail sentence. Eisenstein complains that during the proceedings his lawyer began to blabber, stutter, and crow like a rooster, accusations recalling Richard Wagner's *Judaism in Music* (1850), an essay well known in Viennese musical circles. Wagner asserted that since the Jew has no European language as "mother tongue," he cannot artistically or adequately express himself, "creaking, squeaking, buzzing," and turning phrases into incoherent babble.[17] Although Rosalinde, Eisenstein, and Blind share similar musical material in the first part of the ensemble, Strauss eventually demonstrates Blind's "babble" with a patter-like catalogue of everything he can do as a lawyer. He first recites a list of verbs, all of four syllables ending in *-ieren*, accompanied only by strings. Then he is joined by the full orchestra, Eisenstein, and Rosalinde, who sing a contrasting melody in unison. While Blind repeats his catalogue, the other two sing long, legato phrases over him (see Example 5.2). Eisenstein and Rosalinde are accompanied by violins and flutes, a neutral tone color in Strauss's palette, but Blind's monotone, syllabic recitation is reinforced in the orchestra by horns and trumpets, contributing the blaring, nasal tone Wagner ascribed to Jews.

Example 5.2 *Die Fledermaus*, Act I, No. 2

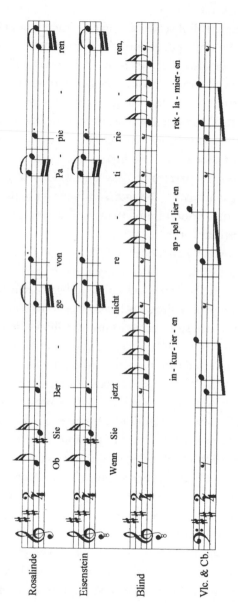

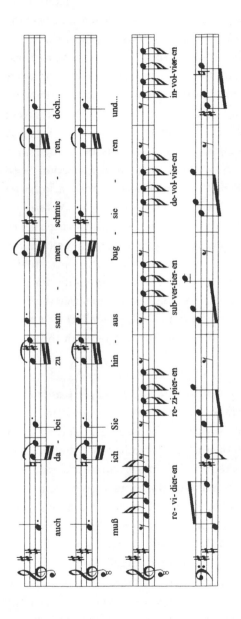

Strauss also uses instrumentation to highlight cultural difference in the figure of Orlofsky. In most operettas the main characters introduce themselves in Act I, but Orlofsky does not appear until after the chorus opens Act II. His character is also unusual in that the role is sung by a woman. Certainly a woman singing a masculine role was not uncommon, especially in operetta, but the reasons for *which* roles should be sung by women are illuminating. Often a breeches role fell to a young man in love, such as Cherubino in *The Marriage of Figaro* or Siebel in Gounod's *Faust*. The title role in Strauss's *Prinz Methusalem*, another love-struck young man, was performed by a woman, and Richard Strauss revived this characterization with Octavian in *Der Rosenkavalier*. The breeches role could also be an eager factotum like Oscar in *Un ballo in maschera* or Niklaus in Offenbach's *The Tales of Hoffmann*, but Prince Orlofsky fits neither of these categories. Suburban theaters regularly featured female choristers or dancers clad in military uniforms or other male garb, providing an opportunity to titillate audiences with the silhouette of women's legs (see Illustration 1.2). In this instance, however, the decision to give the Russian prince a woman's voice may have had more to do with the Viennese perception of Russia than with theatrical conventions.

Habsburg history had been full of tension and antagonism with Russia over territorial claims. Bulgaria had been part of Russia until the Crimean War, and Austria was anxious about the newly independent countries south of her borders, a protective buffer between Russia and Austria's Dalmatia on the Adriatic coast. Indeed, the threat of Russian infringement into Austrian territory provided one excuse for the Habsburg occupation of Bosnia-Herzegovina in 1878. The monarchy sensed Russia encroaching not only to the south, but also to the north where Austria and Russia shared a border in the disputed territories of Poland and Galicia. Austria tried to stabilize relations with both Russia and Prussia by establishing the Three Emperors' League (*Dreikaiser Bund*) in October 1873. When *Die Fledermaus* premiered a few months later, audiences would have accepted a strong, virile Russian prince less easily than one whose potentially threatening verisimilitude was undercut by having "him" played by a woman.

Transvestism occurs frequently in operettas by Strauss and other Viennese composers, both as breeches roles and female characters dressing temporarily as men.[18] When a character appears whose presence is not primarily concerned with gender difference (as Orlofsky's is not), it usually indicates a category crisis elsewhere, displacing the tension inherent in destabilized boundaries, such as nationality or social class, on to a figure that embodies the margin.[19] Act II, precisely the moment of Orlofsky's introduction, presents a flood of blurred national and social boundaries. The Austrian Rosalinde poses as a Hungarian; her chambermaid Adele, dressed in her employer's gown, pretends to be an actress; the bourgeois Eisenstein impersonates a French marquis; and the Austrian prison director, a state employee, is disguised as a French bourgeois.

Orlofsky's couplet plays on the Viennese image of a typical Russian, striving to be polite and sophisticated but essentially boorish and intolerant. Orlofsky warns that when he invites guests to join him in the evening, they often enjoy themselves into the morning hours, but should any of them begin to look bored, he feels free to throw them out the door. They drink bottle after bottle of wine, but since the prince cannot bear to be refused, he breaks the bottle over his guests' heads if they decline a glass, explaining: "'s ist mal bei mir so Sitte, chacun à son goût!" [That's the custom where I come from. To each his own!]. Strauss's music takes the form of a slow march in the unusual key of D-flat major; the muted strings necessitated by the key signature, along with bassoon, horns, oboe, and a single flute, create a dark tone color, while the tambourine and bass drum add a military exoticism. The meter is cut time, and for the first nineteen measures of the piece the orchestra plays a slow anapestic rhythm (short-short-long), a pattern traditionally associated with eastern Europe (cf. Ali Baba's music in *Indigo* or Homonay's "Recruiting Song" in *Der Zigeunerbaron*). Orlofsky's couplet demonstrates Strauss's facility not only in making musical style an integral element of a character's personality but also in expressing a national idiom.

National styles and local identity

Die Fledermaus offers several numbers specifically associated with a variety of countries. Act II brings not only Orlofsky's Russian couplet discussed above, but also Rosalinde's Hungarian csárdás and a ballet that originally included a number of European musical nationalities. More importantly, Strauss's mastery of various national musical styles was accompanied by his synthesis of a specifically Viennese musical identity.

When Orlofsky's guests press Rosalinde to prove her Hungarian patrimony by singing a traditional national song, her number features several genuine and stylized Hungarian characteristics. Its overall form falls into the two sections conventional for a csárdás:[20] a slow opening section in 4/4 (*lassu*) followed by a faster section in 2/4 (*friss* in Hungarian; Strauss marks it *Friska*).[21] The piece begins with a solo clarinet playing a free, winding, chromatically inflected line accompanied by pizzicato strings (see Example 5.3). In the third measure the flute's ascending fourth is echoed first by the oboe, then by the clarinet, while the violin completes the introduction alone with a pizzicato descending octave.

The clarinet's opening, marked *ad lib.* in the score, evokes the style of *hallgató* playing typical of Hungarian gypsies. In this slow, rubato, untexted playing, the gypsy allegedly looked into the soul of his paying patron, perceived his sorrows, and expressed them through his music. The performance thus required a collective effort between the musician and the emoting, actively listening audience.[22] Pizzicato string accompaniment, as in mm. 1 and 4, is also a typical gypsy trait. The strings in m. 2 define the key, B harmonic minor, and a "Phrygian" gesture concludes on the dominant. Although scholars disagree over the existence of a gypsy "scale," they concur that any such scale must include the augmented second associated with the harmonic minor scale, one that Strauss implies by including G-natural and A-sharp in the opening measures. The quick, repeated, ascending fourth figure in m. 3, called the *Kuruc*, is associated with a horn call. Within these four measures, before Rosalinde even takes a breath, Strauss has informed the audience in no uncertain terms that her disguise is complete. His distinctly non-Viennese music has effectively "masked" her true personality.

When Rosalinde begins to sing in m. 5, she reinforces the Hungarian topos through a recurring "short-long" rhythmic motif (eighth-dotted quarter; see Example 5.4).[23] Strauss associated another dotted cadential figure particularly with Hungary, for it not only appears in Rosalinde's csárdás but can also be found in his later "Hungarian" works, *Der Zigeunerbaron* and *Ritter Pásmán* (see Example 5.5). This circling around the first scale degree over tonic-dominant-tonic harmonic motion recalls the "Rákóczy March," probably the best-known Hungarian piece of the nineteenth century.[24] Rosalinde's cadenza in this section is a chromatic descending octave unlike any other in the operetta, further marking the exoticism of the music and, consequently, of her disguise.

In the second part of the csárdás the meter changes to 2/4 as Rosalinde informs her listeners that Hungarians express their fire and love of life through lively dancing. She sings more free syllables in this section (*hei, ho, ha*) and continues her virtuosic performance with long trills, running sixteenth-note passages, and a final high D (d³). When the orchestra alone repeats both parts of the dance, the first violin takes over Rosalinde's part except during her chromatic cadenza, which is played by the solo clarinet whose *hallgató* playing opened the piece.

Strauss and his audience were familiar with the Hungarian idiom not only through its use by western European composers such as Liszt and Brahms, but also from more direct sources. Aristocrats, civil servants, and gypsies alike traveled between the two halves of the empire and their poles, Budapest and Vienna, where for a time it was fashionable to invite gypsy musicians to perform at social gatherings. In fact, at a Russian ambassador's party in 1873 the gypsy musician Jancsi Sági Balog and his orchestra performed in alternation with a Strauss orchestra.[25]

The Act II ballet sequence – although it was always open to substitution and has become the site of modernization in more recent

Example 5.3 *Die Fledermaus*, Act II, No. 10, Csárdás

Example 5.4 *Die Fledermaus*, Act II, No. 10, Csárdás

Example 5.5 Typical Hungarian cadential figure

productions – originally included Scottish, Russian, Spanish, Bohemian, and Hungarian dances. Strauss constructed this finale in the same form as most of his waltzes: five dances separated when necessary by a short interlude to effect a key change, concluding with a recapitulation of Rosalinde's csárdás to represent Hungary. Except for the "Schottisch," a traditional Viennese dance despite its name,[26] all the national dances represent countries which at various times posed threats to the integrity of the Habsburg monarchy. By presenting them within the frame of a Viennese ballroom, Strauss domesticates their power and demonstrates Viennese resilience by having the scene culminate in a waltz.

Example 5.6 *Die Fledermaus*, Act I, No. 5, Finale

Strauss's growing ability to emulate various national styles was matched by his cultivation of an immediately recognizable Viennese tone: bright major keys, parallel thirds and sixths, light orchestration, and melodies based on the tonic triad. Alfred and Rosalinde introduce this style at the opening of Act I, and when Alfred returns for the Finale, he is accompanied by the same serenade-like orchestral texture of his opening aria: pizzicato strings and sparse woodwinds. His melody again includes the sweet, sentimental rising major sixth of Austrian folk-like innocence, and Strauss alternates doubling his melody with violins and clarinets, instruments specifically associated with *Heuriger* and the Vienna woods (see Example 5.6).

The unlikely trio of Orlofsky, Eisenstein, and Adele reestablish contact with a local musical style after Rosalinde's Act II csárdás, when they unite in a paean to champagne. At the end of each verse of their strophic couplet the party guests join them in recognizing the "king of wines." In this brisk polka the piccolo and trumpet double the solo voice lines, giving it a sparkling, piquant tone quality unlike any preceding number. The majesty of the celebrated drink is reflected in the fanfare-like arpeggio as the ensemble sings "Long live champagne!" The choral refrain offers another example of the unresolved sixth scale degree (*la*) as part of the tonic chord, a hallmark of Strauss's style, coinciding here with the word *Land* and thus associating this characteristic melodic flavor with Austria (see Example 5.7).

In the first verse, Orlofsky explains that kings and queens love the sweet grape juice as much as they love laurels, and Eisenstein adds that monks need to refresh themselves so often that their noses become red, a verse reflecting the anti-clerical sentiment prevalent among bourgeois Liberals in the 1870s.[27] The final verse, sung by Adele, suggests an imperial alcohol policy in the starkest terms: "Champagner schwemmt mitunter gar mancherlei hinunter, drum lassen weise Fürsten die Völker niemals dürsten!" [Much can be washed away with champagne, therefore wise rulers never let their subjects go thirsty!]. This is the second number in the operetta to offer alcohol as a means of pacification; not surprisingly, alcoholism became a growing problem in the Habsburg monarchy at the end of the nineteenth century.[28]

The warm, champagne-induced feelings lead Falke to announce that the party guests comprise one fraternity and should address each other as intimate friends.[29] The famous "Du und Du" waltz (op. 367) that follows includes some markers of the Viennese style, but the final extended coda is particularly rich in this respect. The ensemble seems to improvise quietly on the syllables "du" and "la" in a swinging, *Ländler* style, including the rising sixth (both major and minor) in the first two eighth-notes of the bar, parallel thirds and sixths in the melody, prominent sixth scale degree over tonic harmony, lower-neighbor grace notes in the violins, and some pizzicato string

Example 5.7 *Die Fledermaus*, Act II, No. 11, Finale

Example 5.8 *Die Fledermaus*, Act II, No. 11, Finale

accompaniment, a virtual catalogue of Viennese signifiers (see Example 5.8). This flood of sentimental musical effects reinforces the text, in which the characters try to preserve the moment and create a reference point for later nostalgia – "Für die Ewigkeit, immer so wie heut, wenn wir morgen noch dran denken!" [Forever, just like today, when we think back on it tomorrow!].

The final waltz of Act II conveys a feeling of carefree abandon through the lack of the tonic root in the opening chord, its wide melodic swing (encompassing one and a half octaves), and the use of

Example 5.9 *Die Fledermaus*, Act II, No. 11, Finale

the sixth scale degree as part of the tonic chord at prominent interior cadences (see Example 5.9). The text proclaims the *carpe diem* attitude for which the work has become famous and with which the Viennese most wanted to identify: "Liebe und Wein gib uns Seligkeit! Ging's durch das Leben so flott wie heut! Dann bleibet jede Stund' der Lust geweiht!" [Love and wine give us happiness! If only all of life were as fun as today! Then every hour would be dedicated to merriment!].

Musical borrowing and allusion

In his dances Strauss occasionally made subtle reference to well-known songs, such as the Austrian national anthem, the Marseillaise, or contemporary "hits" of the folksong repertoire more difficult to identify today.[30] In *Die Fledermaus*, too, he began borrowing musical ideas from opera and alluding to extra-theatrical musical styles, like the sentimental repertoire of popular men's choruses (*Männergesang-vereine*), the folksong idiom, and funeral music. Whether he intended his audience to grasp specific references is difficult to say, for some audience members may have recognized the intended model, while to others the material may have seemed merely familiar. These allusions served both to align the work with local traditions and to inscribe it into the web of culture at large.

The first voice heard in the operetta is Alfred serenading under Rosalinde's window. He sings to his caged dove, the "noble Rosalinde," with pizzicato string and harp accompaniment imitating a strumming guitar. Unfortunately, his song falls only on the ears of Adele, who throws a coin to him saying, "He must have just come from some *Männergesangverein*." Alfred's music is indeed typical of repertoire sung by men's choruses; in addition to operatic drinking and hunting choruses, the *Männergesangvereine* sang works written earlier in the century by Schubert and his contemporaries. The lyrical line, 6/8 meter, and regular phraseology of Alfred's song recall this popular repertoire.

This scene also suggests an allusion to the first act of Verdi's *La traviata*: the suitors share a name (Alfred/Alfredo); they serenade beneath their lovers' balconies during the first acts in similar meters (6/8 and 3/8 respectively); and the objects of their devotion are both named after flowers (Rosalinde/Violetta). The works are further connected by their carnival ball scenes in Act II, both of which involve disguise and infidelity. In *La traviata*, when the gypsies tell Flora's lover the Marchese that he is not a model of faithfulness, Flora adds, "La volpe lascia il pelo, / Non abbandona il vizio" [A fox will leave his skin, / But not his wickedness]. Strauss's model of marital infidelity, Eisenstein, is introduced at the ball as Marquis Renard, the same aristocratic title and an allusion to the same clever animal of Verdi's opera (fox–Renard–*volpe*). *La traviata*, performed regularly at the Viennese Court Opera, was one of Verdi's most popular works, one with which Strauss and his librettists were undoubtedly familiar. Faced with similar narrative situations, they felt free to borrow details from a successful and well-known model.

Another scene in Act I suggests a moment of musical allusion: the trio involving Eisenstein, Rosalinde, and her maid Adele, all of whom

Example 5.10 *Die Fledermaus*, Act I, No. 4

are preparing for the evening's events. Rosalinde sings how dreadfully she will miss her husband during the next eight days, offering the first occasion for a minor key in the operetta. She is accompanied by strings and clarinet, an instrument associated with funeral music (*Trauermusik*) in the Viennese tradition, where wind bands often accompanied funeral processions to the gravesite. To the text "How will I bear it?" Rosalinde's melody employs the "sigh" motive of a descending minor second, which is echoed in the strings. Her lament serves as a foil to the trio's underlying excitement about the evening's escapades.

After the trio alternates twice between the minor mock-lament and a joyful, anticipatory polka, Adele introduces a short march, assuring her employers that they will see each other again ("Es gibt ein Wiedersehn!"). Her march is marked *maestoso*, the meter changes to common time, and the instrumentation changes from full orchestra to winds and brass with pizzicato strings. In addition to these abrupt changes, the bass writing and texture differs from everything else in the operetta (see Example 5.10). The march lasts only twelve measures, but its marked departure from the surrounding musical material suggests a specific allusion. A similar situation is found in the first act of Mozart's *Così fan tutte*, a work that is itself remarkable for musical references and extra-theatrical allusions.[31]

Example 5.11 Strauss (*Die Fledermaus*) and Mozart (*Cosi fan tutte*)

(orig. D major)

Dorabella and Fiordiligi wave farewell to their men who are, like Eisenstein, under the guidance of a schemer and pretend to leave for compulsory service, only to return in disguise. Although Strauss's characters feign grief over their imminent separation, Rosalinde and Eisenstein are looking forward to a night of illicit freedom; Mozart's Ferrando and Guglielmo also pretend to part with their fiancées in a test of their fidelity. As the couples say their goodbyes, the chorus sings the march "Bella vita militar," just as Adele sings her march tune when Eisenstein and Rosalinde part. Despite pledges of fidelity, all three women succumb to the advances of their respective suitors.

In addition to contextual similarities, the music in both works shares characteristics typical of a march: dotted rhythms, *maestoso* tempo markings, melodic trills, and prominent use of winds and brass. The melodies are also similar in their ascent from the fifth to the first scale degree, then descent from the third to the first scale degree (see Example 5.11). Both marches repeat the opening material at a higher pitch (Mozart's repetition rises a step and Strauss's a third). Moreover, Strauss's writing is noticeably "Mozartean" at this point, including a contrapuntal bassoon line unlike the simple harmonic reinforcement required of the instrument elsewhere in *Die Fledermaus*. The vocal texture of Strauss's trio resembles Mozart's with two sopranos singing over a male voice (after Ferrando and

Guglielmo depart, Don Alfonso waves good-bye to them while consoling the women).

Adele's character may also reflect other elements of *Così*. Her
"Laughing Song" bears resemblance to an aria by Guglielmo, disguised as an Albanian. He, like Adele, implores listeners to observe
various parts of his body, singing "Il tutto osservate: . . . Abbiamo bel
piede, Bell' occhio, bel naso" [Anyone can see that we possess every
merit: . . . beautiful feet, lovely eyes, charming noses!] while Adele
insists, "Die Hand ist doch wohl gar zu fein, dies Füsschen, so zierlich
und klein, die Sprache, die ich führe, die Taille, die Tournüre, derglei-
chen finden Sie bei einer Zofe nie" [My hand is much too fine, my
foot is too delicate and small, my speech, my waist, my dress, such
things you would never find in a maid]. Both arias are in G major and
rely exclusively on tonic and dominant harmony for the singer's first
16 measures. Although their musical similarities are limited, their
narrative functions are not, for both call attention to their characters'
physical features in order to reinforce their disguises.[32] *Così* was infrequently performed in Vienna, but Strauss used these scenes as a
knowing wink to opera lovers.[33]

Strauss's librettists indulged in veiled references as well. In the
toasts that precede the champagne chorus of Act II, two exchanges
underline the artificiality of the stage situation in which the audience
immerses itself. Orlofsky toasts Rosalinde: "To the beautiful Helena
there!" On one level he compliments her beauty in a general way by
comparing her to Helen of Troy. On another level, however, he calls
attention to the fact that Rosalinde is not a real person but actress
Marie Geistinger, who gained an international reputation for her
portrayal of the title role in Offenbach's *Schöne Helene*. In addition to
the allusions included in the score, the actors themselves also took
license to refer to other works in their own spontaneous improvisa-
tions. Alfred's singing in jail in Act III provided a perfect opportunity
for referring to contemporary or relevant operas. (In a recent production he sings phrases from *Rigoletto* and *Die Zauberflöte*.[34])

Strauss makes a subtle but effective allusion to his own compositions during the Act II "Du und Du" chorus. The meter is 3/4, and the

Example 5.12 "Geschichten aus dem Wienerwald" (1868)

chorus sings a grace-note G-sharp to a dotted half-note A for three measures in a row (mm. 924–26), accompanied by the violins an octave higher. This resembles the violin pattern in the first waltz of "Geschichten aus dem Wienerwald" (1868), one of Strauss's most popular waltzes (compare Examples 5.8 and 5.12). Written in the same key, the two dances evoke the same atmosphere of Viennese tradition and *Gemütlichkeit* found in the Vienna woods north of the city and the wine-growing suburbs of Nussdorf and Döbling. The operetta chorus further represents a custom frequently enacted in these suburban *Heuriger*: friends inviting one another to use the familiar form of address. In Strauss's scene, however, the invitation is extended not only between two people who have come to be close friends, but among all the guests in attendance, including aristocracy, foreign dignitaries, chorus girls, and household servants. This erasure of class boundaries (found also in *Eine Nacht in Venedig*) carries over from long-standing carnival traditions. As Mikhail Bakhtin describes it, "All were considered equal during carnival. Here, in the town square, a special form of free and familiar contact reigned among people who were usually divided by the barriers of caste, property, profession, and age. The hierarchical background . . . [was] extremely strong. Therefore such free, familiar contacts were deeply felt and formed an essential element of the carnival spirit."[35]

Finally, Strauss and his librettists alluded to contemporary Viennese theater life when Adele and her sister Ida visit Frank, the jail director, in the final act. Adele, who flirted so energetically with him at the party, must now confess she is not the artist she claimed to be, but rather a maid; still, she tries to convince Frank of her talent for the stage by singing a couplet in which she portrays three standard female roles. When she demonstrates how she would play an innocent girl from the country, the music is in 6/8 with a strumming barcarole accompaniment in the strings, open fifths in the clarinets, and a simple refrain on the syllable "la". Many of the folk plays by Anzengruber, premiered and regularly performed at the Theater an der Wien, involved the troubles of an *Unschuld vom Lande* such as the one Adele impersonates. When she then imitates a queen, the style changes to a march, and Ida and Frank accompany her by pretending to play trumpets and drums. In her final imitation of a woman from Paris, Adele mocks the conventions of popular French dramas: for two acts a young count attempts to seduce the lady of the house, but as soon as he succeeds in Act III, the husband comes home and the wife must beg her husband's forgiveness; the audience sobs as the curtain falls. In this impersonation Adele's vocal writing is the most challenging, with its large leaps and long trills in a high tessitura.

Large-scale continuity

The most striking improvement in this work over Strauss's previous operettas is in large-scale conception, an improvement perhaps related to the speed of its composition. That he wrote the entire score within a short time suggests he conceived it not piecemeal, but as a dramatic and musical whole. Melodies recur throughout the operetta, not for want of new material, but rather to create a psychological and musical continuity. When Adele reads aloud a letter from

Example 5.13 *Die Fledermaus*, Act I, No. 1

her sister at the opening of Act I, inviting her to a ball given by Prince Orlofsky at his country villa, she sings on a monotone b¹ accompanied by strings playing a typical Austrian melody that includes the rising major sixth (see Example 5.13). Strauss illustrates the letter's contents not through Adele's recitation but through the pastoral orchestral material. This melody returns at two significant moments: when Falke persuades Eisenstein to join him at the party instead of going directly to jail, his melody is only marginally interesting, but the tune in the violins alerts the listener to the connection between the ball Adele hopes to attend and the party Falke has in mind. Finally, the melody's implication is confirmed when the chorus sings it at the ball in the opening of Act II. This melody only appears in E major, the only time Strauss uses this key, thus creating large-scale connections in the work.

At the conclusion of Act II, throughout the final exchanges between Frank and Eisenstein, who over the course of the act have become good friends, the cello repeats a slowly descending chromatic line several times – G, F-sharp, F, E. These notes invert the familiar chromatic ascent that opens the overture – E, E-sharp, F-sharp (the G is reached in m. 5). As the guests prepare to leave, the cello line unwinds some of the tensions that initially brought them to the ball. Also, since Eisenstein uses the overture's opening melody in the final act to reveal his identity, it is appropriate that he is associated with its inversion while he is still disguised.

Eisenstein and Frank hear the clock strike six before racing to find their hats and coats. This signal of their curfew had also been carefully prepared in the overture; the passage in Act II replicates measures 41 through 47 of the overture in pitches and instrumentation. The bell is paired with a chorus of trombones and trumpets, which lends a foreboding tone to their whirlwind departure. Unbeknownst to each other, Frank and Eisenstein are due at the same jail, albeit on opposite sides of the bars, and the soloists sing "Auf Wiederseh'n" with knowing irony as they depart together. After seeing the operetta, audience members would recognize immediately the significance of the six bell strokes every time they heard the overture thereafter.

When Frank arrives at his jail, still inebriated from the party, he relives the events of the evening, conveying his thoughts and mood to the audience through music alone. He whistles the waltz sung by the chorus in the previous act as he dances around the room. The march music that had accompanied his assistant Frosch a few minutes earlier returns as Frank extricates himself from his overcoat slowly and with great difficulty, but once he succeeds, the waltz resumes. He begins humming the "Champagne" polka, and continues singing louder and louder until he stops suddenly, hoping no one has heard. As he tries to compose himself to make tea, he is accompanied by the music associated with the party (the music that also accompanied Adele reading her letter and Falke inviting Eisenstein in Act I). He reads the newspaper and whistles as he slowly drifts off to sleep over his desk. His musical reminiscences of the party link all three acts, from anticipation, to event, to memory.

The carnival atmosphere continues at the prison when, in order to discover who was arrested in his stead, Eisenstein changes clothes with Blind and poses as a lawyer. When Rosalinde shows Eisenstein his watch during the course of Act III, he realizes she was the Hungarian countess at the party. The six chimes from the overture foreshadowed not only the morning curfew that called Eisenstein and Frank away, but also the importance of time and a timepiece in proving Eisenstein's guilt and accomplishing Falke's revenge.

When Falke arrives, Eisenstein realizes that the whole evening has been an elaborately planned payback for a previous prank. Rosalinde and Alfred's supper, including the borrowing of his bathrobe, had been pre-arranged, as well as Adele's letter, which was not from her sister at all. The melody in the violins accompanying Falke's explanation of his plan also comes directly from the overture (mm. 74 to 103). Eisenstein asks Rosalinde's forgiveness, explaining that the champagne is to blame for the misunderstanding. The act closes with Rosalinde and the chorus praising champagne in a combination of the csárdás and the "champagne" polka, with each main character singing a phrase or two of his or her signature number. In the final moments, then, Strauss gathers a bouquet of the most memorable tunes of the evening for the audience to take away with them.

THE EXCEPTIONAL AS EMBLEMATIC: *FLEDERMAUS'S* CONTINUED SIGNIFICANCE

Despite its reputation as the example of Viennese operetta *par excellence*, *Die Fledermaus* represents anything but a standard work either in Strauss's oeuvre or in nineteenth-century operetta. Viennese cultural life seems to invite generalizations based on exceptional works: Gustav Klimt's decorative paintings have been used countless times to suggest *fin de siècle* Vienna, yet those works found only a narrow realm of patronage during his lifetime. Pioneering work by Freud in psychoanalysis and Theodor Billroth in surgery are held up as representatives of a progressive medical tradition, yet as late as 1900 physicians at the Vienna General Hospital remained reluctant to interfere with the natural processes of their patients' decline and death.[36] It is only in retrospect that *Die Fledermaus* has come to symbolize its age.

In contrast to Klimt and Freud, Strauss found immediate acceptance and support, but *Die Fledermaus* was no less innovative than their challenging works. The operetta stands alone in Strauss's output for its local, urban, contemporary setting, qualities that most would name as defining features of Viennese operetta. And indeed they became such, but only in this century, beginning with Richard Heuberger's *Der Opernball* [*The Opera Ball*, 1900] and continuing with Lehár's *Die lustige Witwe* [*The Merry Widow*, 1905] and Oscar Straus's *Der tapfere Soldat* [*The Chocolate Soldier*, 1908], among others. Aside from potpourri entertainments alluding to current events, Strauss's contemporaries did not emulate the means to his success with *Fledermaus*, preferring instead settings that were geographically or chronologically distant or altogether fictional.

The international reputation of Viennese operetta, however, has been determined by widespread performances of this exceptional work. *Die Fledermaus* is one of very few Viennese operettas in the repertoire of the Vienna State Opera today. It was first performed in that house, then the Court Opera, on the afternoon of 28 October 1894 as a benefit for the retirement fund of the theater. Tickets cost three times the usual price, and the Opera netted 14,000 fl.[37] The first evening performance took place several years later under the direction of Gustav Mahler. It was performed sixteen times during the 1899/1900 season (the year following Strauss's death) and twenty-one times in 1900/1, making it the most frequently performed and most profitable work of both seasons.[38]

After the turn of the century, *Die Fledermaus* remained the most popular nineteenth-century operetta. Its presence was sustained not only by stage performances but also through the increasingly popular medium of radio. During the 1920s and 1930s, listeners could enjoy live broadcasts from the State Opera or the Salzburg Festspiel. Listeners demonstrated their enthusiasm for operetta and waltzes in general, and for Strauss's works in particular, through regular surveys conducted by Austrian radio (RAVAG). Almost 20,000 listeners submitted their wishes for an all-request concert in February 1931, with Strauss emerging as the clear winner, claiming three of the four top requests: the "Blue Danube Waltz," "Frühlingsstimmen," and the overture to *Die Fledermaus*. The concert, which took place in the Musikverein under the title "Request Concert at Prince Orlofsky's," sold out weeks ahead of time and reached thousands by radio broadcast.[39]

The *Fledermaus* overture was selected again three years later for another radio-sponsored all-request program;[40] the same year, stage and radio celebrated the work's sixtieth anniversary with special performances and articles in the program guide. In recognition of the work's anniversary, fellow Viennese Erich Wolfgang Korngold praised:

> The *Fledermaus* score is equal to the most inspired Lustspiel music of any nation, . . . indeed it need not shy away from the greatest comparison – with Mozart. . . . That Vienna could still give the world Johann Strauss and his *Fledermaus* after Haydn, Mozart, Beethoven, and Schubert, should fill us all with hope for an easier, happier future even in these dark times.[41]

The times were soon to become darker in Austria with the assassination of Chancellor Dollfuss the following summer and the Nazi occupation that followed four years later. *Fledermaus*, along with *Der Zigeunerbaron* and *Eine Nacht in Venedig*, appeared frequently on the State Opera stage during the Nazi occupation (1938–45); in 1939, *Fledermaus* was performed twelve times, a total exceeded only by performances of *Aida* and *Der Rosenkavalier* with thirteen each.[42]

The number of *Fledermaus* performances trailed off during the war, when *Eine Nacht in Venedig* was programed more frequently as a demonstration of solidarity with Italy, Germany's wartime ally. Both works remained popular choices for exclusive viewings (*geschlossene*

Vorstellungen) for the Wehrmacht and Hitler Youth.[43] Despite its association with Nazi occupation, *Die Fledermaus* assumed cultural significance once again as the first stage work by any operetta composer to be performed as a State Opera production in the Volksoper after World War II, a production that was to support and encourage the reconstruction of the State Opera House.[44] Its annual New Year's Eve performance, a tradition that began in the 1930s, is eagerly attended still today not only by tourists but by resident Viennese as well.

Die Fledermaus continues to captivate listeners outside Austria, and has achieved an international recognition unmatched by any other Viennese operetta. Its very popularity, however, has skewed perceptions of the musical context from which it came. The following chapters will examine works that, although they illuminate their own time, have not fared as well beyond the era and atmosphere of their creation.

[*Der Zigeunerbaron*] is no operetta in the ordinary sense. On account of the text, but even more on account of the music, it is a national, a patriotic, a true Austrian and Viennese work of classical character.[1]

Of Strauss's operettas, his *Zigeunerbaron* of 1885 is the richest in extra-theatrical allusions and the most tangled in the cultural-political web of Vienna and the Habsburg monarchy. Music critics and scholars have long regarded this work as evidence of the harmony the empire had achieved by the year of its premiere.[2] Ernst Decsey once declared that the *Zigeunerbaron* accomplished what ministers and delegations could not: "The two halves of the monarchy, embroiled in eternal compromise battles, were fused by musicians."[3] The operetta indeed offers a portrait of mutual cooperation between the two halves of the empire, but although the work is set in Hungary and was written by a Hungarian librettist, its perspective is exclusively Austrian. This fairy-tale story of romance and adventure belies the anxiety many Austrians felt over increasing demands by the empire's non-German population. Premiered at a time of growing political and economic tensions, it propagates an idealized view of Hungary's satisfaction with its role in the monarchy and reveals long-standing national tensions within the divided empire. Despite its innovative use of Hungarian national costume and Gypsy musical elements, the operetta presents a seductive argument for Austrian hegemony under the Habsburg crown.

AUSTRO-HUNGARIAN RELATIONS

Hungary had been recognized as a kingdom within the Habsburg monarchy since the 1867 *Ausgleich*, the political and economic "compromise" between the two halves of the empire. Industrial Austria bargained with agrarian Hungary for optimal trade agreements, while common affairs of military and foreign policy were to be regulated by a central bureaucracy in Vienna. The agreement required that Vienna and Budapest pass identical legislation concerning dualistic affairs such as tariffs, consumption taxes on commodities, regulation of common currency, and operations of the national bank. Tariff revenue paid for common expenditures, and any shortfall was paid from individual governmental budgets, with Austria contributing 70 percent and Hungary 30 percent.[4] Every ten years the contract outlining trade regulations and payment requirements to the common fund was renegotiated, usually with more conflict than reconciliation.

While politicians in Parliament argued over the terms of the *Ausgleich*, Vienna was being transformed. The comprehensive expansion and beautification projects – widening streets, erecting magnificent public buildings along the Ringstrasse, and rechanneling the Vienna river, as well as building new bridges, canals, and schools – did not come cheaply. This intense construction activity tripled the city's costs between 1861 and 1883, for which taxes were raised or created.[5] Taxes were collected not only from Viennese residents, but from all areas of the empire, stirring resentment in outlying areas that their money was being used for the far-off capital instead of closer to home. Understandably, the long-standing rivalry between Budapest and Vienna intensified during this period of urban development.

This large-scale urban renewal in Vienna also created a wealth of new jobs, attracting Habsburg subjects from the rural countryside. Many Viennese who felt threatened by the rapid changes found an easy scapegoat in the influx of Hungarians seeking employment in the city; but a newspaper article in February 1883 also expressed concern that businesses were leaving Vienna for Budapest, where industry was more protected by the local government, or for Berlin, where the economy was experiencing rapid growth. Despite strides made in urban development, the Viennese government passed laws hindering industrial expansion, a stance which many felt was turning the city into a "Krähwinkel."[6] Habsburg subjects on both sides of the Leitha worried that their neighbors were getting a better deal.

The anonymous author of *Das bedrängte Wien* [Vienna Beset], published in 1885, expressed cultural prejudices echoed by many contemporaries when s/he wrote that the empire's non-German population, especially the Hungarians, threatened the political and financial stability of the capital: "Vienna, already weakened by Dualism, suffered because since 1868 neither the Austrian government nor representatives of the Austrian crown took into consideration the changed political relationships, and Vienna was treated less favorably in important public affairs than was Budapest."[7] The author concluded with an exhortation for Vienna, beset by Hungarians, Poles, and Czechs, to engage actively in the cultural battle, and urged the General Assembly (*Gemeindeverwaltung*) to maintain Vienna's premier status at any cost.[8]

At the same time, Budapest received attention at home and abroad for hosting the country's National Exhibition in spring of that year. Journalists came from all over Europe to see exhibits highlighting Hungary's industrial development, artistic treasures, and musical heritage. Librettist Ignaz Schnitzer eagerly hoped that Strauss would finish *Der Zigeunerbaron* in time to precede or coincide with the exhibition. The monarchy's eastern half also received much attention at the time from Crown Prince Rudolf, for he and Mór Jókai, Hungarian novelist and author of the original *Zigeunerbaron* story, had recently begun collaborating on the Hungarian volume of *Die österreichische-ungarische Monarchie in Wort und Bild* [The Austro-Hungarian Monarchy in Text and Picture].[9] By the fall of 1885 the timing could not have been better for an operetta set in Hungary.

DER ZIGEUNERBARON

Strauss visited Hungary several times before he began work on *Der Zigeunerbaron*. He attended the premiere of his latest operetta, *Der lustige Krieg*, in Pest in November 1882 and returned a few months later in February 1883 for a visit. (At this time he also met and played piano duets with Franz Liszt.) He enjoyed Hungary so much during this visit that he promised to write an operetta about it and discussed possible subjects. *Der Zigeunerbaron*, then, occupied most of his attention between 1883 and 1885, a longer genesis than any of Strauss's other works. The work also distinguishes itself in his compositional history for the extent of discussion and exchange between him and his librettist. Together with director Franz Jauner, they developed an integrated and complete vision of the work they hoped to create: a showpiece of Hungarian cultural symbols within the framework of protective Austrian hegemony. Correspondence among the three men during the summers preceding its premiere provides valuable documentation regarding the compositional history of this work.

The operetta's story derives from the novel *Saffi* by Mór Jókai (1825–1904), author and Hungarian national hero.[10] Almost forgotten today, Jókai was a prolific writer in the nineteenth century; he published nearly 100 novels during a period of some sixty years.[11] He had been a Hungarian patriot and fought in the revolution of 1849, but later became a devoted loyalist, serving in parliament for over thirty years. A renowned storyteller, he commanded the same respect in Hungary that Dumas, Sr. or Balzac enjoyed in France.[12] Even the ethnocentric weekly *Der Floh* acknowledged that no Hungarian writer could rival his popularity.[13]

Jókai's novella *Saffi* appeared in November 1883, and Schnitzer wasted no time in creating a libretto based on it. He was already familiar with Jókai's work, having recently translated and adapted for the stage another of his novels, *Der Goldmensch* [The Gold Man].[14] He finished the libretto for *Der Zigeunerbaron* by July 1884 and pestered Strauss constantly thereafter to work harder and faster. Schnitzer wanted the work to open in January 1885 in time for the National Exhibition, but Strauss realized that an operetta on the scale they were planning took time and energy to develop and felt no reason to hurry. As he wrote to his agent and good friend Gustav Lewy in August, "Even when I'm always busy with the *Zigeunerbaron* – with the load of textual problems to overcome and the enormous musical numbers, the work is hardly rewarding – in order to make any progress, I have to work like a robot."[15]

As early as 1884 the press began to report that Strauss's next work would be mounted in the Court Opera, rumors fueled by Strauss's public friendship with theater intendant Baron von Hoffman. Finally, Director Jauner issued a press release stating that the Theater an der Wien owned all rights to the *Zigeunerbaron* and that it would be premiered there in fall of 1885. Jauner not only directed and produced the final product, but also contributed professional suggestions to the operetta as it took shape. His comments reveal much about Viennese theatrical life and its public. In August 1885 he advised Schnitzer that

> The third act is at least *50 percent* too long. The whole thing must be ruthlessly cut so that the length, which holds up the dramatic pace, is trimmed. In the book's current form, we would be there until 11:45! And as you know, every piece that plays past 10 o'clock in Vienna is *lost*.[16]

In the same vein, Strauss asked Schnitzer that summer:

> Have you conferred with Jauner about your introduction to Act III? What has been decided? In the meantime I sketched the march for the market women, etc.; if the introduction is to be handled more simply – then what I have already completed will suffice. Of course it depends on Jauner's willingness to sacrifice – whether to spend a lot or a little money on the introduction.[17]

Strauss further described his vision of the Act III introduction:

> The entrance march must be impressive. Around 80 to 100 soldiers (on foot and horseback). Market women in Spanish, Hungarian, and Viennese costume, *Volk*, children with bushes and flowers – which they strew before the soldiers returning home, etc. etc., the stage opened back to the Papageno Entrance – it must be an impressive scene, since this time we want to imagine an *Austrian* military and *Volk* in a *joyful* mood about a victorious conquest! We emphasize that certain lack in logic that we have been accused of, that desired realization – and the people will attend the *Zigeunerbaron* until this happy moment arrives.[18]

Although the theme of Acts II and III is militaristic, he wanted nothing to do with realism. He wrote that he could not agree to a proposed text having to do with fallen comrades – something else must be "tickled out."[19] Like the Emperor himself, Strauss wanted the spectacle of a large, handsomely uniformed army, with none of the human risk involved in war. In his comments to Schnitzer, he articulated what can be described as "invented tradition," that is, "a set of practices, normally governed by overtly or tacitly accepted rules and of a ritual or symbolic nature, which seek to inculcate certain values and norms of behavior by repetition, which automatically implies continuity with the past."[20]

Impressive pageantry and celebration of re-created history was a regular part of Viennese public life. With his vision of the third act's triumphal march into Vienna, Strauss participated in the same sort of cultural self-projection that governed the historicist architecture of the Ringstrasse itself.[21] Only a few years before *Der Zigeunerbaron*, artist Hans Makart had organized a festival parade, marking "a pinnacle of self-congratulation for Ringstrasse Vienna."[22] Ostensibly celebrating the twenty-fifth wedding anniversary of Franz Joseph and Elizabeth, Makart created a Renaissance pageant in the style of *Die Meistersinger*. The same conflation of history and theatricality governed Strauss's concept of enthusiastic Hungarian participation in imperial politics. By dressing in national costume and singing popular melodies, performers reflected an idealized Habsburg citizenry. As James Johnson writes of opera after the French revolution: "the spectators became the spectacle, and the division between audience and actor was transcended in their common identity in the nation."[23] But Strauss, unlike his French predecessors, was not promoting revolution. The realistic fervor he created with his colleagues served to rouse enthusiasm among performers and audience for the existing empire and its elegant capital.

Strauss and Schnitzer hoped their work would rise to the status of a comic opera, for although it was performed in a *Vorstadt* theater, a venue that at that time rarely offered opera, it was more through-composed than any previous operetta. Many supporters and critics felt that Strauss should be making steady progress toward a performance at the Court Opera, and by designating *Der Zigeunerbaron* as a "komische Oper," he took a nominal step toward that goal. The differences between this operetta and comic operas with spoken dialogue such as Nicolai's *Die lustigen Weiber von Windsor* or *Singspiele* like Dittersdorf's *Doktor und Apotheker* are, in fact, not great. In contrast to Strauss's earlier scores, which were organized around discrete numbers and maintain a light-hearted tone throughout, *Der Zigeunerbaron* encompasses larger amounts of musical material spanning greater lengths of time. Individual numbers frequently give way to scenic complexes in which an aria leads to recitative and then to a chorus with no interruption for spoken dialogue. Strauss's compositional style was gradually moving away from dance music, where articulation is largely a matter of performance convention and therefore less necessary to the score, toward a greater command of his available orchestral resources. He was becoming more comfortable in his role not only as an orchestral leader, but as a composer who could make demands upon performers of his music both in Vienna and abroad.

As an avid listener and performer of contemporary music, Strauss employed Gypsy characteristics in *Der Zigeunerbaron* typical of nineteenth-century opera in general. In Verdi's operas, for example, the Gypsy appears as one who works magic or sees the future (*Un ballo in maschera*, *La forza del destino*, and *La traviata*), and Verdi also glorified the stereotypical Gypsy profession of metal-working in *Il trovatore*. The Gypsy as musician or dancer is found in Thomas's *Mignon*, just as Bizet memorialized the Gypsy lifestyle in *Carmen*, which premiered in Vienna in 1875 with great success. That same year Strauss experimented with Gypsy characteristics in his *Cagliostro in Wien*, in which the chorus avers that the Gypsy's song always includes tambourine and cymbals, and the main Gypsy character, Lorenza, insists that whoever wants to accompany her must play either the cymbals or the fiddle. In sum, the Gypsy stereotypes invoked by Strauss and others include their nomadic lifestyle, their reputed intimacy with nature and the spiritual world, their physical appearance (dark complexion, wild manner, bright dress), and their musical talent.[24]

In *Der Zigeunerbaron* Strauss uses uncommon operetta percussion, including an anvil, a gong, and cymbal crashes, to highlight the difference between cultures. Though he rarely chooses the minor mode for his dance works, he uses minor keys, frequently in combination with the parallel major, when evoking Hungary. (Rosalinde's csárdás in *Die Fledermaus* begins in B minor but shifts abruptly to D major for the faster section. Saffi's "Zigeunerlied" begins in D minor, then shifts to D major.) Melodically, Strauss uses the same chromatically inflected minor scales that typified "Turkish" music generations earlier, often including the raised fourth or lowered second scale degrees, as well as frenzied scalar passages and wide, unconventional leaps. In contrast to much of his dance music, in which orchestration centers on the strings, his works evoking an eastern culture more often feature the clarinet and oboe as solo instruments. The oboe melody of the overture, like Saffi's "Zigeunerlied," is accompanied by pizzicato strings, reminiscent of a guitar, an instrument that suggests not only the freedom and romanticism of the outdoors, but also the less constrained moral code associated with those wandering musicians who typically played it. Strauss uses this orchestral technique in *Der Zigeunerbaron* only for the Gypsies.

Released from the generic requirements of the waltz, Strauss becomes freer with accent, rhythm, and meter in his representations of eastern music. Triple meter is associated exclusively with Vienna, while Hungarians and Gypsies are characterized by a driving duple meter with accented syncopations and *alla zoppa* (short-long) rhythms or by a slow tempo with expressive solo passages marked *ritenuto*. Strauss's use of compositional techniques associated with Hungary do not suggest, however, an ethnographic interest or a studied attempt at authenticity. His distinctions between "Viennese" and "Hungarian" musical styles serve to illuminate differences between characters or illustrate a single character's change in attitude or affiliation from one nationality or set of accepted customs to the other. His adoption of musical "Orientalisms" was aimed specifically at a Viennese audience and was always juxtaposed, explicitly or not, to a western European norm.

Although Gypsy characters figure prominently in operas and

Example 6.1 *Der Zigeunerbaron*, Overture, mm. 1–4

literature from mid-century, anthropological interest in their history, language, and lifestyle began only in the 1880s, contemporaneously with *Der Zigeunerbaron*.[25] Strauss was acquainted with Hungarian artists, intellectuals, and businessmen from living in Vienna and traveling to Budapest, but his personal contact with Gypsies was limited to musical performances. Gypsy ensembles (*Zigeunerkapellen*) were fashionable in Vienna for a time, and he called them the "brown vagabonds" (*braunen Vagabunden*) when they performed during the intermissions of his orchestra concerts.[26] In *Der Zigeunerbaron* Strauss combined his familiarity with Gypsy music and performance conventions with the personal experience of Hungarian librettist Ignaz Schnitzer and the research of Director Franz Jauner; together they offered a more authentic representation of an "exotic culture" than any operetta of its day.

Strauss immediately situates *Der Zigeunerbaron* outside the Viennese bourgeois salon. The overture begins with a chromatic motive in octave unison played by the strings, followed by a cymbal crash (see Example 6.1). A few measures later a clarinet solo recalls Rosalinde's famous csárdás from *Die Fledermaus* (see Example 6.2), the melodic line accompanied by thirds descending not just by whole step, but including the augmented second, lending harmonic uncertainty and exotic flavor. Unison octaves and shifting chromaticism contribute to a sense of tonal uncertainty – in fact, the first authentic cadence does not arrive until measure 20. With the cymbal crash, the winding clarinet solo, and the ambiguous tonality, the overture immediately evokes an "eastern" atmosphere. (Compare this

Example 6.2 *Der Zigeunerbaron*, Overture, mm. 12–16

Example 6.3 *Der Zigeunerbaron*, Overture, mm. 48–53

passage, for example, with the bright opening measures of *Die Fledermaus*, with its major key, standard dance-orchestra instrumentation, and regular meter and periodicity.) Strauss soon calls upon the exotic connotations provided by the oboe. Its solo begins with a turn figure, then has a more extended line featuring seductive triplets and an impudent grace note (see Example 6.3) before offering the first real melody of the work, accompanied by pizzicato strings. The driving duple meter, frequent syncopation, conflation of major and minor, and triplet ornamentation signal a marked departure from familiar Viennese dance genres.

The curtain rises on a scene of the Hungarian Banat during the eighteenth century. The set, as described in the libretto, includes a run-down castle, Gypsy huts, a house with a balcony, and, in the background, a river with a wooden bridge under which boats can be seen floating by.[27] A chorus of boatmen sings a suspiciously Viennese-sounding gondolier song in which they hail the values of marriage and partnership and compare managing a relationship to sailing a boat. This chorus has relevance to the Austro-Hungarian partnership, for the boatmen advise the Gypsy women nearby to "trust your boat without fear, although it may rock" [nur frisch heran / vertrau' dem Kahn / auf schwanker Bahn / dich sorglos an]: the Austrians/boatmen promise protection to the Hungarians/wives and demand their trust but leave no question as to who stands at the helm.

Ottokar's frustrated search for hidden treasure is echoed and supported by the orchestra. The autograph score and original libretto show that originally he did not search alone, but was joined by Zsupán, the local "pig prince" and father of Ottokar's beloved Arsena.[28] It is unclear from these sources, however, whether they worked together or in competition. Zsupán's role was edited out of this scene before the premiere, and the piano reduction of the score and modern productions and recordings feature Ottokar alone. Postponing Zsupán's entrance until he sings his introductory couplet (No. 5) improves the dramatic shape of the act, allowing Ottokar's character and his relationship to Czipra to be established before Zsupán enters the picture.[29] Ottokar leaves after she reveals that the treasure he truly seeks is Arsena. He articulates a popular fantasy and the motto of Viennese operetta in general when he avows, "True love must always be victorious!" [Die wahre Liebe muß immer siegen!]. The chorus repeats the opening gondolier song, thematically connecting his exit with the entrance of Barinkay, the romantic male lead.

Sándor Barinkay is a thinly disguised representation of the "old-money" Hungarian families, whose estates were confiscated after 1848.[30] Like aristocrat Gyula Andrássy, who fled for his life after the revolution but eventually became the empire's Foreign Minister, those Hungarians who were most threatened during the revolution returned to positions of power in the new imperial order under Franz Joseph. Although Barinkay's costume is "half oriental, half Hungarian,"[31] and the text of his entrance couplet links him in several ways to the Gypsy lifestyle, the music belies any exoticism except for the instrumentation:[32] his melody during the two verses is doubled by oboe and accompanied by pizzicato strings, a Hungarian combination found in the overture. In this quick duple section in recitative style he describes his experiences traveling around the world, when he befriended a variety of wild animals, entertained as acrobat and magician, swallowed swords and predicted fortunes in cards, all without any particular training. Contemporary urban audiences would readily have ascribed these talents to Gypsies, a group that traveled according to political conditions and available employment. Barinkay's adventures reinforce prevailing stereotypes of the special relationship Gypsies enjoyed with nature and the animal world, and their predominance as performers.

Although Barinkay's verses are in duple meter, he falls into *tempo di valse* for the well-known refrain, " Ja, das Alles auf Ehr'" [Yes, on my honor]. The instrumentation also changes from the Hungarian pizzicato string and oboe combination to arco strings and horns, a pointed contrast that is surely intended to influence the audience's perception of Barinkay's role in the drama. He describes his previous exploits in one tone, but pleads his sincerity in another: the Viennese waltz. The progression from Hungarian to Viennese musical tropes evokes the progression of political allegiance of wealthy Hungarian families from their homeland to their distant rulers in the capital. Strauss implies to his audience through musical means which of the characters introduced thus far deserves their understanding and sympathy.

As Barinkay finishes, one of Strauss's sharpest satirical figures enters, Carnero, Chief of the Secret Commission for Morals (*Obmann der Geheimen Sittencomission*), who warns Barinkay to be on his best behavior since he is empowered to enforce public morality. The

Gypsy responds: "But this whole chastity or morality commission, as you call it, seems so quaint that I can't take it seriously even with the best intentions. In fact, everyone abroad also makes fun of it."[33] With these remarks Barinkay pokes fun at the official morality of Catholic Austria, for in contrast to the more Protestant Hungary or to common perceptions of "Eastern" morals, Viennese standards of public behavior were notoriously strict. But the Other, whether of a different ethnicity, nationality, or social class, is always portrayed as having looser moral or sexual codes. This serves two purposes for the viewing audience: they can feel morally superior, yet take voyeuristic pleasure in surveying the sexual excess of the Other's culture.

The smug Carnero has come to announce what Czipra already saw in the cards, namely that Barinkay has inherited their land and has come to rule over them.[34] He describes how Hungary has been attacked from all sides during the war of succession: "*We must pull ourselves the hell together! Any minute now the Hungarian army will also be called up.*" To which Barinkay sarcastically replies: "Naturally everyone is enthusiastically following the call."[35] With the Habsburg history of military loss, the army was not a point of pride for the Austrians.

Carnero needs two witnesses to sign over Barinkay's land. He mocks Czipra's "X", the only sign she knows how to make, and calls for Zsupán to serve as the other witness. In his entrance song, Zsupán freely admits he knows nothing of reading or writing ["Ja, das Schreiben und das Lesen, ist nie mein Fach gewesen"], for he has concerned himself from the time he was a child only with raising pigs. The coarse nature of his character is conveyed in performance through use of dialect and unconventional vocal practices, but the orchestra also contributes to his characterization through frequent grace notes in the woodwinds, giving an irreverent tone to his first appearance.

One of Zsupán's trademarks in recordings and live performance is calling various characters, especially Barinkay, a "verfluchter Kerl" [a scoundrel], though the phrase does not appear in either the autograph score or the libretto. It may have been improvised by the original creator of the Zsupán character, Alexander Girardi, in imitation of Strauss's speech habits. Writing to his second wife Lili, Strauss calls Theater an der Wien director Walzel a "verfluchter Kerl" for spending large sums to send two telegrams that essentially cancelled each other,[36] and he used the same phrase as a term of endearment for Girardi a few weeks later.[37] What may have begun as an improvisation based on a private joke became incorporated into the work we know today.

Girardi may also have been responsible for emphasizing those musical and performative elements of Zsupán's character that recall popular images of the Hungarian Jew.[38] A strong correlation between Hungarian political allegiance or family origin and Jewish religious beliefs can be observed in the Austro-Hungarian population at the end of the century. The 1880 census reported that over one-fourth of the Jewish community living in Vienna at the time had been born in Hungary.[39] Similarly, by 1900 Jews comprised 23.4 percent of the population of Budapest but only 8.8 percent of Vienna's and 6.7 percent of Prague's population.[40] Surviving photos and sketches of Girardi as Zsupán show a man displaying a catalogue of Jewish physical stereotypes: a protruding round belly topped by a wide, fringed, silk bow tie; bowed legs with turned-out feet; and thick, curly hair with dark eyebrows and mustache (see Illustration 6.1). Contemporary "scientific" studies of Jews' bodies describe them as soft, round, and "unsoldierly."[41] Zsupán is dismayed when he accidentally volunteers for the army in Act II, and his participation indeed seems preposterous.

Further evidence of the correlation in the popular imagination between Hungarians and Judaism is the currency gained by the catchphrase "Judeo-Magyar" at this time in Vienna. It was wielded frequently by the young Karl Lueger, whose political career rose rapidly in the early 1880s as he used the term to incite support from the Austro-German working classes who feared economic and political antagonism from both Hungarians and Jewish businessmen. He narrowly won the parliamentary elections in June 1885 with attacks on large-scale capitalism as well as on "peddlers" who threatened

6.1 Alexander Girardi as Zsupán, 1885

domestic tradesmen. Although overt anti-Semitism was not yet a part of his platform, the groundwork had clearly been laid.[42] With the premiere of *Der Zigeunerbaron* coming only a few months after this election, the connection between Hungarians and Jews would have been well established with the Viennese public.

Lueger's anti-Semitism had precedents not only in political circles but in musical ones as well. Wagner's notorious assertions about the Jew's inability to express himself clearly are relevant in this instance.[43] Similar allegations might also have been directed toward those Hungarians whose native language was Magyar but who were forced to learn German through government-regulated institutions like school and the army. Zsupán's speech includes a colorful mixture of Hungarian, or Magyar-sounding phrases; and the "gurgle, yodel, and cackle" of which Wagner complains is present in Zsupán's musical material, for his entrance song is introduced and accompanied by piercing reed and brass instruments (see Example 6.4).

Example 6.4 *Der Zigeunerbaron*, Act 1, No. 3, Zsupán's entrance song

Indeed, Strauss may have revised Zsupán's signature melody with the intention of highlighting his religious / racial difference. The sketch for this song is one of the few for which Strauss included the text.[44] It differs significantly from the final version, but he retained the key of G major and the duple meter, and expanded upon the leaps of large intervals (see Example 6.5). Whereas the original melody was predominately diatonic and scalar, the revised melody is chromatic and disjunct. The large descending intervals force Zsupán to swallow syllables and eliminate their vowels, contributing to a "yodeling" effect.

Zsupán also displays the widespread anti-Semitic stereotype of greediness and shrewd capitalism. His characterization as a "gold-digger" explains his original presence in the opening scene with Ottokar, where both search for hidden treasure that does not belong to them. (Although Zsupán was eventually eliminated from this scene, surviving stage photos portray him with pickax in hand.) He is a successful businessman, concerned that his daughter marry well, not for her own happiness, but for his own status and financial benefit. When Barinkay is ennobled in recognition of his bravery in

Example 6.5 *Der Zigeunerbaron*, Zsupán's entrance song

battle, Zsupán decides he may be appropriate for his daughter after all, but Barinkay claims Arsena only on Ottokar's behalf, not for himself. Zsupán gives his permission for the match only reluctantly, telling Arsena, "[Ottokar] gets only cash, no pigs!" Finally, Zsupán exemplifies one of the most vicious anti-Semitic stereotypes – the Jew as vulture – when he boasts after returning from battle that he stole jewelry and pocket change from fallen enemy soldiers.

Although neither Strauss nor Schnitzer explicitly referred to Zsupán as a Jewish figure, his physical appearance, personality, and musical traits suggest such a characterization.[45] Girardi may have had more to do with the character's development than the two authors, for he was known to joke about the eternal covetousness and envy of the Hungarians, vices frequently attributed to Jews.[46] This conflation of Jewish and Hungarian stereotypes carried over into the popular press when *Kikeriki* berated Strauss for his indecision about which theater will host the premiere: "You keep announcing a Gypsy Baron, but compose, it seems to me, a 'wandering Jew' since the operetta wanders from one director's office to another and still isn't finished."[47] If *Zigeunerbaron*'s musical score were the only extant evidence, Zsupán's Semitic traits might be overlooked, but the addition of stage photos and an awareness of national-religious tensions suggest such a characterization.

Barinkay finds himself attracted both to Zsupán's daughter Arsena and to his land holdings, the combination of which results in a marriage proposal. The transaction between the men that is to be sealed with Arsena's hand reflects Hungarian custom: marriages were business decisions made by the parents, in which the children had little say. This was true of the Viennese bourgeoisie as well during the last third of the nineteenth century, when marriages were arranged as business mergers. The Hungarian language reflected a capitalist attitude: an eligible woman was an *eladó lány* (a "girl for sale") and the groom a *vö* (abbreviation of *vevö*, a "buyer").[48] The power of marriage to preserve or augment political and economic power was best exemplified by the ruling family of Austria, "as the tag went, *Bella gerant alii tu felix Austria nube!*"[49] However, the codes of operetta suggest in several ways that the Gypsy Barinkay and the Hungarian Arsena will not be united, (1) because of Ottokar's profession of love for Arsena at the beginning of the work; (2) because of the proximity between Saffi's entrance and her mother's prediction of Barinkay's fortune; and (3) because nationalities are rarely permitted to mix in operetta – although Gypsies, Hungarians, and Austrians may intermarry in real life, the conservative force of the operetta stage required that the groups remain distinct.

Saffi continues the discussion of Gypsy life and habits in her couplet, a csárdás. Among the piece's "Gypsy" qualities are its key – D harmonic minor with a frequently raised fourth scale degree – and the chromatic turn figures played by the violins while the oboe doubles the voice. The chorus of the slow section uses a repeated, exotic-sounding word, "Dschingrah," that means nothing yet conveys a foreign tone and imitates on stage the sound of a cymbal or triangle, both of which accompany her from the orchestra. As Saffi cries "Dschingrah" the strings play open fifths in quick sixteenth-notes as found in the overture, reminding the audience of the primitive sound associated with Gypsy life. In contrast to the introduction, which attested that no one is as honorable and loyal as the Gypsy, Saffi's first verse warns those listening to mind their children and horses when Gypsies are nearby, reinforcing common stereotypes of unlawful Gypsy behavior; but the second verse reverses the warnings of the first, as she now urges the listeners to trust the Gypsy as friend, not enemy. This about-face on Saffi's part is necessary for the resolution of the story. If she and not Arsena is to be the heroine, she must provide the audience with an incentive to sympathize with her, despite her heritage.

Saffi's song has both textual and musical affiliations with the Habañera in *Carmen*, a frequently performed opera in Vienna since 1875. Like all foreign-language works presented at the Court Opera, *Carmen* was translated and performed in German, and the texts of Saffi's and Carmen's songs resemble each other. The women warn listeners to beware since Gypsies are a lawless race; Carmen sings, "Love is like the Gypsy way, there have been no laws made for it" [L'amour est enfant de Bohème, Il n'a jamais, jamais connu de loi]. Her "Prends garde à toi!" becomes "Nimm dich in Acht!", similar to Saffi's "Habet Acht" and "Mann, gib Acht." Musical affinities include key (both pieces begin in D minor then shift to D major), instrumentation (especially the distinctive use of the triangle), and voice part (both songs are for mezzo-soprano). Strauss and Schnitzer would certainly have known Bizet's work and might have hoped to draw on associations already established in the public imagination, bolstering chances for their own success by borrowing subtly from a well-known contemporary.

In the finale Barinkay and Czipra hear "Dschingrah" in the distance and identify the source as Gypsies marching back to their native land. As they approach, the calls of "Dschingrah" become increasingly elaborate and incorporate more exotic elements: accents on off-beats, pizzicato strings, ornamental turns, and brass supplements including horns and trombones. The faster dance section is again in major but uses different melodic material. The standard rhythms and "Strauss sixth" in this dance suggest a Strauss polka more than a Gypsy csárdás, but the exoticism is retained in the instrumentation with the strings playing "Mit dem Holze (umgekehrter Bogen)," that is, with the wooden part of the bow (*col legno*).

Czipra calls on the Gypsies to acknowledge Barinkay as their long-lost leader returned home at last. He accepts their acclamation, and they join in an energetic chorus accompanied by full orchestra. Arsena had been hoping to marry a baron, and now that Barinkay has been named Gypsy baron, he pursues her once again, with the main characters and chorus echoing each other, "He is a baron!" Arsena and Carnero's incredulity at this turn of events is reflected in a deceptive cadence. As Barinkay explains his background, the orchestra recalls Czipra's melody from a few moments earlier when she announced that Barinkay was their leader, while he sings a contrasting melody. Saffi defends his claim in a meter and instrumentation that matches her earlier csárdás, linking Barinkay's childhood directly to Hungary through text and musical gestures. She is accompanied by clarinet and pizzicato strings, giving the orchestra a guitar-like sound. This combination of timbres resembles the *Schrammelmusik* popular in the northern, wine-growing suburbs of Vienna, a musical style that was associated with nature and mobility.[50]

Saffi's song impresses and attracts Barinkay, yet he still asks for Arsena's hand. Only when his petitions have been refused does he choose Saffi as his bride, a change of heart that Saffi suspects is a cruel joke, but he values her loyalty in the face of the others' scorn. Even though *Arsena* refused *him*, the Hungarians take offense at Barinkay's decision to marry a Gypsy; the Gypsies, however, interpret his choice of bride as a sign of faith in them. The two groups, Hungarians around Zsupán and Gypsies around Barinkay, insult each other and prepare to come to blows. The first act culminates in a furious array of as many as four different simultaneous choruses (Gypsies, Hungarians, solo Hungarians, solo Gypsies). The musical confusion reflects the ethnic groups' mutual unintelligibility, for no single line can be heard above the babel, and they remain in a hostile stand-off as the curtain drops. This confrontation makes for exciting theater but hardly represents the state of harmony and cooperation for which the operetta has been hailed.

Act II opens onto the same scene the following morning when Barinkay and Saffi awaken from their night spent together, to which Czipra gives her encouragement and blessing. The ensuing trio, though very simple, offers some of the operetta's most beautiful music. The delicate instrumentation includes small groups of woodwinds, pizzicato contrabass, and the mellow, tenor sound of cellos and horns as melodic instruments. The key of three flats (E-flat major) allows the woodwinds to shine, while creating a rich, covered sound in the strings. As Barinkay urges his "wife" to wake up, Saffi can hardly believe her good fortune, she is astounded and overjoyed that he would interpret their single night spent together as a marriage commitment.[51] Strauss acknowledges their union in the score musically and metaphorically when he writes out only Saffi's line, adding just "col Saffi" to Barinkay's staff, as they repeat their mutual declarations of love in unison to seal their bond.

During the night, Barinkay's father appeared to Czipra in a dream, telling her where buried treasure could be found. Barinkay digs while she and Saffi imitate the sound of tapping stones under which it might be hidden, with the text "Klopfe, klopfe, klopfe" reinforced by the glockenspiel. He indeed finds the long-buried treasure, and the three celebrate their collective good fortunes with a waltz, accompanied by full orchestra.[52] The dance is ternary: in the first section they admire the golden treasure while singing in unison, but in the contrasting section the tone becomes more sentimental as Saffi and Czipra sing in parallel sixths and thirds that love is allied with loyalty more than gold or money are. Therefore, hours spent with one of true heart should be valued over all else – an observation that could be shared by the more impecunious audience members in the balcony as well as those enjoying box seats.

The following ensemble brings the Gypsy chorus to the stage as they prepare for the day's work. Their Eastern identity is immediately established by two strikes of the gong. A leader calls them to attention with horn flourishes, then the chorus responds with Strauss's "Anvil Chorus" (see Example 6.6). As they sing about their professional duties, forging keys, dishware, nails, and knives from iron, the full orchestra accompanies them, including strikes on the anvil. The contrasting section of this ternary chorus is for women alone, as they praise their happy lifestyle: "Cling and clang! Iron makes us sing!" [Kling und Klang! Eisen macht Gesang!]. Although most Gypsies' lives were filled with tedious work for little pay, Strauss fulfills the urban fantasy of a naïve folk with simple desires. The full chorus recapitulates the initial "Anvil Chorus," emphasizing that when the country is threatened, their swords will be most valued.

This chorus number shares several characteristics with Verdi's "Chi del gitano i giorni abbella?" from *Il trovatore* (1853), an extremely popular opera in late nineteenth-century Vienna and a staple of the Court Opera repertoire. Verdi's chorus is also sung by Gypsies at work, and the instrumentation of both includes full orchestra and anvil. In the introductions to both choruses the orchestra plays in unison a distinctive melody which includes accents, trills, and strings of triplets. In both cases the introductions are in a minor key, but the music turns to major as the choir enters. The choruses are structurally parallel, appearing at or near the beginning of their respective second acts. They share a ternary form with the repetition of the chorus separated by a section in contrasting key for women only or a single woman (Azucena in Verdi's work). The texts are also similar, with both groups of Gypsies claiming to find their lives happy and free.

Carnero eventually inquires about Saffi and Barinkay's relationship, since he had earlier forbidden their union. Their response, "Who married us?" [Wer uns getraut], has become one of the work's best-known duets. The Hungarian combination of pizzicato strings and clarinet accompanies them. With a pun on the German word for bullfinch (*Dompfaff*, or "cathedral priest"), the couple asserts that the bird has married them and that two storks served as witnesses. The chorus echoes Barinkay's opening phrase of each verse; in the autograph, the chorus mocks him, "The bullfinch, he married them, ha, ha, ha," but the mockery was changed in later versions to affirmation ("ja, ja, ja"). Barinkay's flippant response to authority reflects the irreverent tone characteristic of the Liberal attitude toward the conventions of Catholicism; indeed, the Liberal press of the 1880s regularly ridiculed the *Pfaffen* and other trappings of the church.[53]

This light-hearted reply to Carnero's inquiry accomplishes two things. First, it reinforces the romantic image of the Gypsy's relationship to nature. Second, it comments directly on Strauss's own marital

Example 6.6 *Der Zigeunerbaron*, ACT II, No. 10

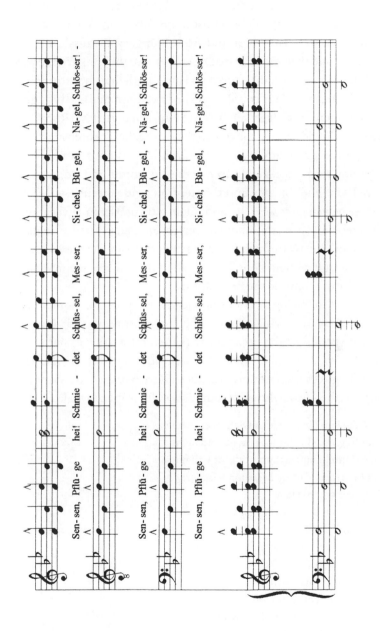

situation. During the time he composed *Zigeunerbaron*, he became closely acquainted with Adele, whose father, like many Viennese Jews after mid-century, had emigrated from Hungary. Strauss's divorce from his second wife was final by December 1882, but remarriage was not allowed in the Catholic church and inter-faith marriages were not allowed in Austria. Many couples escaped these limitations through a "Siebenbürgen" marriage: in this area of what is now Romania, couples could most easily convert to the Evangelical church and wed. Although the procedure was fairly common,[54] these ties were not always honored once the couple returned home; indeed, Strauss received no end of unwanted attention and speculation from Viennese newspapers when he and Adele returned from a "vacation" in the Siebenbürgen as a married couple. He addresses the media's harassment directly through his characters, who are devoted to each other although without benefit of legal union and, despite intervening problems, reunite in the final chorus.

A couplet following this duet provided an opportune moment for substituted or improvised verses, and the censor's records include one such version on the occasion of the operetta's twenty-fifth performance, 17 November 1885. Girardi, in the role of Zsupán, acknowledges the connection discussed above between the Viennese public and the *Zigeunerbaron*'s Commission for Public Morals:

> In Wien lebt ein Krösus, an Schätzen schwer,
> Gibt freigebig her, immer mehr und mehr,
> Der Mann kann's ja thun – er gibt sich nie aus
> (*Im Parterre und in den Logen umherspähend*)
> Sitzt hier wo im Haus . . .
> (*Plötzlich vor das Dirigentenpult tretend*)
> Ich mein' . . . unsern Strauss!!
> Sein Lied, das so feurig und lieblich quillt
> Bezähmt selbst die Wilden, macht Zahmen (*tanzend*) wild . . .
> Ihm sprudelt die Quelle, die nie versiegt –
> Die Welt macht er froh und vergnügt!
> Bleib rührig, wack'rer Musensohn,
> Nur fort in diesem Ton –

Wie der "Zigeunerbaron," –
Der unbestritten
Wohlgelitten
(*Das Publikum apostrophirend*)
Bei *dieser* Sitten-Commission!

[In Vienna lives a Croesus, full of treasures,
Gives generously of them, always more and more,
The man can do it – he'll never run out –
(*Searching the parterre and loges*)
He sits here in the house . . .
(*Suddenly steps in front of the conductor's stand*)
I mean . . . our Strauss!!
His song that murmurs so fiery and sweet
Tames even the wild, and makes the tame (*dancing*) wild . . .
In him runs the spring that never runs dry –
He makes the world happy and satisfied!
Keep active, brave son of the Muses,
Just continue in this tone –
Like the "Zigeunerbaron," –
The undeniable,
Long-suffering
(*indicating the audience*)
Before *this* Morality-Commission!][55]

Girardi brings audience members across the footlights by explicitly implicating them as enforcers of morality. Rumors circulated frequently during Strauss's lifetime that he was fed up with Vienna and was preparing to move to another large European city. The Berlin premiere of *Eine Nacht in Venedig* a few years earlier had frightened his Viennese audience into believing that he might not return. With this verse inserted into the appropriate couplet, Girardi publicly acknowledges that he has been the object of gossip and criticism for his personal life and asks him to stay in Vienna despite it.

Carnero and the remaining ensemble are surprised by the arrival of Count Homonay, who informs them that he has come to recruit soldiers for the Austrian army in their fight against the Spanish. Using dance as a military metaphor, he explains, "We want to march to Spain soon and let the gentlemen there dance a csárdás." Carnero, who still opposes Barinkay and Saffi's marriage, greets the Count, "You got here just in time to witness how we caught the recently returned 'patriot' as a criminal *in flagrante*." Barinkay, however, supports the monarchy by donating his new-found wealth to the king and his army. In the most heavily censored passage, Homonay mocks Carnero's Morality Commission, responding to Carnero's complaints about Barinkay's immorality with the declaration:

> Your Highness seems to forget that we find ourselves on Hungarian ground! That means that in Hungary a girl may not fall around the neck of her lover (without (~~your~~) organization checking) if a misdemeanor hasn't been committed . . . or that in order for me to give a cute young lady a kiss, I first must call the (police) to observe! Short and sweet, Your Highness, this whole weird Commission might be appropriate . . . *skeptically evaluating Carnero's appearance* (~~for people under your Constitution – the Hungarian Constitution~~) has completely different rules![56]

The censor routinely objected to any specific reference to government or royalty, and here the words "police" and "Constitution" drew attention. This passage highlights the differences between Hungarian and Austrian views of morality – Hungarians find Austrians too prudish and their government agencies too intrusive, while Austrians view their neighbors as indulgent and immoral. Once again the conflicting attitudes between the two halves of the empire are emphasized over their mutual understanding and respect for each other's mores.

At the time of *Zigeunerbaron*'s premiere, the Hungarian regiment, the Honvéds, were recruited and conscripted for each military engagement,[57] and Habsburg residents had only to look back to 1878 for a precedent for military action, the occupation of Bosnia-Herzegovina. This move was intended to prevent Serbia and Montenegro from expanding, thus creating a Slav state in the Balkans and threatening Habsburg Dalmatia. The occupation required concerted participation from Hungarians and Austrians alike before the

6.2 Hungarian and Austrian soldiers (*Der Floh*, 25 August 1878)

Bosnian occupation was secure. The cover of *Der Floh* on 25 August 1878 celebrated their common victory with a Hungarian soldier and an Austrian soldier standing before an eastern-looking city labeled Sarajevo, each with one arm around his colleague and the other arm held aloft in victory (see Illustration 6.2). This illustration reflects several stereotypes found in Strauss's operetta: the Hungarian soldier's uniform is far more ornamental than the Austrian's; the saber is the weapon of choice for the Hungarian while the Austrian carries the more modern rifle; the Hungarian's mustache is longer and thinner than the Austrian's; and in his free arm the Austrian holds aloft a banner with the empire's insignia while the Hungarian holds up his flask. The thematic similarity of the Bosnian military engagement to events in *Der Zigeunerbaron* is clear – soldiers from both halves of the empire cooperate to defeat a common enemy.

Homonay's song, reinforced by the chorus, imitates a familiar Hungarian military custom and musical genre: *verbunkos* music. The *verbunkos* (the *Werberlied* or Recruiting Song) was traditionally used by military recruiters traveling through small villages and attracting eligible young men to enlist through song, dance, and wine. As the dance progressed from a slow, steady tempo to a whirling, inescapable pace, the recruits were increasingly seduced by the romance of military life.[58] The covenant was sealed by drinking out of the recruiter's cup, a custom used to comic advantage when the ever-"thirsty" Zsupán unknowingly accepts Homonay's offer.

Homonay's song uses typical tactics of military propaganda to attract recruits. He refers to the manly strength of the Hungarian divisions: "Es muß das Ungarheer siegen oder sterben! Lieber möge unser Blut seine Erde färben, eh' die Hand im Kampfe ruht" [The army of Hungary must win or die! Better our blood should color its earth than let our hand rest in battle]. He continues his appeal in the faster pace of the csárdás, promising that all young women love Husars, and it is the Husars' duty to kiss them. The emphasis on Hungarian tendencies toward violence and passion reinforced stereotypes commonly associated for the Austrians with their eastern neighbors. The accented short-long pattern adds rhythmic flavor to this section and may imitate the sound to Austrian ears of a forceful, persuasive speech by an impassioned Hungarian.[59] According to a report in the *Fremdenblatt*, Jókai gave Strauss the march melody for the Recruiting Song as an authentic tune from the "Freedom War" (the Hungarian revolution of 1848–49) in which

Jókai had participated as a rebel.[60] By appropriating a piece of Hungarian *Kulturgut*, one originally used for revolutionary purposes, and placing it in the service of a government institution, Strauss, wittingly or not, carries out the work of cultural imperialism.

The second act finale brings anticipation of a reunion in Vienna, new information about Saffi's heritage, and a celebration of military strength. Arsena and Mirabella begin the waltz-chorus praising Vienna: "So voll Fröhlichkeit gibt es weit und breit keine Stadt, wie die Wienerstadt, keine so fein" [There is no city far and wide as full of happiness as Vienna]. The text continues, "[everyone in Vienna] wants song, women, and wine!" alluding to one of Strauss's most famous waltzes, "Wein, Weib und Gesang."[61] This apotheosis of Vienna, which only prefaces the further praise found in Act III, directly contradicts general Hungarian sentiment about the imperial capital.

The waltz meter is abandoned when Carnero renews his complaints about the immoral Gypsies. He and Homonay argue once again whether Saffi and Barinkay's marriage is legal and under whose jurisdiction the question falls. Carnero orders his men to arrest Barinkay, Saffi, and Czipra, but Homonay stops him. He takes Saffi and Czipra into custody himself saying, "As children of this nation I take you under protection." But Carnero warns: "This nation is also the subject of the King who sent me!", reminding listeners once again of Hungary's subservience to Austria.

Zsupán, Mirabella, and Arsena join Carnero's attack on the Gypsies' values, but Czipra soon interupts them with an announcement. She surprises everyone by presenting a previously unknown document showing that Saffi is not her child but rather the daughter of the last Pasha of Hungary.[62] The news disappoints Barinkay, however, who explains that he fell in love with the poor Gypsy girl, not the princess. The blow this strikes to Saffi is made even more poignant by his use of the tune and accompaniment first heard in the Act I finale when Saffi pledged loyalty and trust to him on behalf of the Gypsies. To the accompaniment of Homonay's Recruiting Song, Barinkay reaches for the cup of wine to seal his decision.[63] Barinkay feels he must leave her, and the music reveals his decision before he can articulate it for himself.

The jumbled state of the autograph score reflects the many revisions and discussions involved before finalizing the original order of events at the end of Act II. But Strauss had learned something about dramatic writing by this point in his operetta career and made suggestions to Schnitzer regarding the structure of the second finale:

> The action (*now* excellent) must take place in *one number*, namely in the second finale. It is impossible that the main themes of the finale appear already in the numbers coming *before* the finale – what musical stimulus would the closing number then have – on which the main success of the operetta depends? Recruiting March, Drinking Song (Barinkay) and waltz are the pillars of the II. finale. These themes could be repeated in the finale, but must not appear in the preceding pieces.[64]

Strauss understood the importance of the second act finale for the overall success of the operetta. Indeed, he believed the Act II finale to be even more important than the Act III finale, for the energy and tension remaining after Act II determined whether or not the audience, including critics, would stay for the final act.[65]

In the original finale, Homonay's *Werberlied* followed the Viennese waltz, but the later version, in which the waltz appears after the forces have been recruited, is more effective dramatically. The original finale also concluded with the waltz with which it began, but Strauss rewrote the ending, surprising audiences at its twenty-fifth performance. The revised conclusion, which uses the Recruiting Song, part of the earlier "Anvil Chorus," and an orchestral reference to the Rácóczy March, has remained the more popular. A return to the "Anvil Chorus" at this point reinforced the Gypsies' earlier assertion that the fatherland will appreciate their swords now that they are going to war.

The tragic ending of the second act, though innovative at the time, was soon widely imitated and eventually became a hallmark of "Silver Age" operetta. Critics like Hanslick heartily protested about the tendency to create tension after the second act in this manner, leaving the audience to wonder how the crisis would be resolved in the third. In *Der Zigeunerbaron*, the conflict comes not from mistaken identity, as was often the case in more comic operettas, but rather from intolerable class differences. Barinkay's decision to leave Saffi because he suddenly feels unworthy of her appears only in Schnitzer's version, not in the original story by Jókai. Hanslick complained that it was completely out of character and the audience loses all respect for the hitherto sympathetic hero.[66] He felt that Barinkay should go to war only out of patriotism like his comrades; he should not leave Saffi because she is the daughter of a Pasha, but because he is the son of a proud nation. The crisis splits the mood between festivity and anguish.

The Entr'acte sets the scene of Act III with a full instrumental repetition of the waltz sung by Barinkay, Saffi, and Czipra when they found the buried treasure in Act II. The *Schatzwalzer* is appropriate also in this context as a fitting introduction for troops returning with war booty. As the curtain rises on the Kärntnertor, a familiar Viennese landmark, the chorus celebrates their victorious return. The realistic stage setting comes into play once again when the boy suggests that they run to meet the returning soldiers: "They must come from there across the Wieden. There we'll see them sooner." The Theater an der Wien, built in the district of Vienna known as Wieden (IV. District), was commonly referred to as the Wiedner Theater. When the back doors of the stage were thrown open to admit the returning throngs of soldiers, the audience could imagine themselves taking part in precisely such a scenario.

Zsupán acts as spokesman for the Hungarian regiment and reports his exploits in the immediately popular march, "Von des Tajos Strand." Strauss demonstrated his stage experience once again in his conception of this song. In a letter to Schnitzer on 26 July 1885 he argued: "We can't leave the March couplet in *this* length; it should be kept short enough so that if it is pleasing, it could be done 3 times. Remember the March Trio by Suppé from *Fatinitza*, which was repeated 3 or 4 times almost every time. It would never have achieved this success if it were arranged longer than it is."[67] His judgment proved correct: Zsupán's march was also demanded three times on opening night and at almost every performance thereafter.[68]

This song served as military propaganda, much as Homonay's Recruiting Song did. Arriving on stage astride a Lipizzaner,[69] a symbol of Austrian power since their victory over the Spanish, Zsupán is pleased to return from battle without scars or wounds, only a little sunburned; he even got away with pilfering jewelry and pocket change. By having a Hungarian return from a war on behalf of the Habsburg monarchy not only unhurt but wealthy, Strauss and Schnitzer endorse the value of a common military organization for the two halves of the empire. Hungarians had long wanted an independent standing army, and negotiations with the crown became increasingly heated until finally in 1889 they were allowed to form their own regiment using commands in Magyar, but Franz Joseph retained control over their artillery.[70] At the very time Hungarians were lobbying for their own army, the operetta insists that such a division is unnecessary.

Zsupán's proud display of his spoils again engages anti-Semitic stereotypes and taps a common concern at the time, natives of Transleithania coming to Vienna and threatening long-standing urban business practices. The number of legally registered peddlers in Vienna, many of whom were poor Hungarians and Galician Jews, jumped from 927 in 1866 to over 1600 in 1878–79.[71] Tension between established shopkeepers and the peddlers escalated, until the City Council agreed to hold public hearings in 1880. Behind thinly veiled anti-Semitic motives, all the guilds favored a complete prohibition of peddling. One of those who spoke at the hearing was Josef Buschenhagen, a poor watchmaker who felt that the foreign watches being sold by Jewish peddlers on street corners and restaurants were ruining his business.[72] Later he called several rallies and engendered much public sympathy for the guilds' cause. When the Hungarian Zsupán returns to Vienna with dozens of watches from fallen soldiers, he touches on a negative image already very much alive in Viennese public life.

The waiting crowd and the returning soldiers sing together in fanfare of their conquest. Even the reluctant Ottokar enjoyed and excelled at soldiery once he experienced it first-hand. Barinkay is reunited with Saffi, who sings a few bars of her signature melody, including a descending harmonic minor scale. The crowd and Czipra hail him as their Gypsy baron, and the operetta concludes with a chorus of his entrance couplet, "Ja, das alles auf Ehr'." That is, the text ends there, but the orchestra gives the Hungarians the last word with a final return to duple meter and *alla zoppa* rhythm. This happy end reinforces the message that if only the Hungarians comply with the wishes of the monarchy, all subjects will find wealth, courage, and personal fulfillment. The operetta indeed celebrates cooperation, as previous scholars have asserted, but it is the Hungarians who are urged to cooperate with the Austrians – the reverse would have been unthinkable.

PERFORMANCE: INNOVATION AND EXTRAVAGANCE

One of the most influential theater phenomena of the late nineteenth century was the theater troupe from Meiningen. The troupe had visited Vienna in 1875 and 1879, and performed again in October and November 1883, the period when Strauss began work on *Der Zigeunerbaron*. They excelled in elaborate set and costume design, but, more importantly, they revolutionized the theater world with their extraordinary coordination of crowd scenes.[73] Their method embodied a kind of *Gesamtkunstwerk* in which they balanced the various elements of set, costume, text, music, performance. The function of the performers received new value above all in the confrontation between the individual and the crowd.[74] Indeed, many critics complained that their work overemphasized the decorations and crowd coordination and that the text provided only an excuse for the other aspects.[75]

The Meiningen group used the Theater an der Wien for their guest appearances in Vienna, as it was the only house large enough to accommodate their productions. One of their fundamental innovations was the horizontal division of the stage, adding depth and perspective to what had been perceived as a two-dimensional space,[76] and the set for *Der Zigeunerbaron* used this technique. As the largest of any of the *Vorstadt* theaters, both in physical space and available seating room, the Theater an der Wien was well suited to introduce these innovations to Vienna. The stage extended to the street behind the theater allowing horses and carts to enter from the street, thereby enhancing the realism on stage. It was also one of the first theaters to install electric lighting (even the Court Opera used gas until 1887).[77] The new equipment allowed unprecedented stage effects, as when the beginning of *Zigeunerbaron's* Act II brightened gradually from dawn to morning.

Although Jauner was officially banned from work in the theater after being found guilty of negligence in the Ringtheater fire of 1881, it was widely recognized that his talents lay behind the consortium running the Theater an der Wien. Following the Meiningen model, he took special care with the details of production. He asked Strauss to bring him pictures from Pest of the Hungarian national dress and went to rural Hungary himself to research folk life there.[78] The steps toward realism in costuming, set design, and lighting which he introduced in *Der Zigeunerbaron* set an example that would be followed for the next decade.

RECEPTION

Although secondary literature has often hailed *Der Zigeunerbaron* as a symbol of the contentment then shared by the two halves of the Habsburg monarchy, contemporary Hungarian theater-goers seem not to have shared this opinion. A telling barometer of Hungarian national sentiment is provided by the reception of *Die Fledermaus* at its premiere in Budapest in 1882, only a few years before the *Zigeunerbaron*. Actors in the Hungarian national theater troupe, the *Népszínház*, had always performed in national dress; but because wearing the requisite tuxedos in *Die Fledermaus* would have been such a novelty, the director Lajos Evva completely changed the setting of the operetta to eighteenth-century China and all the characters to visiting Italians. He feared that the patriotism and the anti-Austrian sentiment of his public could easily become dangerous![79]

For this production, the director also added the following discussion to the dialogue following Rosalinde's csárdás in Act II:

ALL (*clapping*): Wonderful! Eljen!

MELANIE (an invited guest): But please, that is certainly no Hungarian song! I was myself Hungarian in my childhood, I should know! That must be a fiery Spanish song!

MARQUIS CARICONI: That is an insult! I forbid it! That is no Spanish song, rather it is English!

MURAY (an American, *angrily*): Not English! A Chinese or Japanese song perhaps!

RAMUSIN (diplomatic attaché): No, no, neither one!

ORLOFSKY: What then? If not even the specialists can agree!

KRAPOTI: It must be one of those waltz-dependent dualistic csárdás![80]

The added dialogue suggests that Hungarian public opinion was far from satisfied with the conditions of dualism.

When *Der Zigeunerbaron* premiered in Vienna three years later (24 October 1885), its success was recognized by critics from both halves of the empire, but explanations for that success varied. The *Neue Freie Presse* declared it to be an "Austrian operetta," although only the last act took place in Vienna.[81] The Viennese *Fremdenblatt* emphasized the novelty and significance of the Hungarian setting:

> For Hungary, last night's event meant the acquisition of a national opera, and Strauss should prepare himself today for the storm of enthusiasm with which the hot-blooded Magyars will celebrate him . . . The Hungarian element is used in the opera for the first time . . . It is surprising how precisely and successfully the national color was achieved in melody and instrumentation . . . What Hungarian composer surpasses him?! . . . Fully half of the operetta had to be repeated, in fact, many times the audience could not be satisfied with a single repetition.[82]

The Austrian reviewer generously offers the most Austrian of composers as the creator of the Hungarian "national opera." The condescension inherent in such a suggestion typified the Austrian attitude

toward Hungary: patronizing, but with a show of generous enthusiasm.

Der Floh also noted the work's Hungarian setting; its front page on
the day of the premiere was entitled "Magyars in Vienna" and portrayed the two leading women dressed in national costume with
Strauss and Jókai in the background playing the violin and bass. The
article inside clarified the journal's disapproval of Strauss's behavior:
"The members of the Hungarian delegation may be proud of their
countryman from the Siebenbürgen, Strucz János – or as the
Viennese and the other Europeans customarily call him, Johann
Strauss."[83] This reviewer no doubt reflected the opinion of many
readers for whom "Europe" did not include Hungary.

The *Neues Wiener Tagblatt* was not misled by the operetta's eighteenth-century setting. Critic "W. Fr." recognized its timeliness as the
two halves of the empire renewed *Ausgleich* negotiations:

> It is set in the middle of the previous century during the time of the
> second war of succession, never dropping however the connecting
> thread to the present, and if it did not sound so stark and dry, one could
> say that the author or authors have, in the face of the *Ausgleich* negotia-
> tions already in progress, fixed the quotas between the two halves of the
> empire. Only thereby a reversed relationship comes to light, in which
> through the two first specifically Hungarian acts of the *Zigeunerbaron*,
> the eastern half of the empire receives 70 percent and the western,
> only 30.[84]

Under the ever-contested terms of the *Ausgleich*, the responsibility
for contributions to the common imperial fund was, as this journalist
noted, exactly the inverse of the operetta's distribution.

The reviewer from the *Vorstadtzeitung*, Isidor Fuchs, entitled his
article "Johann Strauss's Ninth," alluding to one of the most famous
works of the nineteenth century:

> Until now whoever spoke of the "Ninth" with a tone of delight, had
> expressed himself clearly enough to awaken the image of the most pow-
> erful musical creation of the century in every educated person. From
> now on, however, there is, in addition to Beethoven's Ninth, also a Ninth

by Johann Strauss; i.e., *Der Zigeuner-Baron* . . . Were it possible for contemporaries to judge a work of music after a single performance, one
would not doubt for a moment which of the two "Ninths" deserves
priority. Without question, the Strauss operetta.[85]

The *Vorstadtzeitung* had a limited readership, but the reviewer
thought it reasonable not only to compare Strauss's work to that of
Beethoven, but to prefer it. The reviewer's comments also reflect a
class distinction, for if the prestigious, inner-city districts can claim
Beethoven's Ninth, the *Vorstadt* is happy to claim *Der Zigeunerbaron* as
a parallel cultural symbol.

Hanslick prepared himself for the premiere of this new work, as
was his habit for all premieres. In the same letter in which he
requested tickets for his wife, himself, and two friends, he requested a
libretto or a score from Strauss a few days before the dress rehearsal.[86] His review in the *Neue Freie Presse* praises the music for being
"authentic and natural," with orchestration that had the "inimitable
Straussian sound." He hailed the *Zigeunerbaron* as an advance for the
composer toward mastering larger forms and toward finer and more
characteristic dramatic handling. He did not recognize much original
in the music, but he commended the composer for borrowing
material only from himself. That fact alone differentiated him from
other operetta composers who in their most successful numbers
imitate, if not annex, Strauss. However, Hanslick opposed even the
slightest suggestion that operetta was moving in the direction of
grand opera, a tendency he foresaw in *Der Zigeunerbaron*; he felt such
a style taxed the singers beyond their vocal capacity and made performances at provincial theaters impossible.

The premiere of *Der Zigeunerbaron* in Pest took place on 26
November 1885, not simultaneously with the Viennese premiere, as
Jókai had hoped. Jauner guided that performance as well and sent
positive reports back to his colleagues who had stayed in Vienna to be
present at the author's benefit, the twenty-fifth performance. He
exclaimed: "Yesterday the orchestra pit had to be cleared, and many
hundreds had to go away without a ticket. That pleases *me* very

much!"[87] Despite good box office receipts, this premiere lacked the journalistic support found in Vienna. In Budapest Barinkay was played by popular Hungarian actress Ilka Palmay, but her star appeal was not sufficient to gain critical acclaim. The Hungarian press also objected that Schnitzer had changed Jókai's story to suit Viennese tastes, while others protested against the "waltzification" of patriotic Hungarian music.[88]

The Hungarian critic "lb" offered explicitly political grounds for the success of *Zigeunerbaron*:

> According to our premises, we explain this success in a cultural-histori-
> cal manner not from the higher value of the Strauss–Jókai collabora-
> tion, but rather from the serendipitous coordination of timely events,
> which made the Viennese-German audience receptive to a "dualistic"
> libretto. Jókai was already long popular in Vienna, and it was possible
> for his genial poetic nature to set the stark politics of dualism in harmo-
> nious, social tones. The misfortune of the German Constitutional Party,
> the agreement during the Budapest Exhibition, the *Goldmensch* as prede-
> cessor prepared the ground for the unprecedented success of
> *Zigeunerbaron*.[89]

The "dualistic" libretto was acceptable to the Viennese-German audience, but was not embraced by the Hungarians as a symbol of their satisfaction with the dualistic arrangement. Commencing a tradition that has continued well into this century, Austrians preferred to regard the operetta as a reflection of Hungary's satisfaction with the division of assets and liabilities as they stood.

Der Zigeunerbaron, which was performed eighty-seven nights running, meant an important boost for the profits of Theater an der Wien. After *Die Fledermaus*, it has become the most performed of Strauss's operettas; between 1896 and 1921 it was performed 7420 times on German-speaking stages, the third most frequent of any operetta written between 1855 and 1900.[90] The operetta was the first to celebrate its 300th performance in Vienna,[91] and Alexandrine von Schönerer chose to close her long career at the Theater an der Wien on 30 April 1900 with a performance of *Der Zigeunerbaron*, her greatest success.[92]

Der Zigeunerbaron has taken its place in the history of operetta and in the career of Johann Strauss. Although it was not performed in the Viennese Court Opera until eleven years after his death,[93] Strauss made his own entrance into the bastion of high-art music only seven years and two works later. As countless friends and critics had noticed, his musical and dramatic language was becoming ever more suited to the requirements of the Court Opera. The journalist organization "Concordia," in an attempt to convince him that he could write a work for the opera, sponsored a performance of *Der Zigeunerbaron* at the Theater an der Wien in which all the major roles were sung by performers from the Court Opera.[94] His next work, with the help of his librettist, took further steps toward an operatic style and his only opera soon followed.

Richard Wagner and Johann Strauss – these names evoke opposite poles of nineteenth-century music: one, a world of Teutonic gods and thundering brass, and the other, a world of waltzes and champagne. However different their music may have been, these composers shared the spotlight as popular cultural personalities in the 1870s and 1880s, a period in which Wagner's works became standard fare at the Court Opera and Strauss celebrated his fourth decade performing for the Viennese public. A Wagner museum opened in Vienna; the Academic Wagner Society was founded; and hopeful Wagnerian epigones sought recognition from Viennese listeners. Operetta composers also began experimenting in the 1880s with medieval or Renaissance Germanic settings, tragic characters, and thick musical textures – all hallmarks of Wagner's operas. The trend toward a more earnest style began with Strauss's *Der Zigeunerbaron*, and continued with his *Simplicius* (1888) and *Ritter Pásmán* (1892), each of which represents a step toward through-composition, heavier orchestration, a more chromatic harmonic language, and a greater mixture of tragic and comic elements. Despite protests from Hanslick and other critics who preferred a strict division between opera and operetta, composers continued to mingle Freia with Fledermaus in hopes of artistic – and commercial – success.

Wagner's and Strauss's status as pillars of art music and popular music remained unchallenged through the end of the century. In fact, the end of their reign in their respective musical realms could be placed in 1905 with the premieres, within three weeks, of Richard Strauss's *Salome* (in Dresden) on the one hand and Lehár's *Die lustige Witwe* (at the Theater an der Wien) on the other.[1] These events were not as unrelated as they might seem, for not only do both works evince anxiety over women's roles in the new century, audiences for the two musical styles overlapped; the Viennese bourgeoisie who made the pilgrimage to Bayreuth also prided themselves on having box seats for Strauss's operettas.

Enthusiasts of both operetta and music drama discovered in these genres the means to a similar end, escape from daily concerns through nostalgia for a bygone era. What ensured the composers' success, however, was that the escapism was carefully engineered to reinforce hegemonic cultural and political ideals. Wagner's rise in popularity in the 1880s was matched by increasing displays of German nationalism and anti-Semitism, and by growing interest in the literature and religion of the German Middle Ages. Strauss's librettist, Victor Léon, actively drew on these elements as well, not only to attract audiences but to make claims for the status of Viennese operetta as German art. An examination of contemporary political events and Wagner's reception in Vienna will provide new perspective on Strauss's goals and achievements at the end of the nineteenth century.

GERMAN NATIONALISM IN VIENNA

Many Viennese born in the late 1840s and the 1850s were deeply affected by Austria's loss of influence in the German empire to Prussia in 1866, and they associated this loss with the post-revolutionary Liberal government.[2] The *völkisch*, German national movement had begun among university students with the establishment in 1871 of the Society of German Students in Vienna (*Leseverein der deutschen Studenten Wiens*), a group that based much of its philosophy for the regeneration of German culture on the ideas of Nietzsche and Wagner. The founding of the Academic Wagner Society two years later strengthened student interest in Wagner's theoretical writings. Their generation shared with Wagner an enthusiasm for the ideas of Schopenhauer, and the Society espoused their belief in music as the direct expression of the undifferentiated Will. These student groups sparked discussions and ideas that would shape the members' later political and artistic careers.

The Society of German Students was dissolved by the government at the end of 1878 as a danger to the state. At that time it included not only students but 135 professors, among them eighteen imperial counselors (*Hofräte*) and twenty-four members of parliament. Its list of members ranged from music patron Nicolaus Dumba to budding German nationalist Georg von Schönerer (brother of theater director Alexandrine von Schönerer). Feelings of German artistic and political nationalism belonged not merely to those of a fringe group or transient students, but rather reached into the upper echelons of Viennese society. During the last year of the Society's existence one of its members, Siegfried Lipiner, gave a lecture, "On the Elements of a Renewal of Religious Ideas in the Present," in which he equated religion with transcendent emotion, and as a show of respect the Society published his speech at its own expense.[3] In 1881 a few of the more artistically inclined former members of the Society of German Students formed their own group, the Saga Society (*Sagengesellschaft*), devoted to German myth and music.[4] Of their members, Lipiner went on to write the libretto to Karl Goldmark's *Merlin* and Richard von Kralik worked throughout the 1880s and 1890s on editions of German sagas and folk stories of early Christianity.

An elaborate wake held by German-national university students in March 1883 marked the occasion of Wagner's death. Wagner's extreme popularity extended even to those students who did not belong to the Academic Wagner Society, for as Hermann Bahr wrote, "every young person was a Wagnerian then. He was one before he had even heard a single measure of his music."[5] The closely policed event attracted 4,000 mourners from all ranks of society. German national fervor was inspired by the music performed, such as the battle hymn from *Rienzi*, *Wach' am Rhein*, and selections from *Tannhäuser*, and by charismatic speakers like Georg von Schönerer and the young Bahr, who was later expelled from the university for his participation in the almost treasonous event. The kind of passionate politics practiced by these young men, filled with appeals to cultural patriotism and emotion, marked a deliberate departure from the cooler, more rational methods of their Liberal forefathers.

The Wagner wake occurred at a time when nationalist sentiment was running high owing to growing dissatisfaction with the pro-Slav policies of Prime Minister Eduard Taaffe and his conservative coalition in parliament. In 1880 Taaffe passed ordinances allowing official documents in Bohemia and Moravia to be in Czech or German, and requiring all government officials in these provinces to be bilingual, thus giving Czechs more opportunities for positions in the civil service. Czechs at the university in Prague had long campaigned to have Czech declared the official language, and on 11 April 1881 the school was divided by imperial decree into two insitutions, one German-speaking and one Czech-speaking. Tax reforms passed a year later redrew districts in favor of the Bohemian landed curia and lowered the required taxes, enfranchising the "5–Gulden men."[6] Austrian Liberals felt threatened by these developments and regarded them as a sign of imminent cultural decline. Léon and his contemporaries worked against the perceived "de-Viennization" by absorbing and propagating their collective German heritage.

Nationalist sentiment, along with the popularity of Wagner's *Die Meistersinger von Nürnberg*, spurred an interest in the music of the German Renaissance. Robert Hirschfeld, a student of Hanslick at the University, finished a dissertation on Johannis de Muris in 1884 and, in the same year, organized programs of *a cappella* works for small ensembles. In this way he hoped to demonstrate authentic roots for Wagner's works and to reestablish German preeminence in Austrian concert life.[7] A similar historicity marks Makart's fascination with the Dutch Renaissance, an interest evidenced not only by the *Meistersinger*-style parade he organized for the Emperor's wedding celebration in 1879 but also in his enormous, detailed paintings. Hirschfeld, Makart, Léon, and others of their generation felt the allure of pre-capitalist, pre-industrialist societies; having experienced the economic collapse of 1873 and the ensuing depression at a formative age, they were disillusioned with the conditions that precipitated it.

Many operetta composers and librettists were indeed attracted to German nationalism, a sentiment that their works both conveyed and stimulated. Seeking to eliminate traces of the genre's French heritage, operetta's creators focused on German mythology, history, and military might. Leading male roles in the 1880s were frequently soldiers or military heroes, as opposed to servants and aristocrats as they had been in the past, or artists and bohemians as they would be in the twentieth century. Millöcker's *Feldprediger* of 1884, for example, invokes the power of German military unity: "If the German Reich is united in brotherhood with Austria, then God have mercy on the enemy, but also on the false friend" [Wenn deutsches Reich / Mit Österreich / Im Bruderbund vereint, / dann gnade Gott dem Feind, / Aber auch dem falschen Freund].[8] Whereas the military had once served as the object of mockery (in Offenbach's and Strauss's early works), it now became elevated to a heroic ideal.

Another cultural manifestation of this pan-German enthusiasm was the renewal of interest in German romantic opera, a phenomenon so widespread that Hugo Wolf lamented in 1885 that German composers set only libretti that deal entirely with German myths, sagas, or history.[9] A celebration of the centennial of Carl Maria von Weber's birth brought *Der Freischütz*, *Oberon*, and *Euryanthe* to the Court Opera in 1886, and works by Heinrich Marschner once again enjoyed popularity. *Hans Heiling* (1833) was frequently performed in the 1880s, and Court Opera director Wilhelm Jahn recovered *Der Vampyr* (1828) from the archives and revived it with great success in 1884.[10]

When Goldmark's *Merlin* premiered at the Court Opera in 1886, the popular press noted its coincidence with the premiere of Adolf Müller's operetta, *Der Hofnarr*. The cover of *Der Floh* that week featured "The wise man and the fool" and remarked: "A court sage and a court fool are the heroes of the musical novelties this week. The court advisor to King Arthur, Merlin, the Magician in the opera house, and the 'Court Fool' of the operetta in the Wiedner Theater: Winkelmann the Wise, Girardi the Fool."[11] The following week's issue featured a fictional review that mixed elements of the two performances (plot, characters, performers, etc.) in its account of the simultaneous premieres. Despite its mocking tone, the newspaper report demonstrates that mythological and German Renaissance topics provided fodder for authors working on both sides of the Ringstrasse; creators of art music and of popular theater drew on similar raw materials, differing only in the final product. Composers of both genres found inspiration in the model of Wagner's theoretical ideas and their manifestation in his stage works.

WAGNER RECEPTION IN VIENNA

Wagner's relationship to Vienna was full of promises and disappointments.[12] He arrived in the city in 1861 expecting *Tristan* to be produced at the Court Opera that fall, but after seventy-seven rehearsals the Opera abandoned the project in spring 1863. While in Vienna for these rehearsals, the composer wrote the libretto to *Die Meistersinger*. When he read the work to an assembled group on 15 November 1862, Hanslick was among the first to hear Wagner parody his pedantry in Veit Hanslich, the figure who became Beckmesser.[13] During his stay in Vienna, Wagner frequented what would soon become the birthplace of Viennese operetta, the Theater an der Wien, and gave three benefit concerts there at Christmas and New Year 1862–63 including premieres of selections from the still unfinished *Meistersinger*, *Rheingold*, and *Walküre*. After a Christmas concert in 1863, he left the city and his outstanding debts behind, only to return nine years later seeking investors for his Bayreuth Festival. *Der Floh* noted his return to Vienna with a cartoon showing Wagner in his ever-present beret astride a swan, holding a lyre and distributing "Bayreuth shares" while Court Opera director Johann Herbeck, dressed as a ballerina, drops flower petals in Wagner's path (Illustration 7.1).[14] Despite high ticket prices, the benefit concert was sold out.[15] The anti-Semitic and anti-Wagnerian *Kikeriki* commented on the success of Wagner's concert with a full-page cartoon showing him conducting in a theater full of Jewish listeners, caricatured by large, crooked noses and balding foreheads – ironically, features of Wagner's own profile:

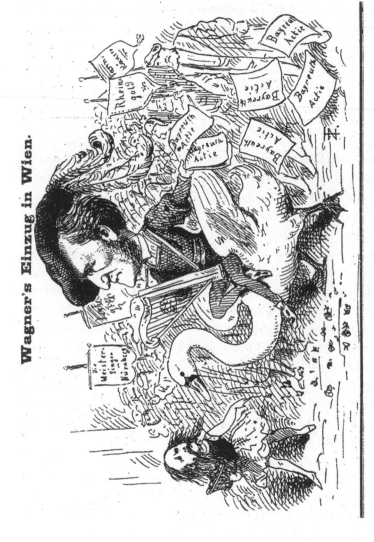

7.1 Wagner's arrival in Vienna (*Der Floh*, 12 May 1872)

"Judaism in music as it appeals to Richard Wagner. Namely, when they pay 25 fl. for a reserved seat" (Illustration 7.2).[16] However vehemently Wagner may have objected to Jewish participation in musical affairs, he fully appreciated their support in his business affairs.

Because relations between Wagner and the Court Opera had been strained ever since the failed attempt to produce *Tristan*, when Franz Jauner became director in 1875 one of his first projects was to restore relations with the composer. Jauner, a shrewd businessman, recognized that Wagner's monumental later works would help to fill the coffers depleted under the previous director's administration (Johann Herbeck, 1870–75), and paying Wagner the royalties owed him went a long way toward reconciliation. During his five-year tenure at the Court Opera, Jauner hired Hans Richter as musical director, and together they mounted all four *Ring* operas, first separately, then as a cycle in May 1879.[17] Wagner returned the consideration by engaging many Viennese singers to perform at Bayreuth – almost all the leading roles in *Parsifal* (1882) were sung by Viennese.[18]

Enthusiasm for things Wagnerian escalated in the 1880s and culminated in establishing a museum in the composer's honor, an institution that attracted endless abuse from the musical press. One paper announced its opening and speculated on possible items in its collection: the hair Wagner found in Beethoven's music, a "note" from a Swiss hotel that became part of an endless melody, and a drawing of the "shoulder" over which the master looked at all other musicians.[19] Despite its inauspicious beginnings, the museum stayed in business and expanded its services into a reading library devoted to Wagner-related publications.[20]

Germanic operas by composers such as Goldmark, Victor Nessler, and Engelbert Humperdinck also satisfied public demand for Wagneriana. Though less frequently performed today, works such as *Merlin*, *Der Trompeter von Säkkingen*, and *Hänsel und Gretel* achieved enormous success in their time. These works drew heavily on the tradition of German romantic opera begun earlier in the century with Weber, but the adjective "Wagnerian" was often invoked to connote a variety of characteristics: roving harmony, endless melody,

7.2 Wagner conducting in Vienna (*Kikeriki*, 12 May 1872)

leitmotivs, powerful orchestra, a plot drawn from German myth or legend, and a moment of redemption. The modernist view that cultural influence runs only from high to low was gainsaid by at least one nineteenth-century critic, who felt that Nessler had appropriated more than his share from the operetta stage: the front page of *Kikeriki* featured mock letters from Robert Planquette (composer of the popular *Die Glocken von Corneville*), Suppé, and Strauss "thanking" Nessler for using their work in his *Trompeter* and, in Strauss's case, asking for royalties.[21]

An extensive parody of *Der Trompeter von Säkkingen* in the popular press demonstrates the grasp this work held on its Viennese public. *Der Floh* "reported" that because this opera had achieved such success, several other Viennese theaters would be producing their own versions of it,[22] then listed the cast of characters and a brief plot summary for mock performances at the Burgtheater, the Carltheater, the Theater an der Wien, and the Theater in der Josefstadt. *Der Floh*'s announcements suggested the manner in which each theater might adapt the work to suit its own needs and style: thus the Burgtheater's version was a tragedy; the Carltheater presented a *Volksstück* with Mirzl (instead of Maria) and Damiancek from Bohemia (instead of Damian); the Theater in der Josefstadt offered a localized comedy (*Lokalposse*) in which Damian is a "Rascal [*Mistbub*] from Ottakring" (a working-class suburb of Vienna); and the version at the Theater an der Wien was an operetta with the leading male role played by a woman, another character the Herzog von Schönau-Carrara-Ferrara-Mortara,[23] and Damiano a run-down virtuoso (to be played by Girardi). The rest of the cast comprised a chorus of trumpeters, all with male names and all played by women, reflecting the popularity of both trumpet choruses and trouser-clad women on the operetta stage.

Parodies were not limited to newspaper articles: several Wagner operas were parodied on suburban Viennese stages long before the operas themselves were premiered in Vienna, creating the unusual situation of an audience familiar with the satire before its source. Such was the case with a parody of *Tannhäuser* written in 1853 by the *ne plus ultra* of Viennese comic actors, Johann Nestroy. In Nestroy's version, Venus is the proprietress of an underground delicatessen, and instead of journeying to Rome, Tannhäuser becomes a tenor at an opera house "of the future." The music by Karl Binder combines the themes and accompanimental patterns of *Tannhäuser* with new meters and text; for example, Tannhäuser's duple-meter song at the end of Act I as he takes his leave of an irate Venus becomes, in Binder's hands, a triple-meter *Ländler* with Venus urging him to go (Example 7.1). Binder also stylizes Mozart and Weber *à la* Wagner when Tannhäuser plans to sing a "Zukunfts-Zauberflöte" (a "Magic Flute of the Future") and fits Max's text (from *Der Freischütz*) to the music of the Pilgrim's Chorus (Example 7.2). Although the instrumental accompaniment includes the persistent sixteenth-notes and prominent brass of Wagner's *Tannhäuser*, several choruses end with the "duliäh," "juchhe," and "la la la" syllables typical of Viennese *Volkslieder*. When Wagner's *Tannhäuser* finally received its Viennese premiere in 1857, Hanslick recalled that as the real opera reached points the audience knew as humorous, the out-of-town singers were bewildered by the audience's laughter.[24]

The Nestroy/Binder parody was far from an isolated incident. Suppé composed his own *Tannhäuser* parody (1852) and also collaborated with Nestroy to produce *Lohengelb* (1859).[25] A review of *Prinz Methusalem*, Strauss's operetta of 1877, suggests that Strauss too may have participated in the business of parodying Wagner. A reporter for the *Fremdenblatt* remarked that

> It must have occured to everyone who attended both the dress rehearsal and the first performance that the first performance lacked an aria for Herr Eppich [Trombonius, a composer], which was particularly successful and aroused lively merriment in the dress rehearsal on account of its Wagnerian style and its parody of the "Lohengrin" motive. Did Strauss . . . eliminate the aria from his work at the last minute, or did the director of the Court Opera, who is at the moment preparing *Die Walküre*, exercise his influence and intervene with Strauss, in order to keep the memory of the Bayreuth composer unsullied by laughing satire from the Carltheater stage, where couplets about Wagner are repeatedly dashed off?[26]

Though no musical or textual evidence of the missing couplet is extant, the review suggests that Strauss experimented with incorporating Wagnerian elements, if only in jest, a full decade before he attempted composing his genuinely Wagnerian works.

WAGNER AND VIENNESE OPERETTA: PARODY OR HOMAGE?

Distinguishing between parody and genuine Wagnerian homage challenged viewers and critics then as now, for many of the works one might charitably assume to be failed parodies were in fact serious efforts. Composers and librettists alike seemed fascinated by the possiblities offered by Wagnerian music drama, but few achieved the desired success. The pathos and tragic drama associated with the *Gesamtkunstwerk* were unsuited to the talents and limitations of operetta performers, and despite repeated attempts, the *Mischform* made few inroads with operetta audiences.

The prolific Adolf Müller, Jr. climbed on the Wagnerian bandwagon with his comic opera *Der Liebeshof* [The Court of Love].[27] Librettists Hugo Wittmann and Oskar Blumenthal may have inspired him with their text, which draws on several obvious Wagnerian tropes. The work premiered on 14 November 1888 at the Theater an der Wien where Müller served as Kapellmeister. With its slow duple meter, and orchestration including harp, percussion, a full complement of brass, and triple stops in the strings, Müller's overture recalls that of *Die Meistersinger*. The similarity continues in the first act when the oblivious cuckold, Roger von Ventadoux, slowly and deliberately writes poetry with feather in hand: (pedantically scanning his verse) "Long-short, long-short, long-short, oh how sweet to write a Minnesang, one seeks the rhyme, counts the feet: long-short, long-short, long-short, long!" In an ensemble with harp and pizzicato string accompaniment, the five main characters sing "O noble, beautiful *Minnezeit*, song of the troubadour!" But Marion, Roger's wife, complains that he is too poetic and loves her too theoretically ["Du bist zu poetisch, Du liebest mich zu theoretisch."].

Example 7.1 Nestroy and Binder, *Tannhäuser*, Act I, No. 2

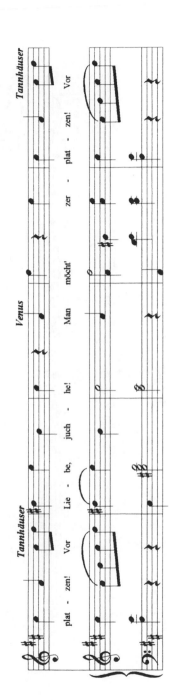

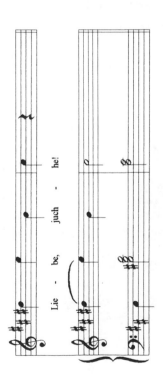

Example 7.2 Nestroy and Binder, *Tannhäuser*, Act III, No. 20

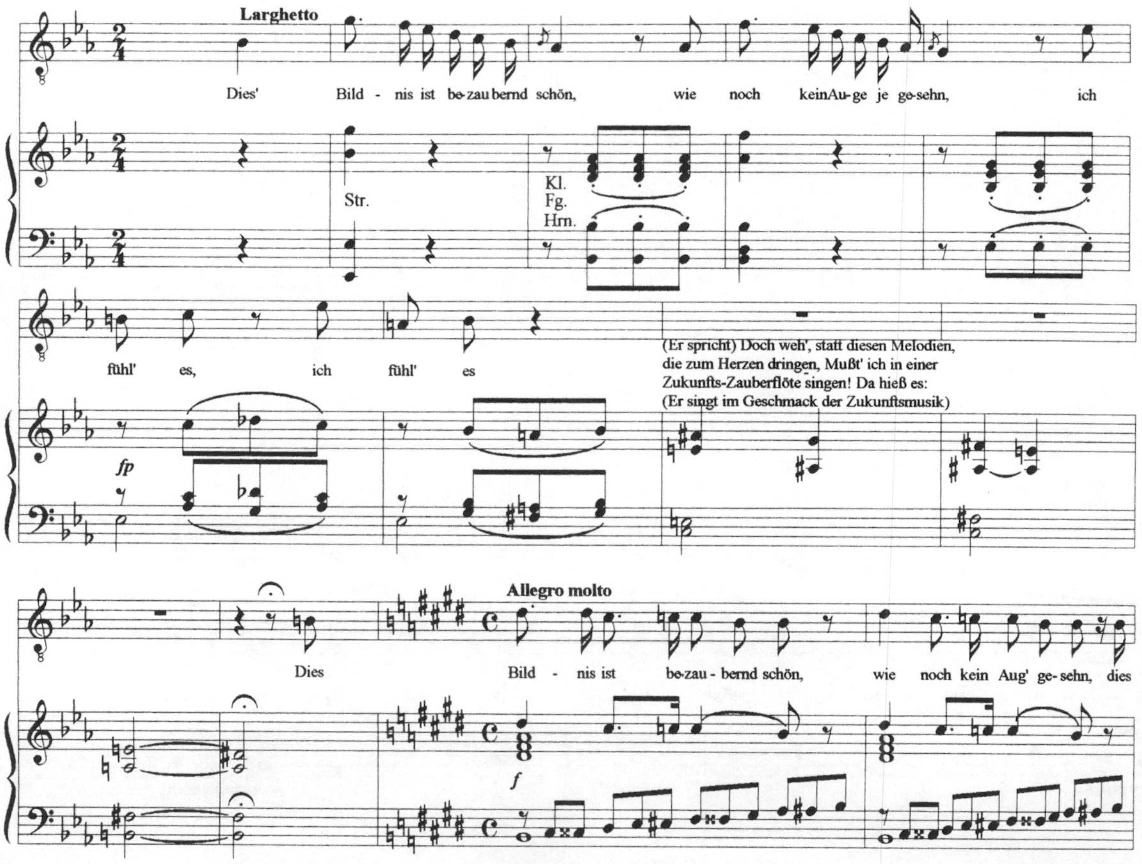

These scenes fall between the chairs of biting satire and sincere emulation.

The second act follows the German romantic convention of including a hunting chorus, complete with sixteen natural horns on stage. The popularity of on- or off-stage horns and trumpets began with such works as Weber's *Freischütz*, continued with Wagner's *Der fliegende Holländer* and *Tristan und Isolde*, and became ever more frequent after 1886 with the success of *Der Trompeter von Säkkingen*. In addition to Müller's *Liebeshof*, the device can also be found in his *General Gogo* (1896), in Carl Zeller's *Der Vogelhändler* (1891), and in Strauss's *Waldmeister* (1894), *Simplicius*, and *Ritter Pásmán*.[28]

Although Müller and his librettists included elements of the Wagnerian music drama, they also retained the satiric tone and contemporary allusions germane to operetta. In Act II a group of state-employed detectives spy on a thief they believe is hiding in the castle, as the refrain of their chorus explains, "We're the civil servants of the secret police" [Denn wir sind die Beamten der Geheimpolizei]. At the end of the act a journalist (!) tells stories of political corruption and politicians' philandering under the transparent guise, common to the operetta, of a foreign setting, assuring listeners that "such a thing could only happen in Baghdad." Despite clever passages, audiences were unsure what to make of the work, and its life on the stage of the Theater an der Wien was brief.

Another Wagnerian operetta, *Der Doppelgänger*, was written by Victor Léon, a future collaborator with Strauss. With a score composed by Alfred Zamara, this work demonstrates Léon's first attempt to incorporate the tone of comic opera with a Wagnerian subject. It premiered in the Theater an der Wien under Jauner's typically generous direction and stage design in the fall of 1887. Combining elements of *Der fliegende Holländer* and Lortzing's *Zar und Zimmermann*, the story revolves around men coming home from the sea and the impersonation of a Danish king. Similar in name and manner to Wagner's Erik, Léon's Eriksen greets the ship as it arrives in the harbor with "Hoiho!" The text for the opening chorus of *Der Doppelgänger* betrays him immediately as a Wagner enthusiast: "O höret, hört der Tuba Ton, des Königs Barke nahet schon" [Hear, o hear the tuba's sound, the king's bark is approaching]. The archaic vocabulary ("Barke" instead of "Schiff") and the self-conscious use of the genetive case (preceding the noun it modifies) suggest that Léon had mastered the manner, if not the substance, of Wagner's self-conscious poetic style.

The opening of Act II presents another key ingredient of German romantic opera, one Wagner used on several occasions: a men's chorus. The men pay tribute to their queen with an *a cappella* "Ave Maria" (stylistically similar to Bruckner's choral works), after which they honor the queen individually with their own songs of courtly love, a scene that recalls Tannhäuser's song contest on the Wartburg. *Der Floh* praised the work:

> Designed with Jauner-like verve and gripping style, the operetta *Der Doppelgänger*, the promising first work of our young Zamara, fills the house every night at the Theater an der Wien . . . We hope that the talented composer, whose name already has a good reputation, will soon let us – in the truest sense of the word – *hear* from him again, if only a little less Wagnerian![29]

Encouraged by their first success, Léon and Zamara intended to pursue their Wagnerian inclinations further in their next collaboration, but they were not destined to finish the work together. Although most of the first act had been composed, Léon broke his contract with Zamara in order to offer the libretto to a more prestigious composer, Johann Strauss.

STRAUSS'S ENGAGEMENT WITH *ZUKUNFTSMUSIK*

By the late 1880s, Strauss had long been familiar with Wagner's music. He and his brothers introduced music from Wagner's operas to Vienna in their *Volksgarten* concerts years before the works reached any Viennese stage. His orchestra performed selections from *Tannhäuser* in 1854, three years before its Viennese premiere at the Thalia-Theater and five years before its appearance at the Court

Opera. When he conducted the Entrance March from *Tannhäuser* and the entr'acte from *Lohengrin* at a *Volksgarten* concert in March of 1855, none of Wagner's stage works had yet appeared in Vienna, and music critics, including Hanslick, praised Strauss for his "enrichment of current musical life."[30] Johann's brother Josef was an avid Wagnerian who performed selections from *Tristan und Isolde* and arrangements from *Das Rheingold* for the composer when he came to Vienna in May 1861.

Through personal conducting experience, Johann was more familiar with the pre-*Ring* Wagner than with his later works. Wagner's theoretical writings were known in Vienna before his music or stage productions, but Strauss was in no sense a bibliophile. In fact, his engagement with the written word limited itself largely to libretti and newspapers, and he surely would not have endured the intricacies of Wagner's lengthy prose.[31] His letters give no indication that he gave much consideration to aesthetics, compositional process, or contemporary theoretical issues, and his method of working independently of his librettist precludes any connection between word and tone as outlined in Wagner's *Oper und Drama*.

Strauss and Adele traveled to Bayreuth in the summer of 1884, where they saw *Die Meistersinger von Nürnberg* and *Parsifal*. Soon thereafter, he informed *Zigeunerbaron* librettist Ignaz Schnitzer that he wanted to compose an operetta with a German subject,[32] a choice that may have been influenced not only by his first-hand experience with Wagner's works, but also by the enormous success the Germanic works like *Hans Heiling* and *Merlin* were enjoying at the Court Opera. Strauss began work on a new Schnitzer libretto, but soon dropped it in favor of one by the young, idealistic Léon.[33] The *Wiener Allgemeine Zeitung* alluded to Wagner already at this stage when it reported that Strauss was so happy finally to have the long-awaited book, he did not even ask "Woher er kam der Fahrt?"[34] Although the broken contract cost him his friendship with Schnitzer, it opened a new path for him and Viennese operetta.

VICTOR LÉON

Léon (1858–1940) was born within six years of both Gustav Mahler and Victor Adler, and his nostalgia for the *volkstümlich* betrays a disillusionment with Liberal ideals common to their generation.[35] He attended Gymnasium in Vienna, where he later pursued his career as writer and librettist; as a young man he associated with Hermann Bahr and other members of the literary circle Young Vienna (*Jung Wien*) at the Café Griensteidl, a popular locale for budding intellectuals, authors, and artists. Frequently the object of satirist Karl Kraus's scathing wit, these young men gathered to smoke small cigarettes, drink small cups of coffee, and immerse themselves in lengthy discussions of aesthetic beauty and literary style.

Strauss and his friends, always on the lookout for a suitable libretto, must have seen promise in the young author of *Der Doppelgänger*, for Léon was approached soon after its premiere and asked if he would work with Strauss. He was thrilled at the opportunity to collaborate with the established composer. His high regard for Strauss (already noted in chapter 3) appears repeatedly in his letters, which invariably address him as "Most honored Master" and close with similarly polite formulations. His obsequious attitude was combined, however, with an arrogant confidence in his own talent. Although he had achieved a single moderate success when he and Strauss began working together, he refused to accept a collaborator under any circumstances.

A letter from 29 June 1887 is worth quoting at length, for it gives an impression of what working with the young author must have been like:

> Most honored Master!
> Herr Priester was good enough to pass on to me your opinion of the second act.[36] I must admit, your letter aroused more astonishment than anything else. It is not authorial vanity that prompts me to speak up, but more the conviction that I have written the second act suitably for the stage and effectively throughout – it is both original and poetic. Director Jauner himself found fault only with details. It is inconceivable to me

that you can call this strict and logically structured, thoroughly motivated whole, a "patchwork," equally inconceivable that you miss the unity with the first act. Does the second not bring enough new elements and intensification? I refer you only to the first scenes, the bell scene, and the finale. Does the plot not move constantly, powerfully forward? Is the interest not equally divided among all the characters? These impressions are not just mine alone. Far be it from me to sing my own praises, but as author the judgment must also be entrusted to me whether something is patchwork or organic, whether it is effective for the stage or not. And just as, after long and completely selfless examination, I am most strongly convinced that the present second act is good overall, my conviction is no less that it could only grow worse through changes in content, structure or form. Except for details, text changes, etc. in which I want to and will observe your impressions completely, I can – for the sake of the *thing* – under absolutely no condition, agree to change the act; just as it is unthinkable to me – even when I would not be materially injured – that I would let a strange hand, as they say, "collaborate," on my finished, completely original, well-thought-out and carefully crafted work.

I am happy to concede that improvements may be needed in verse and prose. Do you request that? How easily it could be done in a thousand other ways! Even if this or that scene does not meet your subjective impression, which I value highly in any case, I ask you to tell me and I will gladly see what can be done, just as I have always done everything desirable, and what I have acknowledged as desirable. However, I can just as little substantially revise the present second act as take on a collaborator, which could only ruin and not improve. To submit to this you could not and should not expect of me, in the work's interest and in yours.

You will receive the third act in 8–10 days.

With the request to remember me to your gracious wife, I sign myself in eminent admiration and with greetings full of deep respect to you, honored Master, forever your humble servant

Victor Léon[37]

Although some of Léon's excessive phrases were standard conventions of nineteenth-century epistolary style, he carried such formulations to the extreme. Yet Strauss's difficulties with Léon's work were not merely a matter of differences in generation or social stature, but differences in basic aesthetic and artistic goals. Léon, under the heady influence of Wagnerism, wrote a libretto replete with religious overtones and German national sentiment. Strauss simply hoped to continue his path to the Court Opera, while repeating the commercial success he had achieved with *Der Zigeunerbaron*. Given these fundamental but largely unspoken disagreements, *Simplicius* was destined for neither critical nor popular success.

SIMPLICIUS

Strauss composed most of the music for *Simplicius* while in Coburg, Germany, awaiting permission to divorce his second wife, and he dedicated the operetta to Ernst II, Duke of Sachsen-Coburg-Gotha, as a show of gratitude for his cooperation and assistance.[38] The Duke, himself an accomplished composer, was a devoted patron of German opera, particularly Wagner's works. (He earned the nickname of "opera Duke" for his passion and hobby.[39]) His opera *Santa Chiara*, whose premiere Liszt conducted at Weimar in 1854, was performed widely in Germany, earning even Meyerbeer's praise in Paris, where it received sixty performances.[40] Strauss's dedication of *Simplicius* (and *Ritter Pásmán* as well) to a particularly nationalist German nobleman and Wagner patron marks a public acknowledgment of his debt to German operatic traditions.[41]

Strauss's residence in Germany during the work's creation required him and Léon to conduct lengthy correspondence by mail, and their letters reveal a great deal about their collaborative habits and the compositional process. In a letter of 20 June 1887, Léon conveyed to Strauss the reactions and recommendations of director Franz Jauner.[42] Both composer and librettist relied on Jauner's extensive theatrical experience, although they did not always agree with him or follow his advice. In the margins of this letter Strauss's wife Adele commented, "this opinion of Jauner's [Johann] does not share" and later, "Jauner again incorrect." In another letter a few months later, Léon described his wish to bring operetta to a higher artistic

niveau (just the kind of aspiration Hanslick disdained).[43] A nationalist wish to rid the genre of dependence on French libretti along with
the popular interest in the German Middle Ages inspired him to write
stories of human conflict set in south Germany within the context of
strong Catholicism; he expressed conflict between good and evil
through the naïve, *volkstümlich* hermit and the institutional, urban
army. The religious allusions and hostility to modern capitalism in
Simplicius find an obvious precedent in *Parsifal*.

In a letter written the same day to Strauss's friend Josef Priester,
Léon further confirms the work's aspirations to the status of
Wagner's *Consecration Festival* when he emphasizes that the audience
should leave the theater at the conclusion of each act *without applaud-
ing*. The public must have time to appreciate and review the final melodies and the total effect without disturbance.[44] When the audience
at Theater an der Wien predictably applauded, Léon did not take a
curtain call. His failure to appear, considered by some to be further
proof of his snobbishness,[45] not only reflected an allegiance to
Wagner's *Parsifal* but also emulated the convention at the
Burgtheater, where only guest performers or jubilee honorees
appeared in front of the curtain and neither the author nor the actors
responded to applause.[46] By governing his own and the audience's
behavior, Léon hoped his work would be considered worthy of conventions associated with high art.

Léon's vision of *Simplicius*, based on the seventeenth-century tale
Simplicius Simplicissimus by Jacob Grimmelshausen (1625–76), comprised a dramatic prologue (a *Vorspiel*) and two acts.[47] The dramatic
prologue has precedents in German romantic opera such as *Hans
Heiling* and the original version of *Der Freischütz*. The latter seems to
have been especially suggestive, since it featured a hermit praying in
the woods before a rude cross, exactly as in the opening scenario of
Simplicius. Wagner had used the term *Vorspiel* in the sense of "overture" since *Lohengrin*, but he included a dramatic *Vorspiel* only in
Götterdämmerung.[48] These German works served as structural
models for the young Léon.

Critics quickly recognized the work's resemblance to Wagnerian precedents and derisively dubbed Simplicius the Parsifal of the seventeenth century.[49] One reviewer commented further:

> In fact, there is something of the "reiner Thor" [innocent fool] about him. Léon has moved the action of his libretto from the Spessart to the Sudeten, relocated the battle camp in Olmütz and thus translated or, as they say, localized, the adventures of his hero into Austrian; and so really nothing remains of the original except – "Simplicius" and the development of his character.[50]

The devout hermit or *Einsiedler* who guides Simplicius' spiritual life in Léon's story recalls Gurnemanz, also described as an *Einsiedler* in the final act of *Parsifal*, who offers spiritual guidance to Parsifal. The first scene of *Simplicius* shows the hermit bent deep in prayer before his hand-made cross when trumpet calls from behind the scene interrupt his meditations, and a trombone fanfare similarly disturbs Gurnemanz's morning prayers in the first scene of *Parsifal*. In both cases the brass heralds the arrival of knights. Léon's hermit, like Gurnemanz, had once been a knight himself and chose to reject the hierarchy, artificiality, and worldly temptations of society in favor of a life immersed in nature and spirituality. In the *Vorspiel* he confesses, "O, Simplicius, my son, how I thank my Lord and Creator that I am no longer what I was, that I still have you, my child, whom I dedicate in devotion and innocence to the service of the Lord, far from the world."[51] Clearly this language marks a departure from the festive carnival atmosphere of *Die Fledermaus* and from the exotic Hungarian countryside of *Der Zigeunerbaron*.

Both Simplicius and Parsifal have been raised in the wilderness by single parents, away from society, and their solitary lives are changed at the sight of men on horses, ready for battle. While Parsifal wants to become like the armored men, Simplicius assumes they are devils come to take him away to hell.[52] Just as in *Parsifal* the knights taunt Kundry for looking wild and unkempt, saying "Was liegst du dort wie ein wildes Tier?" [Why do you lie there like a wild animal?], knights similarly mock Simplicius and the hermit, "So lebt Ihr wie ein wildes Tier?" [So you live like a wild animal?].

As the trumpet sounds, a terrified Simplicius enters. In Simplicius' frightened calls to his father, Léon pays homage to Goethe with what a reviewer for the *Wiener Tagblatt* described as a "textual reworking of the Erlkönig."[53] He cries, "Vater, O Vater!" to which the *Einsiedler* replies, "Du rufst mich, mein Sohn!" [You call me, my son!] and encourages him to confess his fears. The troops then kidnap Simplicius in hopes that he can guide them through the woods and back to their camp. In Act I (after the Prologue) he emerges from the tent where he has been kept, calling for his father in verse that recalls the "Erlkönig" even more strongly:

> Vater, Vater – hörst Du mich nicht? . . .
> Ich hab' sie erblickt, ich hab' sie geseh'n –
> O Vater, mein Vater, 's ist um mich gescheh'n! . . .
> Hussah, Hurrah, der höllische Troß,
> Vater, siehst Du, des Teufels Genoß –
> Es funkelt sein Körper, es streckt sich sein Arm,
> Die Höll' jagt nach Seelen, daß Gott sich erbarm'!
> Der wilde Jäger, er kam heran –
> O Vater, er faßte, er faßte mich an!
> Hui, nun durch das Dickicht, über Felsengerölle,
> Da schleppt mich der Teufel hinab in die Hölle![54]

> [Father, father – don't you hear me? . . .
> I've spotted them, I've seen them –
> O father, my father, what has happened around me! . . .
> Hurray, hurray, the hellish camp,
> Father, do you see the Devil's company –
> His body sparks, he stretches out his arm,
> Hell hunts down souls that God would forgive!
> The wild hunter, he came closer –
> O father, he grabbed, he grabbed me!
> Ho, now through the thicket, over rocky plains,
> The Devil dragged me down into Hell!]

This blatant allusion to Goethe's poem did not go unnoticed by Viennese critics. Julius Bauer questioned, for example, "Why should the innocent Goethe be parodied *seriously* in an operetta! We would have expected entirely different words from the mouth of a yet unwashed 'reiner Thor,' who shortly before mistook the riders for wolves, just as Parsifal mistook them for gods."[55]

Far from satirizing Goethe, Léon wanted to show his respect for the poet, and at the same time assert his work as part of the heritage of great German literature. None of his writings suggests the sort of critical distance necessary for parody. On the contrary, he took himself and his work quite seriously, joining others of his generation in linking aesthetic goals to those of German nationalism. As he explained to Strauss:

> You know, my most honored Master, and we all realize that the genre of the operetta finds itself going the way of all flesh, and this already well represented. It is up to us, if we want to save it, to give it other forms, more lasting and more noble shapes. So I have regarded it my literary assignment, my artistic duty – if I may say so – to help guide it away from the superficial and vapid operetta genre handed down by the French, one directed only to the lowest amusement of the senses, in order to steer us out of this swamp of baseness into better waters, into the clear streams of German taste.[56]

Although he does not mention Goethe explicitly in this letter, Léon's familiarity with Goethe's ideas emerges when describing his intentions regarding the role of Simplicius. He adopts Goethe's vocabulary of *Pflanzenkunde* [botany] when he describes his desire to portray Simplicius' development from his *Urzustand* [original condition] through all his phases until he becomes a man. He wants to show what kind of *Keime* [germ] lies within him and under which influences he develops. These ideas and their vocabulary, taken from Goethe's observations of the plant world, fascinated many Viennese thinkers at the end of the nineteenth century, though Strauss was not among them.[57]

Musically, Strauss continued the path in *Simplicius* that he had established in *Der Zigeunerbaron*, away from set numbers and a conventional dance orchestra toward a more through-composed style and enlarged orchestral resources. Although he still worked within the standard genres of couplets, choruses, and dances, he more often connected them with recitative or melodrama. Strauss composed more choruses and more melodrama in this work than in previous operettas, but most of his stylistic changes are in details of rhythm and orchestration.[58] Despite Léon's enthusiasm for Wagneriana, Strauss remained true to his own musical heritage. He wrote to a friend that he was "secretly slipping in real Austrian shouts of joy."[59] This statement suggests both that he was less enamored of German nationalism than his collaborator and that he felt a need to be secretive about his musical allegiances.

In *Simplicius* Strauss called upon the brass, woodwind, and percussion sections of the orchestra far more than in previous works. In contrast to most of his music that relies heavily on the violins to lead the orchestra and to supply the melody, the first moments of the overture and of the dramatic *Vorspiel* are characterized by timpani and solo clarinet. He left the remainder of the introduction and accompaniment solely to the woodwind, horn and timpani, and the opening scene with the hermit praying alone is also dominated by woodwind rather than strings. Strauss emulated Wagnerian instrumentation in his increased use of the harp throughout the operetta, both as part of the tutti orchestral texture and as a featured instrument. In Simplicius' romantic duet Strauss used the horn as a solo melodic instrument and the harp as accompaniment.[60] For this piece he also chose the unusual key (for him) of D-flat major, a key more favorable to the wind and brass than to the strings.

Strauss followed musical fashion of German romantic opera when he provided opportunity for brass and percussion performance on stage like the works mentioned above (*Der Freischütz, Der Trompeter von Säkkingen, Der Liebeshof*). At the end of Act I (following the Prologue) *Simplicius* includes a march for men going off to war, requiring trumpets, horns, and snare and bass drums on stage. This scene also recalls Strauss's previous triumph in *Der Zigeunerbaron*: in both cases the central act closes with men cheerfully leaving home to fight for their country. In Léon's version the tone expresses his combination of religiosity and nationalism when the men join the battle crying, "Für's deutsche Reich! Mit Gott für Kaiser und

Vaterland!" [For the German Empire! With God for Emperor and Fatherland!].

Léon was undoubtedly more familiar with the basic theories of the Wagnerian leitmotiv than Strauss was. He wrote to Strauss during the early stages of the work suggesting that the end of Act II would be more effective if the hermit were led across the stage while the orchestra played his motif (the *Einsiedlermotiv*) rather than having him sing a few bars,[61] a technique Wagner used frequently in *Parsifal* and the *Ring* operas. However, no leitmotivic usage, so important for Wagner's theories and music, can be detected in this work in even the broadest sense. Strauss's own musical personality was far too evolved at this point in his career to be won over entirely to *Zukunftsmusik*.

Despite the pretentious text and lofty aims of his librettist, Strauss's Viennese spirit shines through, but the juxtaposition of librettist's and composer's goals often creates a paradoxical effect, as when Simplicius sings of his terror at the iron devils who startled him in the woods to a charming waltz in B-flat major (see Example 7.3). Even in this operetta, the most popular song, "Ich denke gern zurück, an mein entschwund'nes Glück" [I like to think back on my vanished happiness], is a wistful, nostalgic waltz, qualities that characterize the memorable songs from Strauss's earlier operettas like "Ja, so singt man" from *Indigo* or "Brüderlein" from *Die Fledermaus*. Although he incorporated some Wagnerian elements and continued his efforts more successfully in his next stage work, ultimately the combination of Viennese dance music and the Wagnerian music drama was unconvincing.

Simplicius enjoyed an enthusiastic response at its premiere on Friday, 16 December 1887. Julius Bauer's review expressed the general sentiment: "A Strauss operetta can be more or less pleasing, but it must be seen and heard by everyone."[62] *Kikeriki* reported that Strauss composed "not in the light style of operetta music, but in that of grand opera. Almost throughout, serious and melancholy tones fall on our ears, alternating with battle fanfare and melodrama." The review continued, however, that the theater celebrated its greatest triumph with the "rich, grand, and impressive" stage design.[63] *Der*

Example 7.3 *Simplicius*, Act I, No. 3

Floh reported that "the persistent friends of Maestro Strauss shove the Wagner-Beret on his head in overbearing honor and want to proclaim him the Richard Wagner of operetta."[64]

The work's success was short-lived, and it soon disappeared from the theater's repertoire. One critic cited the work's lukewarm reception as evidence of a false trend: "When even a *Strauss* operetta cannot 'make' more than 28 full houses in a row, then the proof is finally here that *serious* motives, whether musical or textual, do not have their place in the operetta."[65] Although *Simplicius* failed in Vienna, Strauss remained confident in the operetta's possibilities and worked diligently on two revisions, one for Budapest and another for the German Theater in Prague (under the direction of Angelo Neumann). Since he could not convince Léon of the need for revisions, Strauss engaged the services of the Hungarian playwright and civil servant Ludwig Dóczi. Their collaboration led to Strauss's most ambitious project yet, a comic opera.

RITTER PÁSMÁN: "A SOCIAL GESAMTKUNSTWERK"

Simplicius quickly faded from public memory, but Strauss soon accepted the Wagner-beret nonetheless and prepared a work suitable for performance at the Viennese Court Opera. Dóczi's play *The Kiss* had enjoyed a run at the Burgtheater, and it was upon this play that the libretto was based. The story takes place in Renaissance Hungary, where the first two acts are set at the country castle of the title character, Ritter ["Knight"] Pásmán. His wife and servants scurry to prepare a meal welcoming him and his merry band home from the hunt, but one of the hunters becomes enamored of Pásmán's wife and kisses her forehead while her inattentive husband is carousing. As the hunter and his servant leave, Pásmán finds out about the kiss, curses his wife, and runs off to the king to demand justice. Act III takes place at the king's castle, to which Pásmán has been followed by his wife and her maid. He demands a kiss from the anonymous hunter's wife as revenge, and when the king admits that it was he who kissed Pásmán's wife, Pásmán wins a kiss from the queen. This simple plot took over three hours to run its course.[66]

Even before the first downbeat, an astute opera patron would have several reasons to suspect Wagner's influence. This work, like *Simplicius* before it, was dedicated to the Wagner enthusiast and German opera patron Duke Ernst II of Coburg.[67] A glance at the cast of characters further suggests a Wagnerian touch: the maid Kunigunde, nicknamed Gundy, recalls Kundry, the single female role in *Parsifal*,[68] and Eva, the female lead, shares her name with the heroine of *Die Meistersinger*. A reviewer for the *Wiener Allgemeine Zeitung* remarked: "'O Eva, schlimmes Weib!' We cry it out once again; and this time we think of Richard Wagner's pretty jewelry maker's daughter from Nürnberg, who must have haunted our Maestro Strauss endlessly when he worked on the musical sketch and design of his honorable Lady Eva."[69]

Wagnerian models are evident in *Pásmán*'s music and narrative structure as well. The stage action at the beginning of *Pásmán* Act I, like the beginning of *Der fliegende Holländer* Act II, features a spinning song performed by a chorus of women. Both are in duple meter and feature similar accompaniments; strings play a repeated pattern while horns or flutes punctuate the off-beats imitating the spinning wheels (see Examples 7.4a and 7.4b). The choruses imitate the wheels' sound by the same syllable, "Summ," and in both scenes the women acknowledge their duty to stay home and spin while their men roam the world.[70] The spinning music is in major keys, and the vocal melodies are harmonized with parallel thirds and sixths. Indeed, Strauss's melody strikingly resembles Wagner's in some places (see Example 7.5). The two scenes have similar narrative structures in that the spinning refrain is sung twice with a conversation involving the heroine's maid (Gundy/Mary) intervening. The women conclude by consoling themselves with thoughts of the prize they will win for working hard at home: either a man (in Strauss's version) or his money (in Wagner's). Both Strauss and Wagner draw on the particularly German metaphor of the woman who, like a spider (*Spinne*), spins her net in hopes of ensnaring her victim, the unsuspecting man.[71]

Immediately following the spinning song (and Senta's ballad in *Der fliegende Holländer*) in both operas a secondary male character (Mischu/Erik) enters breathlessly and announces the men's return for whom the women hurriedly prepare the unexpected feast under the direction of the heroine (Eva/Senta) and her handmaid

Example 7.4a *Der fliegende Holländer*, Act II

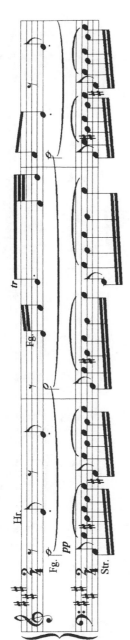
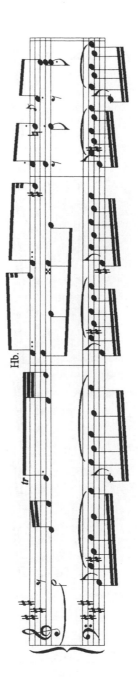

Example 7.4b *Ritter Pásmán*, Act 1

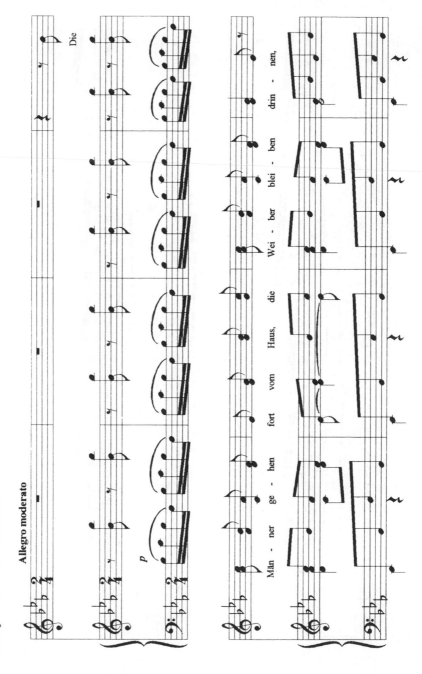

Example 7.4b (cont.)

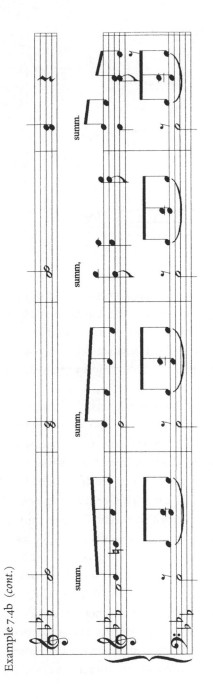

Example 7.5 Melodic similarities

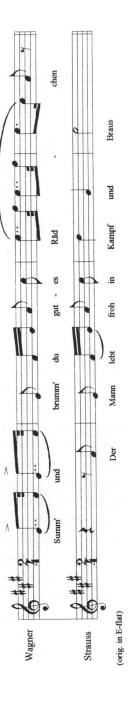

(orig. in E-flat)

Example 7.6 *Ritter Pásmán*, Act II, "Tristan chord"

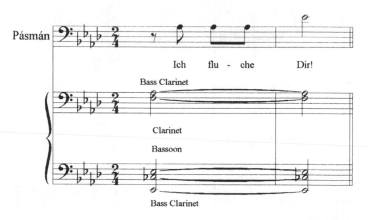

(Gundy/Mary). A love duet between the messenger (Mischu/Erik) and one of the leading women follows this scene, but Strauss differs from Wagner in that the maid Gundy, not the heroine, sings the duet. The music also differs in style, for while Strauss's piece is in 3/4 and the two sing simultaneously, Wagner's is in common time and Erik and Senta sing only in alternation.

These scenes offer the most extended structural parallels between the two works, but Strauss also imitated Wagner's harmonic style by using more diminished-seventh harmonies and fewer authentic cadences. The harmonic language is much more rich and varied than that found in his stage works for the Theater an der Wien. Keys change frequently and unexpectedly through German augmented sixth chords. The half-diminished seventh chord (or "Tristan chord," the signature sonority of Wagner's *Tristan und Isolde*) even appears in a few significant places; in the first act when the king asks if he should fall to his knees and swear his love, Eva's shocked "Nein" is accompanied by the loud tremolo of the chord (here spelled F, A-flat, C-flat, E-flat).[72] This sonority also accompanies Pásmán when he curses his wife at the end of Act II (see Example 7.6). Strauss shared his post-Wagnerian contemporaries' penchant for using excessive instrumentation and chromatic harmonic language to underscore simple

Example 7.7 *Ritter Pásmán*, Act II

scenes, and often exaggerated the emotional weight of his characters' exchanges, such as when the king and Eva conclude their duet
("Wouldn't it be nice") to the accompaniment of the full orchestra,
including two harps and full brass. In another instance, Pásmán
shocks the assembly by kissing the queen at the end of Act III accompanied by the entire orchestra on a tremulous G-minor chord.

Although Strauss used no leitmotivs in the Wagnerian sense, he
did use instruments in a leitmotivic fashion. (Repetition of melodic
material, though necessary to establish leitmotivs, may have been
counterintuitive for a composer known for his wealth of melodic
invention.) The bass clarinet is strongly associated with Pásmán from
the beginning, when a solo bass clarinet provides a counter-melody
to his entrance song, and soon after, the instrument doubles his
melody, an unusual practice for this work. When Pásmán discovers
his wife's "unfaithfulness" in Act II, the bass clarinet has a short solo
after Pásmán cries "Du ehr' vergess'nes schändliches Weib!" [You
shameful woman, forgetting of honor!] (see Example 7.7). The
context (marital infidelity) and the melodic contour (ascending
minor sixth followed by a short scalar descent) is reminiscent of
Tristan's opening measures. Indeed, the association between the bass
clarinet and the cuckolded husband finds precedent in Wagner's
opera, for a solo bass clarinet also accompanies King Mark's discov-
ery of Tristan and Isolde's illicit tryst in Act II. In true leitmotivic
function, the bass clarinet presents Pásmán's opening melody when
he is the topic of discussion, but absent himself; the page Rodomonte

sings about Pásmán in Act III before he arrives at court, while appropriating Pásmán's entrance melody and signature instrument. Likewise, the king is often accompanied by the English horn, an instrument also associated with Tristan (cf. the opening of Wagner's third act). Had Eva been aware of the orchestral music at the beginning of Act II, she would have been alerted by the English horn that the man in the helmet was not her husband but rather the king, hoping to steal a kiss.

Although Strauss alludes to and borrows from Wagner in these musical elements, he was far less concerned with the relationship between music and text than was Wagner. His habits of working at some distance from his librettist, established over the course of more than twenty years, precluded any possibility for a close integration of the two elements most essential to Wagner's *Gesamtkunstwerk*. As we have seen, it was common practice in the operetta trade for librettists to fit their text to the composer's music. Millöcker, for example, requested of librettist Hugo Wittman, "Above all I must ask you to text the end of the 1st Finale (it's already orchestrated)."[73] Léon wrote similarly of *Simplicius*, "for the prologue and first act I have fitted the text to your music, as far as I notated and remembered it."[74] In a letter to Simrock written while composing *Pásmán*, Strauss revealed his musical independence from the text: "In an opera themes are thrown in but then thrown out again because there is no time to develop them. Something occurs to you – but it comes to nothing because in the most beautiful moment of creation for the musician, the text stops!!!"[75] Not only did the text fail to *inspire* music in Strauss, it became a *hindrance* to composition. When faced with the task of composing three hours of continuous music, he could conceive it only in terms of dance music, "absolute music," without text.

Dóczi, like Léon, proudly displayed his familiarity with Wagner's literary style in his libretto, which features end rhyme and regular meter similar to that found in *Der fliegende Holländer* but no pretensions to *Stabreim* or internal rhyme (the alliteration of lines like "Dem Ritter ist's Warten wider wärtig" appear only as unfortunate coincidences). Dóczi frequently made archaic choices in vocabulary, using "Weib," for example, instead of the more contemporary "Frau." His use of the genitive also suggests medieval linguistic practices, as in the line above, or most amusingly: "Kahlheit ist der Weisheit Siegel, hoher Würde klarer Spiegel" [Baldness is a sign of wisdom, a clear mirror of great worth]. The libretto's plodding action was matched on the smaller scale by simplistic text, such as when Eva and the party search for her missing ring, the chorus sings: "Ein Ring, ein Ring, ein rundes Ding, will gern sich verstecken, in Winkeln und in Ecken" [A ring, a ring, a round thing, likes to hide itself in nooks and crannies]. Any trace of intentional parody is sadly missing.

Occasionally, Strauss responds musically to the text, as examples of word painting show. While the men discuss night-fishing, the orchestra illustrates the increasing agitation of the fish with low, repetitive murmuring triplets, then sixteenth-notes. Strauss similarly illustrates the eruption of a volcano with ascending triplets and an "eruption" into full orchestra on the word "Feuer" [fire]. Act III brings more text painting with quick 32nd-note runs in the flute and *sforzando* chords illustrating "Funken" [sparks], and accented woodwinds (on a half-diminished seventh chord!) echoing Pásmán's knock at the door. The text setting of Pásmán's entrance song is quite awkward, in what may have been a deliberate effort to reflect the clumsiness of his character (see Example 7.8).

Although Strauss and his librettists sought to emulate Wagner in various ways, they failed to grasp the essence of Wagner's aesthetic ideal represented by the *Gesamtkunstwerk*. Instead, Strauss's attitude toward the text reveals his pragmatism born of experience in the faster paced, more factory-like atmosphere of the operetta theater. Giving little regard to staging, set design, or the text, Strauss produced isolated moments of musical beauty but fell short of securing a permanent place for himself in the Court Opera repertoire.

In the preparation *Ritter Pásmán* received for its premiere at the Opera, Strauss and Dóczi felt their work fell victim to negligence and unfortunate circumstances. The premiere's scheduled date of 18

Example 7.8 *Ritter Pásmán*, Act I, Pásmán's entrance song

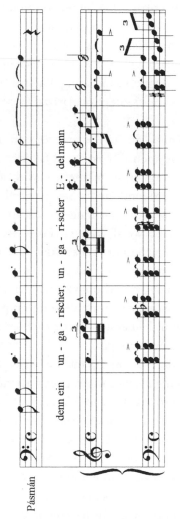

Pásmán

denn ein   un - ga - rischer,   un - ga - ri-scher   E - delmann

November, Empress Elizabeth's name day, was an occasion for wide celebration. The text of the third act finale, "Hail! Hail our Queen! She protects us with her high and noble sense!" would have been especially apropos on that date, but due to performers' illnesses and the vagaries of Wilhelm Jahn's direction, the premiere was postponed. Dóczi and Jahn had little confidence in each other, the former continually warning Strauss that he should not let himself be manipulated by Jahn's suggestions: "The responsibility for success lies finally with you alone . . . and when the work achieves a great success – as I am completely convinced – it will be won through Strauss's genius and not through Jahn's cuts, and it should not then be said that *he* made the success possible."[76] Only a few months before the premiere, Dóczi complained: "I have convinced myself at this occasion [a meeting regarding casting] that Jahn has hardly interested himself in the work at all; he knows it neither in general nor in detail. Therefore I have decided that in rehearsals he should stick to what is given and leave the responsibility to us."[77] Strauss, too, was displeased with the preparation and direction Jahn gave the work. It premiered on New Year's Day 1892 and received only eight more performances at the Court Opera before vanishing from the repertoire. He wrote to Simrock after the third performance that Kapellmeister Fuchs gave the public a more authentic impression than Jahn had: "Jahn would truly have killed the opera with his poor understanding of the tempi."[78] His impressions of Jahn's neglect, even ill will, were reinforced by a letter from Simrock, who had spoken with Ludwig Hartmann, a leading German music critic in Dresden. Both men encouraged Strauss to conduct *Pásmán* himself in Prague to ensure an adequate performance. Simrock gossiped: "Hartmann wants to write about *Pásmán* (*after* Prague) and wants to *rehabilitate* the opera. He told me *a lot*!! He told me that Jahn spoke *badly* of *Pásmán already weeks before*. It's unbelievable what was done in *Vienna* to *kill Pásmán!*"[79]

Strauss chose not to conduct the Prague premiere, but he did prefer the production it received there (April 1892) where he felt the tempi were more appropriate. Despite his approval of the performance, he mocked Prague conductor Karl Muck in a letter to his friend Josef Simon: "He is terribly taken with himself. With that he has the soul of a true Wagnerian swine, who tries to be inconsiderate in order to count as pure Wagner blood."[80] These comments suggest that Strauss was not as enamored of Wagner and his followers as many of his colleagues were, although Wagner had held Strauss's musical genius in high regard.[81] Strauss rarely discussed current musical events in his correspondence, but the very absence of Wagner's name, particularly during his collaboration with the ultra-Wagnerian Léon, speaks volumes. Perhaps his friendships with Brahms and Hanslick colored Strauss's personal attitude toward Wagner, but it did not prevent him from imitating those elements of Wagner's musical style he thought would contribute to his work's success.

RECEPTION: A BRILLIANT FLOP

As was the case for any Strauss premiere, *Ritter Pásmán* was sold out months before opening night. The opera not only attracted more attention than any of his other operetta premieres, it attracted more attention than most other *opera* premieres.[82] Strauss had finally made it to the pinnacle of high art in Vienna and, by extension, the Habsburg Empire. As one journalist exclaimed:

> Strauss in the Court Opera for the first time! An event for our city, a musical event, a first-rate social event, and one might say, a family event that transports each one of us into a state of the greatest expectation . . . From the fourth gallery: Yesterday, the *Straußianer* left just as little to be desired of enthusiasm and loving understanding, of happy belligerency and proud victorious joy, as the most die-hard Wagner veteran.[83]

Ludwig Speidel, theater critic for the *Fremdenblatt*, provided the most colorful description of the evening:

> Since the beginning of time the Court Opera has not been the site of such a crush of humanity as it was yesterday, the first *Pásmán* evening. For weeks and months every little place in the house has been reserved;

yesterday loges and seats, had they been available, could have brought five to ten times their price. And from the early afternoon on, the doors to the standing room area were besieged by a mass of people whose perseverance hunger and thirst could not shake.[84]

Speidel continued this thought in the next issue:

> The appearance of Johann Strauss in our opera is a Viennese event in itself. There is no artist in Vienna – with the exception of Strauss, Sr. and Lanner, there never has been one – who enjoys the same popularity as Strauss does through all levels of the population.[85]

This diverse audience included the crown princess widow Stefanie, several archdukes, the oldest and most honorable court advisors, presidents, and managers of various businesses.[86] Highly regarded musicians from both the art music and popular music worlds attended the premiere and wished Strauss well.[87] One reviewer alluded to the aesthetic heritage of the opera in his description of opening night: "Today we engage ourselves with the anxiously awaited premiere which *Ritter Pásmán* and the performing artists, but also the composer himself and the public in brilliant cooperation, made into a social Gesamtkunstwerk."[88]

Although the premiere was a shining social event, few critics showed enthusiasm for the work itself or predicted a long tenure in the opera house. The reviewer for the *Wiener Abendpost* complained that the characters were not sufficiently distinguished musically; Pásmán has a few superficially Hungarian traits in his entrance aria, but for him the rest of the music is too sentimental. Several critics, including Hanslick, Robert Hirschfeld, and Theodor Helm of the *Deutsche Zeitung*, objected to the frequent changes in tempo and meter, saying it gave the opera a nervous feeling. As was often the case, the banality of the text was universally condemned. In a note wishing Strauss good luck for the premiere, Léon archly suggested that the libretto would have been better if he had written it.[89]

Another common complaint was the ambivalence of Pásmán's character. As critic Richard Heuberger noted, he is a comic figure in the first act, but "in the second act, as he learns of the kiss, he changes suddenly into a tragic figure, into a Hungarian King Mark, singing, like this character, long, very long monologues."[90] The critic for the *Illustriertes Wiener Extrablatt* acknowledged Strauss's debt to Wagner but felt that Strauss betrayed his own true character in this work: "The Waltz King appears before the public incognito, avoiding every pregnant rhythm, every foot-spinning melody, every theme sure to head for the ear, and moves in a musical manner of expression that in many places affects the music dramas of Wagner, but unfortunately is not at all like Strauss, i.e. individual."[91] Alluding to the contemporary hit by Mascagni, another critic wrote: "Whether this new *Cavalleria ongarese* will become a leading work of our Court Opera for a longer period of time, is surely difficult to decide."[92] Despite their differing musical styles, Strauss's work superficially resembled Mascagni's in their common theme of "rustic chivalry."

The strength that composers and critics most frequently acknowledged was Strauss's talent for instrumentation.[93] Heuberger noticed that "in the csárdás, Strauss used the dulcimer to the greatest effect – for the first time in an opera by a German. Just as Strauss is one of the finest experts on the art of instrumentation, so is the majority of *Pásmán* full of beautiful, unusual tone colors."[94] Singled out for praise by many critics was the innovative obbligato for solo violin in a "duet" with the queen in Act III. The critic for the *Wiener Abendpost* cited this solo, performed by concertmaster Arnold Rosé, as one of the few places Strauss's muse shone through.

The pro-Wagner journal, the *Neue Zeitschrift für Musik*, gave this premiere special attention. While most Viennese papers showed only mild enthusiasm for the work, the reviewer for the *NZM* hailed it as a "turning point in the history of the German Spieloper."[95] Lortzing, Nicolai, and Götz hardly appeal to the taste of the current public, he wrote, but Strauss's work combines the spirit and grace of the French *opéra comique* with German depth of feeling and the joy of melody typical of the Austrians from Schubert and Haydn on. Having positioned Strauss's work in the line of honored Germanic composers, he proceeded to ally it more closely to the most honored, and most German, of composers, Wagner:

Only in the lyric parts and mood scenes does the music of *Ritter Pásmán* move within a closed form, otherwise the music only characterizes the word. If this also happens in the presentation of many melodies, the melody appears, however, never for its own sake, but rather serves to illustrate the stage action . . . Thus, we have here a music drama in the truest sense, passing before us in the genre of a musical comedy.[96]

He felt compelled to justify his favorable opinion in the face of skeptical Viennese critics:

The judgment Strauss's music has received from most Viennese artistic critics stands in great contrast to its significant intrinsic value. The Viennese critics have always regarded Strauss only as the greatest waltz composer and cannot accustom themselves readily to the fact that his compositional talent reaches farther than 3 / 4 time.[97]

Not surprisingly, Hanslick disagreed with the Wagnerian's assessment. Acknowledging the wealth of musical ideas and fine instrumentation in his opera, Hanslick reserved trenchant criticism for the libretto, a sticking point in his evaluation of almost every stage work. Despite his praise for the music, Strauss felt he was unduly harsh and that his criticism hurt attendance, lamenting to his publisher Simrock:

Dear friend, I must tell you straight out that Eduard H[anslick] has hurt *us* enormously in his damnation of the libretto in such a horrible way (which it certainly did not deserve). I could thank him neither personally nor in writing for his duty of love. He should have criticized the libretto more mildly for your sake and for mine . . . [In the margin he notes:] Certainly the article in the *Neue Freie Presse* influences show business.[98]

Simrock agreed about the harm Hanslick's review caused the opera's reception and noted Hanslick's friendship with Jahn, insinuating a collaboration on their part to bring the work to an early end.[99]

Although Strauss and Hanslick eventually mended their differences, Hanslick returned to the problematic opera in his obituary for Strauss in 1899:

With a really comic opera in the older form, like *Zar und Zimmermann* for example, Strauss too would have penetrated the Court Opera. But the stretched-out, entirely sung verse, broken up by neither recitative nor spoken dialogue, forced the composer into a continuous arioso, out of which discrete musical numbers only seldom sharply distinguished themselves.[100]

Nor could Brahms muster enthusiasm for his friend's ambitious composition. He commented to Heuberger that "[the opera] wanders and drags on and on . . . and comes to nothing . . . I fear very much for its success, and yet wish so much that it could have one!"[101]

Strauss was well aware of the opera's shortcomings, which he noted to his brother Eduard a few months after the work's premiere: "Nothing against Dóczi, but to make such a scandal over a few innocent pecks does not suit the current corrupt society. *These* days they would have been more sympathetic had the king *seduced* the knight's honorable wife."[102] Strauss was, after all, competing for attention at the opera with the new *verismo* style. Mascagni's *Cavalleria rusticana* was extremely popular in Vienna, reaching 100 performances at the Court Opera within only two years of its premiere. His *L'Amico Fritz* was in production at the Court Opera during the same time as Strauss's work, and journalists did their best to generate competition between the two men (and sell newspapers to avid audiences) by propagating rumors about which composer had received the more generous honorarium.[103] Hanslick lent his wry observation of the Mascagni mania:

> Finally the Viennese will have the chance to see the young Mascagni! His *Cavalleria rusticana* just reached its 100th performance in the Court Opera, and that pathetic *Intermezzo* has already achieved the rank of a national plague. And on top of that there is the cult of personality. Never before on German soil has a composer been celebrated with such a fit of homage as Mascagni in these Viennese September days [1892]. The curiosity of the public pursues him on the street and detains him after the theater . . . but if an English admiral in red uniform and tall feather hat stepped on to a newly discovered south sea island, he would receive no more wonder from the natives than Mascagni did from the Viennese.[104]

Ritter Pásmán offered neither the metaphysical overtones of Wagner's works nor the explicit treatment of love and betrayal found in late nineteenth-century Italian opera. Although Strauss enjoyed enthusiastic local support, his work did not achieve a broad or lasting audience.

Strauss, too, had misgivings about the work even before the premiere. Despite his many successes, he was always pessimistic and insecure about his stage works, with the high-profile venue of the Court Opera only intensifying his doubts. Regarding *Ritter Pásmán*, he wrote in August 1891, "First I'll finish Pásmán, then come the horrific birth pains, the delivery (unthinkable without a cesarean section) of the corpus delicti, which will have the misfortune of drowning right after its first bath."[105] His gloomy intuition accurately predicted the opera's fate. Strauss also complained to Josef Simon about *Pásmán*'s weaknesses: "Give me a powerful stage work! [It would give me] great joy to make something of it! But I want to earn money and not waste years with one project – I'm not young anymore. I don't want to deceive you, I would rather you deceived me. Give me money, I ask no more of you dumb folk."[106] As much as Strauss may have wanted to limit his concerns to the business end of composition, he occasionally admitted the pride he took in having written an opera. After the premiere of *Pásmán* in Berlin, Strauss admitted: "The smallest success of an opera by me stands higher in my eyes than many other accomplishments." But he quickly regained his nonchalance: "It pleases me to have fooled the world and myself. It was for me much more a caprice, for which unfortunately my friend Simrock felt the urge to pay 40,000 fl."[107]

Strauss went on to compose four more operettas after *Ritter Pásmán*, but in these last works he abandoned his experiments with Wagnerism and returned to the "salon operetta" style of *Die Fledermaus* with which he had achieved so much success. He was disappointed that his contribution to the Court Opera repertory was not long-lived, but, as he confessed to his brother, "I don't want to strive for a fortune with [this work] – I only wrote it to prove that a man can write more than dance music."[108] Strauss unquestionably exceeded this modest goal, not only with his achievement in the Court Opera but with his long, successful career, creating a legacy of Viennese operetta to be enjoyed and emulated by generations to come.

Epilogue

On a June afternoon, the funeral procession left Strauss's house in the Igelgasse and wound its way through the inner city, stopping at the Protestant church in the Dorotheergasse and at the Gesellschaft der Musikfreunde, before heading outside the city limits to the Central Cemetery. The hearse was drawn by eight black horses, driven by men dressed in Renaissance Spanish costume, and was followed by six carriages overflowing with flowers and wreaths; members of Concordia and the Gesellschaft der Musikfreunde, Conservatory professors, artists, and deputies accompanied the procession with flags and torches, six of them carrying red satin pillows bearing his medals, his baton, a lyre, and his violin, whose strings had been sprung in recognition that it would never again be played. More carriages followed, carrying the grieving widow and female friends. More than forty representatives of parliament and the city council, along with Mayor Karl Lueger, Gustav Mahler, and Arnold Rosé, gathered at the church, where the pastor spoke a few words: "In our time, which is so torn by dissonance, a man like him was a divine gift."[1] Crowds gathered in the streets to pay their last respects, with some ardent devotees following the cortège all the way to the cemetery. Lueger spoke at the graveside, where Strauss was given a place of honor next to his friend Johannes Brahms.

Public speeches and newspaper articles were filled with metaphors tying Strauss and his music to the city in which he lived. The day of the funeral, Guido Adler devoted his music history lecture at the university to his career: "Strauss's melodies strengthen the feeling of home for Viennese, for Austrians. One could say, 'Vienna lives in his sounds.' They are the musical reflection of the Viennese soul."[2] Another eulogist reflected, "Now that he is dead, this great, kind Viennese master, it is as if one of the old, world-famous landmarks of *Alt Wien* has disappeared from the city's physiognomy, demolished by death. Johann Strauss belongs to Vienna like the Prater or St. Stephen's."[3] His role as Austria's genial ambassador was invoked by another mourner: "In all parts of the world, on all seas, the name Johann Strauss was like our flag . . . We bury more than a composer. A proud piece of our fatherland is laid to rest."[4]

Strauss's extravagant funeral replicated several facets characterizing his life and career in Vienna. The Viennese penchant for spectacle that made his operettas so successful is found here in their appreciation of an elaborate burial. The high drama of horses, carriages, flags, and costumes resembles a carefully choreographed scene from the repertoire of the Theater an der Wien. Not until the Emperor's death seventeen years later would the city again witness such a "schöne Leich." The gathered crowds themselves became an inextricable part of the production for they acted as both observers and participants. Commerce played a part here too, as bold entrepreneurs sold hundreds of picture postcards featuring Strauss's portrait.[5]

The easy comingling of art music and popular music in Vienna, at least in the nineteenth century, also finds representation in this scene with the participation of Mahler, Rosé, and members of the Gesellschaft der Musikfreunde, an organization to which Strauss left a substantial inheritance.[6] The two strands of cultural life are perpetually interwined in the Central Cemetery, where the "great heroes of classical composition" lie side by side with Strauss and, later, other leading members of theatrical life: Jauner, Girardi, Gallmeyer, and Geistinger.[7]

To this day, Strauss continues his role as an international symbol of Viennese lightheartedness and grace. The centennial of his death in 1999 was celebrated by numerous new productions of his works, historical museum exhibitions, and noteworthy publications and recordings. Nikolaus Harnoncourt has devoted particular attention to Strauss's works recently, with his production of *Die Fledermaus* opening the Vienna Festival in this year.[8] Another production of this work, set in the 1920s, premiered at the Volksoper on Easter Sunday, commemorating its original premiere. Strauss's persona remains a vital part of the city's marketing plan, from the Johann Strauss Café that greets visitors in the airport to Austrian Airlines' airplanes themselves, emblazoned with the forty-foot image of his face and violin on its fuselage and tail.[9]

Despite the commercialism, Strauss's music continues to thrive, and our understanding of his life, his music, and the audience for which it was created will ultimately benefit from renewed popular attention. Popular music has long been considered the purview of sociologists or, more recently, ethnomusicologists. However, historical musicologists have also begun to examine popular genres like operetta more closely, unearthing much provocative material, both on its own account and for the way it intersects with and responds to events in the art-music world.[10] This attention to popular genres can only enhance our view of musical life at large.

Much work remains to be done in the field of operetta, a genre that could benefit from a wide range of approaches and analytical methods. A broader knowledge of operettas by Strauss's colleagues and competitors would provide a fuller context for understanding his works as well as those of contemporary opera composers. Autograph works by Millöcker, Suppé, Müller, Genée and others are deposited in the Vienna City Library, the wealth of which material has barely been touched. Many more stage works by Strauss himself await in-depth research. For example, the operettas he composed after his failure to gain a permanent place in the Court Opera repertoire suggest his reluctant retreat to a style more familiar and comfortable for him: *Fürstin Ninetta* (1893), *Jabuka* (1894), *Waldmeister* (1895), and *Die Göttin der Vernunft* (1897) are conceived once again as a collection of numbers connected by spoken dialogue. He was disappointed that his works in a more serious style were unsuccessful. As he confessed to his friend Josef Simon only a few months following the premiere of *Ritter Pásmán*,

> I am already scribbling around with this operetta [*Fürstin Ninetta*], but I can't deny it, it's difficult for me to get used to this common doodling again. Operetta texts today have nothing that even comes close to

poetry. Just ordinary rubbish! I'm writing on this work without inspiration. It will truly be trash, you can depend on it.[11]

As we have seen, Strauss was rarely inspired by the text in any of his
works; many of his operettas had libretti far worse than *Fürstin
Ninetta*'s, yet he only began complaining about texts after his disappointment at the Court Opera. He discounted the effort and genius it
took to create a brilliant, light work like those of his earlier career.

The issue of Strauss reception in the twentieth century promises
several fascinating avenues of research, such as the political use of his
life and work as a means of maintaining, then recreating, the feeling
of empire. Austrians clamored for his operettas during the First
World War, but his music assumed even greater significance after the
dissolution of the empire, as they promoted a nostalgia for the
monarchy's former power and grandeur. Studying the reception of
his works and the manipulation of his image – and official documents
– during the Nazi occupation would contribute a great deal to the
topics of Nazi propaganda and the Nazi conception of degenerate
art.

Another topic worth further investigation is the high opinion of
Strauss's work shared by the most eminent Viennese composers and
theorists. Heinrich Schenker used examples from the "Blue Danube"
in *Der freie Satz*, and Schoenberg paid tribute to Strauss in his article,
"Brahms the Progressive" (1947): "Real popularity, lasting popularity,
is only attained in those rare cases where power of expression is
granted to men who dwell intensely in the sphere of basic human
sentiments. There are a few cases in Schubert and Verdi, but many in
Johann Strauss."[12] Webern, too, conducted many of Strauss's works
in his various positions as Kapellmeister, and although he complained about the poor quality of other operetta composers' works,
he remained enthralled by his musical gifts. Their regard for him was
not based solely on patriotic grounds; rather they showed a genuine
admiration for Strauss's wealth of melodic invention and talent for
effective instrumentation.

Indeed, the interaction between "high-brow" and popular arts, touched upon in chapters 2 and 7, remains to be more thoroughly investigated. From libretti by serious journalists like Max Kalbeck and Theodore Herzl to operettas by Josef Hellmesberger, Jr. (leader of the string quartet bearing his name and a professor of violin at the Vienna Conservatory), the genre clearly aroused more than cursory interest from some of Vienna's leading minds. Strauss attracted particular admiration from many of his contemporaries, both from composers now in the canon of Western art music (Liszt, Brahms, Wagner) and from those critics instrumental in establishing that canon (Hanslick, Schenker).

In sum, operetta offers an invaluable window on to the urban and cultural life of which it was a part. It provides rich fodder for discussions of musical style, the interaction between art music and popular music, representations of empire, reactions to public policy and immigration, and countless further topics. Late nineteenth-century Vienna witnessed a whirlwind of changes in the ethnic, political, and physical landscape of the city, and the Viennese happily clung to a reassuring emblem of their collective identity. They found such a figure in Johann Strauss, a composer whose career began years before the seemingly immortal Franz Joseph came to power. Strauss retained that role for many Austrians throughout the century following his death. Many might still agree with Richard Specht's observations that concluded his 1909 biography of Strauss: "This music is something unusual: pleasure itself. A small piece of fulfilled longing for life's joy. And: in its sounds is Austria . . ."[13]

Indigo und die vierzig Räuber

Adapted from the stories of 1001 *Nights*, this loosely constructed story takes place on the exotic island of Makassar, ruled by King Indigo. As the curtain rises, his harem and their leader Fantasca are being guarded by the eunuchs Falsetto and Soprano. Ali Baba the mule driver introduces himself and observes that aristocrats and husbands are also mules, a fact they would do well to acknowledge. When Janio, Indigo's advisor, describes his homesickness, Fantasca soon joins him; although she recognizes that the island is a tropical paradise, they both would prefer to be in their hometown on the Danube. In the finale, Fantasca speaks flatteringly to Indigo (but warns the audience not to believe her). Because a band of robbers has been threatening the countryside, Indigo offers a prize for capturing them, and Fantasca volunteers to be the prize, a reward both Indigo and Janio are eager to claim.

Act II takes place in the woods, where the harem women have disguised themselves as robbers in order to escape King Indigo's tyranny. Janio, in search of the thieves, finds Fantasca in the woods and sings her a love song, but she soon asks him to leave. A passing group of soldiers sing quietly, hoping not to awaken the enemy. Ali Baba, drunk and feeling sorry for himself, attempts to hang himself from a tree, when Janio saves him by cutting the rope. Meanwhile, the women drink and entertain themselves until Janio appears on the scene; they suspect he is a spy, while he believes he has found the robbers' den. As the women continue to drink, Janio and Fantasca spend the night together.

Act III opens on the marketplace back in the capital where vendors hawk their wares. Ali Baba has become wealthy, and his behavior with the local women causes trouble with his wife, whose forgiveness he wins temporarily by purchasing her a shawl. The soldiers return, happy that their battle was cancelled owing to inclement weather. Janio enters with the "thieves" tied up in sacks, hoping to claim his prize; however, much to everyone's surprise, the harem women emerge from the sacks. When a ship appears in the harbor, the women and Janio – hearing the sailors singing the waltz tune of his homeland – make their escape. Ali Baba joins them, after offering King Indigo a souvenir in a sack – his wife.

Die Fledermaus

The operetta begins in the bourgeois salon of Gabriel von Eisenstein. Outside the window Alfred serenades Rosalinde, his former lover and now Eisenstein's wife. But his songs are heard not by Rosalinde but by her maid Adele, who has just received a party invitation. She asks for the night off, but Rosalinde refuses because Eisenstein is to begin his jail term that night and she does not want to be left alone. As Adele disappears, Alfred slips in through the window, and although Rosalinde refuses his advances, he promises to return that night after her husband has gone. Eisenstein arrives with his incompetent lawyer Blind, complaining that his sentence has been increased to eight days, a term he must begin that night or be arrested. As Blind leaves, Eisenstein's old friend Dr. Falke arrives and persuades Eisenstein to attend Prince Orlofsky's ball with him that night before he begins his jail sentence. Eisenstein dresses for the evening, Rosalinde gives Adele the evening off after all, and the three of them sing with barely repressed glee of how sad they soon will be. As soon as Eisenstein and Adele depart, Alfred returns and makes himself at home in Eisenstein's smoking jacket. He and Rosalinde are enjoying champagne together when Frank, the jail director, arrives to escort Eisenstein to jail. When Alfred protests, Rosalinde insists that he must keep up the charade for the sake of propriety, and he leaves with Frank.

Act II takes place at the sumptuous home of the young Russian

Prince Orlofsky, to whom Falke explains the drama planned for his entertainment, "A Bat's Revenge." Adele arrives, followed by Eisenstein; they try to hide their alarm when they spy one another, but Eisenstein admits that she looks like his chambermaid, a *faux pas* Adele makes light of in her well-known "Laughing Song." Falke introduces two more players in his evening's entertainment, a French chevalier (Frank) and a masked Hungarian duchess (Rosalinde). Eisenstein flirts with the Hungarian, unaware that she is his wife, while she nabs his watch to be used later as proof of his infidelity. Questioning her identity, the party guests ask her to remove her mask, but instead she demonstrates her Hungarian nationality by singing a csárdás. As the party continues, Falke entertains the guests with his story of the bat: last carnival, Eisenstein and Falke attended a costume ball where Falke had dressed as a bat, and Eisenstein left him asleep on a park bench the next morning still in costume. Orlofsky, amused, calls for a toast, and all waltz and drink champagne until the stroke of 6 a.m., when Frank and Eisenstein rush off to the jail.

Act III begins with the antics of Frosch, the perpetually inebriated jailer, who is annoyed at the constant singing of a prisoner, namely, Alfred. Frank arrives, also tipsy and tired from the evening's events, and promptly falls asleep. Adele and her sister follow close behind, for Frank, in his disguise as the French chevalier, has promised Adele to help her find a job as an actress. She demonstrates her talents by performing various roles, but he must admit that he is a prison director and not a wealthy Frenchman. Frosch escorts the sisters out as Eisenstein enters, surprised to see his new friend at the jail. Frank is equally surprised that someone else claims to be Eisenstein, the prisoner he thought he had arrested the night before. While Frank trundles off to retrieve the alleged Eisenstein, Blind arrives and Eisenstein forces him to swap clothes in order to find out who is impersonating him. When Rosalinde arrives, she and Alfred try to explain their predicament to the lawyer, but Eisenstein's fury betrays his disguise. He accuses her of unfaithfulness, an accusation that loses its impact when she produces the watch he gave her while flirting at the party. He realizes that she was the Hungarian duchess, while Falke enjoys his revenge. Soloists and chorus conclude the operetta by forgiving everyone and blaming the whole mess on champagne.

Der Zigeunerbaron

Set during the reign of Maria Theresa, *Der Zigeunerbaron* opens on to the marshy Hungarian countryside. At the beginning of Act I, the Hungarian Ottokar searches for hidden treasure while the old Gypsy woman Czipra laughs at his efforts. Just as she assures him the rightful owner will soon return, Sandor Barinkay arrives to claim his property. He entertains the gathered Gypsies with tales of his adventures far and wide, and Czipra's daughter Saffi falls in love with him. Zsupán, Barinkay's neighbor and a wealthy Hungarian pig farmer, enters; Barinkay asks with amorous intention about his daughter Arsena, but Zsupán does not approve of the Gypsy Barinkay, and Arsena prefers Ottokar. Saffi sings a Gypsy ballad, after which Czipra reveals that Barinkay's father was the Gypsies' former leader and that Barinkay has inherited the right to rule. Spurned by Arsena, Barinkay chooses Saffi for his bride.

Act II begins the following morning. Having dreamt about the location of buried treasure, Czipra tells Barinkay, who unearths it. Saffi and Barinkay have spent the night together, and Carnero, the Chief of the Secret Commission for Public Morality, harasses them about their illegal union. When Count Homonay arrives recruiting volunteers to fight in the war against Spain, the men leaving for war, as well as the women staying home, talk with great anticipation of meeting in Vienna for the victory celebration. Carnero and Homonay insult the Gypsies, but Czipra surprises them with a document proving that Saffi is the daughter of the last Pasha of Hungary. To Saffi's disappointment, Barinkay now feels that he too must leave because he is unworthy of marrying a prince's daughter and joins the army.

Act III takes place in Vienna after the war, where a crowd of Austrian, Hungarian, and Gypsy women and children greet the returning soldiers. Zsupán proudly expounds upon his war exploits and his bravery. He grants Arsena permission to marry Ottokar, who has also returned a successful warrior. Barinkay becomes ennobled for his performance in the war; with that, he has indeed become a Gypsy baron and happily returns to Saffi.

Simplicius

As the *Prologue* begins, a hermit prays alone in the woods before a simple wooden cross. His prayers are interupted by trumpet calls, which remind him of a riding song from his previous years as a knight. His adopted son Simplicius arrives, terrorized by the figures he has seen on horseback, believing they are devils who will take him away. The soldiers follow close on his heels, and, while mocking the hermit's primitive lifestyle, they abduct Simplicius in hopes that he will direct them out of the woods.

The first act takes place in the soldiers' camp near Olmütz, where the chorus praises the military life. Baron von Grübben, an astrologist, arrives with his telescope, while Simplicius still longs and prays for his father. Meanwhile Arnim, the university-student-turned-soldier, is reunited with his love, Hildegarde. Children sing a chorus in imitation of the soldiers, pounding with kitchen utensils on pots, pans, and other improvised instruments. As the act closes, the soldiers, joined by Simplicius, march off to war.

Act II begins a year and a half later. Simplicius is still living a soldier's life, and although the hermit appears, they do not recognize each other until later in the act. Tilly flirts with Simplicius, amused at his naïveté. An ensemble of bells accompanies some dancers, while the chorus sings about the Danube-nymph, a conscious parallel to the Lorelei. Simplicius recounts the events of the operetta and admits his love for Tilly as everyone agrees that love has won the day.

Ritter Pásmán

Act I begins with the women of Pásmán's house spinning and singing together, regretting the fact that men are allowed to roam the world while they must remain at home. Mischu, Pásmán's assistant, arrives to announce the imminent arrival of Pásmán and his fellow hunters, who will be eager for dinner. The women prepare a feast, and as the men arrive, the king (in disguise) immediately falls in love with Pásmán's wife, Eva. The men sing a drinking song, toasting the wine of various countries, and as they carouse, Pásmán trades his helmet for the king's beret. When the men prepare to go night-fishing and leave, the king returns, hoping to find Eva alone. In the dark, he mistakes her maid Gundy for her and tries to kiss her. She runs away, locks the door, and the act ends with the king calling Eva's name.

The next act begins where the previous one left off, but now Eva spies the king (still wearing Pásmán's helmet) and, mistaking him for her husband, allows him to kiss her goodnight. When she realizes her error, she cannot bear her guilt and plans to throw herself at her husband's feet to beg forgiveness. The king reveals his identity to her but begs her not to tell her husband; when she relents, he kisses her on the forehead. Mischu has overheard the last scene, but because the king has still been wearing Pásmán's helmet, he has mistaken the couple for Pásmán and Eva. When Pásmán returns and asks Mischu for his helmet, however, Mischu reminds him that he was wearing it when he kissed his wife a few minutes ago. Meanwhile, the king and the other men leave Pásmán's estate quickly and quietly and ride back to the castle. Pásmán plans to follow them and kill the rogue who stole a kiss from his wife. Before he leaves with Mischu, he curses his "adulterous" wife.

The final act takes place at the king's castle where celebrations are underway in honor of the new queen. When Pásmán arrives (followed closely by Eva and Gundy in disguise), he demands to know the identity of the man who kissed his wife. Because the king and his jester have exchanged costumes in advance of his arrival, Pásmán addresses his concerns to the jester and is interrogated about the nature of the kiss. Mischu, the eyewitness, admits that it was a kiss on the forehead, so the jester decides that it would be fair for Pásmán to kiss the perpetrator's wife on the forehead as well. The king disagrees, but when Pásmán recognizes and threatens him, the queen steps up in his defense. She presents herself as his wife and asks that the punishment be carried out. Pásmán kisses her, but when the king orders him arrested, she gives Pásmán his kiss back, proving that she did it only for the sake of his penitence. The opera ends with the chorus extolling the queen and her kiss of mercy.

NOTES

INTRODUCTION

1 See Leon Botstein, "Music and Its Public: Habits of Listening and the Crisis of Musical Modernism in Vienna, 1870–1914" (Ph.D. dissertation, Harvard University, 1985).

2 The *Ausgleich* was the political and economic "compromise" between the two halves of the empire that created the kingdom of Hungary, and thus the dual monarchy. See chapter 6 for more about the ramifications of this agreement.

3 See Schorske, pp. 24–115.

4 *Wiener Tagblatt*, 1925. Quoted in Norbert Linke, *Johann Strauß (Sohn) in Selbstzeugnissen und Bilddokumenten* (Reinbek bei Hamburg: Rowohlt Taschenbuch Verlag, 1982), p. 167.

5 Webern wrote to Schoenberg from Stettin (6 October 1912): "Yesterday I heard an operetta by Joh. Strauss, *Eine Nacht in Venedig*. That instantly revived me. It is such fine, delicate music, really I was completely enthusiastic. Do you know this operetta? I now believe that Johann Strauss is a master." Copy, Arnold Schönberg Center, L24W3.

6 Webern arranged the "Schatzwalzer," op. 418 from *Der Zigeunerbaron*; Berg arranged "Wein, Weib und Gesang," op. 333; and Schoenberg arranged the "Lagunenwalzer," op. 411 from *Eine Nacht in Venedig* and "Rosen aus dem Süden," op. 388 from *Das Spitzentuch der Königin*.

7 Hanslick's obituary for Brahms ("Johannes Brahms, Die letzten Tage. Wien, 3. April 1897," *Am Ende des Jahrhunderts, 1895–1899, Der "Modernen Oper*," VII. Teil, Berlin: Allgemeiner-Verein für Deutsche Litteratur, 1899) reports that Brahms, already weak when Strauss's new operetta *Die Göttin der Vernunft* appeared, nevertheless instructed Hanslick repeatedly to reserve a seat for him in his loge: "For Johann Strauss, with whom he also liked to socialize in Ischl, Brahms felt the warmest sympathy and was still gladdened by his last work, *Waldmeister* . . . On 13 March he also appeared in the Theater an der Wien right on time for

the premiere of *Göttin der Vernunft*, but felt too ill to remain until the end . . . It was the last time Brahms attended the theater."

I   THE BIRTH OF A GENRE

1 See David F. Good, *The Economic Rise of the Habsburg Empire, 1750–1914* (Berkeley: University of California Press, 1984).

2 Schorske, pp. 24–115.

3 Since the English translation of *Vorstadt* ("suburb") calls to mind American housing developments and shopping malls rather than the distinctive neighborhoods surrounding Vienna's inner city, I have preferred to use the German term.

4 See *Fremdenblatt*, 2 December 1887 and 11 December 1887.

5 "Italienische Opern in der Wiener Musik- und Theater-Ausstellung," in *Fünf Jahre Musik (Der "Modernen Oper," VII. Teil)*, 2nd edn (Berlin: Allgemeiner Verein für Deutsche Litteratur, 1896), p. 62.

6 "Towards a New Awareness of Genre," *Science Fiction Studies* 28 (1982), 322.

7 Tzvetan Todorov, *Genres in Discourse*, trans. Catherine Porter (Cambridge: Cambridge University Press, 1990), p. 15.

8 Jeffrey Kallberg, *Chopin at the Boundaries: Sex, History, and Musical Genre* (Cambridge, MA: Harvard University Press, 1996), p. 32.

9 Binder and Nestroy also collaborated on an enormously popular parody of *Tannhäuser* (see chapter 7).

10 Alexander Faris, *Jacques Offenbach* (New York: Charles Scribner's Sons, 1980), p. 105.

11 See chapter 4 for more on Strauss's decision to compose for the stage.

12 *Kikeriki*, 9 October 1871.

13 *Illustriertes Wiener Extrablatt*, 2 December 1888.

14 *Ibid.*

15 For example, Strauss suggested to Adolf Müller, who conducted the premiere of *Fürstin Ninetta* at the Theater an der Wien, that the leading woman "should begin her imitation of [Eleanora] Duse [a famous Italian actress] a bit later" (September 1894). Quoted in Strauss, p. 123.

16 P. Walter Jacob, *Jacques Offenbach in Selbstzeugnissen und Bilddokumenten* (Reinbek bei Hamburg: Rowohlt Taschenbuch Verlag, 1969), p. 111.

17 For more on Strauss and anti-Semitism, see chapter 3.

18 Anton Bauer, *150 Jahre Theater an der Wien* (Zurich, Leipzig, and Vienna: Amalthea Verlag, 1952), p. 129.

19 His list of characters describes Venus as the owner of a subterranean deli. The story takes place simultaneously in several centuries. The first act is set near a champagne spring, the "second somewhere else, and the third after the second."

20 "Martha, oder Die Mischmonder Markt-Mägde-Mietung."

21 See chapter 7 for more about Wagner parodies.

22 "Die Musik in Wien." Quoted in Margarethe Egger, *Die "Schrammeln" in ihrer Zeit* (Vienna: Österreichischer Bundesverlag, 1989), p. 150.

23 See the anthology *Wiener Lieder und Tänze*, ed. Eduard Kremser (Vienna and Leipzig: Verlag Gerlach and Wiedling, 1911).

24 "Eine Opernsängerin singt so hochdeutsch, daß man gewöhnlich von dem, was sie singt, kein Wort versteht; eine Lokalsängerin singt aber so, wie ihr der Schnabel gewachsen ist, man versteht nicht nur, was sie singt, sondern sie gibt einem noch eine Menge mehr zu verstehen." Quoted from Gallmeyer, "Lokalsängerin und Postillon," in Erika Döbler, *"Josefine Gallmeyer. Der Ausklang des Wiener Volksstücks"* (Ph.D. dissertation, University of Vienna, 1935), p. 120. See Chapter 2 for more about Gallmeyer.

25 Adam Müller-Guttenbrunn, *Das Wiener Theaterleben* (Leipzig: Verlag und Druck von Otto Spamer, 1890), p. 7.

26 The *Fremdenblatt*, 2 December 1881, reported that Franz Steiner, director of the Theater an der Wien, had taken steps with the appropriate authorities to prevent folk singers from performing Girardi's popular song "Nur für Natur" from Strauss's *Der lustige Krieg*.

27 *Kikeriki*, 18 November 1886.

28 Johann Strauss to Johann Schrammel, 4 March 1884. Quoted in Egger, *Die "Schrammeln,"* p. 95.

29 See chapter 6 for more about *Der Zigeunerbaron*.

30 *Wiener Extrablatt*, 14 August 1886. Quoted in Egger, *Die "Schrammeln,"* p. 132.

31 *Wiener Spezialitäten*, 15 August 1886. Quoted in Egger, *Die "Schrammeln,"* p. 131.

32 See Christian Glanz, "Popularmusik: Ein Brennspiegel für Identität und Gemeinschaft," *Österreichische Musikzeitschrift* 10–11 (1996): 722–26.

33 Andreas Koepp, "Viennese Soul Music," *Austria Kultur* 9 (July/August 1999): 9–10.

34 Glanz, "Popularmusik," 725.

35 Venice, ceded to the Habsburg empire at the Congress of Vienna, was lost in 1855, and the Habsburgs relinquished Lombardy in 1866. Dalmatia, an Italian-speaking strip of the Adriatic coast and home of Franz von Suppé, belonged to the empire until World War I.

36 Quoted in Richard Traubner, *Operetta: A Theatrical History* (Garden City, NY: Doubleday, 1983), p. 155.

37 Quoted in Otto Schneidereit, *Franz von Suppé: Der Wiener aus Dalmatien* (Berlin: VEB, Lied der Zeit, Musikverlag, 1977), p. 132.

38 Published in *Deutsche Revue über das gesamte nationale Leben der Gegenwart* 9 (1885): 163–73. Quoted in Marion Linhardt, *Inszenierung der Frau – Frau in der Inszenierung: Operette in Wien zwischen 1865 und 1900* (Tutzing: Hans Schneider, 1997), p. 14.

39 *Wiener Zeitung*, 11 October 1880. Review of Richard Genée's operetta *Nisida* (premiered at the Carltheater, 9 October 1880).

40 Eduard Hanslick to Johann Strauss, 2 November 1887, WSLB-HS, IN 118.760.

41 Linhardt, *Inszenierung der Frau*, p. 115.

42 *Fremdenblatt*, 26 November 1881.

43 See chapter 7 for more about the influence of German romantic opera traditions on Strauss's works.

44 See chapter 7 for more about Wagner's reception in Vienna.

45 *Der Floh*, 9 October 1887.

46 *Figaro*, 14 January 1893.

47 Victor Tilgner to Johann Strauss, 11 February 1893, WSLB-HS, IN 127.586.

48 Linhardt, *Inszenierung der Frau*, p. 260.

49 *Ibid.*, p.268.

50 *Hugo von Hofmannsthal and His Time: The European Imagination, 1860–1920*, trans. and ed. Michael P. Steinberg (Chicago and London: University of Chicago Press, 1984), p. 62.

51 *Ibid.*, p. 38.

52 Quoted in Schneidereit, *Suppé*, 30.

53 "Die culturelle Macht der Bühne," *Österreichische Musik- und Theaterzeitung*, Bd. III/No. 18–19 (1891), 9.

54 Adam Müller-Guttenbrunn, *Wien war eine Theaterstadt* (Vienna: Verlag von Carl Graeser, 1885), p. 63. Müller-Guttenbrunn complains specifically about the situation of Vienna's Stadttheater following Heinrich Laube's retirement.

55 Quoted in Norbert Nischkauer, "Bemerkungen zum Thema Johann Strauß und die Zensur," *Die Fledermaus* 4 (March 1992): 12.

56 "Macht der Bühne," *Österreichische Musik- und Theaterzeitung.*

57 Hermann Bahr, *Wiener Theater* (Berlin: S. Fischer Verlag, 1899), p. 253.

58 *Königliche Private Berlinerische Zeitung (Vossische Zeitung)*, 5 October 1883. Berlin, however, had no native operetta composers, a fact made clear by the curtain at the newly redecorated Friedrich-Wilhelmstädtischen Theater in Berlin: it showed portraits of Strauss, Suppé, Millöcker, Zell, and Genée – all Viennese.

59 *Neues Wiener Tagblatt*, 2 January 1892.

60 András Batta, *Träume sind Schäume: Die Operette in der Donaumonarchie*, trans. from Hungarian by Maria Eisenreich (Budapest: Corvina, 1992), p. 25.

61 *Kikeriki*, 14 March 1867.

62 *Kikeriki*, 5 December 1880.

63 *Kikeriki*, 1 December 1881.

64 *Kikeriki*, 15 January 1882.

65 *Kikeriki*, 29 November 1885.

66 *Fremdenblatt*, 3 January 1892.

67 See chapter 2 for more about the individual theaters and their directors.

68 *Johann Strauß* (Vienna: Österreichischer Bundesverlag, 1925), p. 8.

69 John W. Boyer, *Political Radicalism in Late Imperial Vienna: Origins of the Christian Social Movement, 1848–1897* (Chicago and London: University of Chicago Press, 1981), p. 249.

70 Silvia Ehalt, "Wiener Theater um 1900," in *Glücklich ist, wer vergißt. . .? Das andere Wien um 1900*, ed. Hubert Ch. Ehalt, Gernot Heiß, and Hannes Stekl (Vienna: Hermann Böhlaus Nachfolger, 1986), p. 329.

71 Hermann Menkes (1909), quoted in Christopher Hailey, "Between Instinct and Reflection: Berg, Opera and the Viennese Dichotomy," in *The Berg Companion*, ed. Douglas Jarman (London: Macmillan, 1989), p. 224.

72 *Der Floh*, 1 May 1870, noted that lower socio-economic classes arrive at

the theater box office as early as 4 a.m. in order to be the first to buy blocks of tickets.

73 *Der Zwischenakt*, 10 February 1871.

74 *Fremdenblatt*, 3 October 1880.

75 Max Kuybensz, "Die Einwirkungen der Börsenkatastrophe von 1873 auf das sociale Leben in Wien," *Deutsche Rundschau* 3 (April 1875): 117.

76 Johann Strauss to Friedrich August Simrock, in Strauss, p. 74.

77 See the *Neuester Plan und Führer durch Wien und nächste Umgebung* (Vienna: R. Lechner's k.k. Hof- und Universitäts-Buchhandlung, 1883), p. 35, for a chart comparing ticket prices at various Viennese theaters.

78 WSLB-DS, 172.817, Mappe 12. Review of the *Simplicius* premiere (December 1887).

79 Rudolph Lothar, *Das Wiener Burgtheater* (Berlin and Leipzig: Schuster and Loeffler, n.d.), p. 48.

80 Directors Franz Jauner and Friedrich Strampfer, composer Franz von Suppé, and performers Josephine Gallmeyer and Alexander Girardi are only a few of the most prominent figures who worked at several *Vorstadt* theaters over the course of their careers.

81 Ignaz Schnitzer, *Meister Johann: Bunte Geschichten aus der Johann-Strauß-Zeit*, vol. 1 (Vienna and Leipzig: Halm und Goldmann, 1920), p. 251. Schnitzer published similar comments during Strauss's lifetime in the *Fremdenblatt*, 16 October 1884, under the title "Wie Johann Strauss arbeitet" (quoted in Mailer, vol. 3, p. 262).

82 Schnitzer, *Meister Johann*, vol. 1, p. 190.

83 In 1881 Vienna had forty-five shops selling music and five commercial lending libraries. Botstein, "Music and Its Public," p. 481.

84 *Ibid.*, p. 711.

85 *Neue Freie Presse*, 3 March 1875.

86 *Kikeriki*, 7 January 1877.

87 *Fremdenblatt*, 4 December 1881.

88 "Das Zeitalter der Deutlichkeit," in *Gegen den Strom: Flugschriften einer literarisch-künstlerischen Gesellschaft* 14 (Vienna: Carl Graeser, 1887), 25.

89 Anonymous, *Wien und die Wiener: Ungeschminkte Schilderungen eines fahrenden Gesellen* (Berlin: Verlag von Eduard Rentzel, 1892), p. 74.

90 Schneidereit, *Suppé*, p. 47.

91 *Kikeriki*, 17 January 1870.

92 The Strauss–Simrock correspondence regarding *Ritter Pásmán*, housed in the Coburg city library, offers an example of this negotiation.

93 Schnitzer, *Meister Johann*, vol. 2, p. 77.

94 Hanslick, *Am Ende des Jahrhunderts*, p. 32.

95 *Johann Strauß* (Breslau and Berlin: S. Schottlaender, 1885), p. 13.

96 Strauss complained to his publisher Simrock about the damage caused by Hanslick's unfavorable review of *Ritter Pásmán*: "The article in the *Neue Freie Presse* definitely influences stage business!" Letter, Johann Strauss to Friedrich August Simrock, 12 January 1892, in the possession of Paul Pfändler, Zurich.

97 Hanslick, *Am Ende des Jahrhunderts*, pp. 110–11.

2   CREATORS AND PERFORMERS OF VIENNESE OPERETTA

1 Preface to *Der Grandprofoss*, 1787. Quoted in Kurt Honolka, *Papageno: Emanuel Schikaneder, Man of the Theater in Mozart's Time*, trans. Jane Mary Wilde (Portland, OR: Amadeus Press, 1990), p. 56.

2 Letter, Johann Strauss to Alexander Girardi, 18 September 1894, WSLB-HS, IN 135.803.

3 WSLB-MS, MH 3518.

4 In 1898, however, Herzl's work appeared once again on a Viennese stage; at the Carltheater Franz Jauner produced his *Das neue Ghetto*, an agit-prop play advocating Zionism. See Bahr, *Wiener Theater*, p. 495.

5 Genée's handwriting is evident throughout the autograph scores of *Indigo und die vierzig Räuber* and *Die Fledermaus*, among others.

6 Carl Millöcker, *Gasparone*, text by F. Zell and Richard Genée, ed. and intro. by Anton Würz (Stuttgart: Philipp Reclam, Jr., 1970), p. 4.

7 Letter, Johann Strauss to Max Kalbeck, summer 1894, WSLB-HS, IN 127.594.

8 Letter, Johann Strauss to Max Kalbeck, 7 July 1893, WSLB-HS, IN 121.591.

9 Letter, Richard Genée to Johann Strauss, 22 June 1883. Quoted in *Johann Strauß (Sohn) Gesamtausgabe . . . Eine Nacht in Venedig*, ed. Fritz Racek (Vienna: Doblinger and Universal Edition, 1990), p. 519. Genée often "filled in" instrumentation in full score that Strauss had indicated in a short score.

10 Letter, Adolf Müller to Richard Genée, 11 May 1892, WSLB-HS, IN 125.312.

11 Schneidereit, *Suppé*, p. 151.

12 Strauss, p. 108.

13 Otto Keller, *Die Operette in ihrer geschichtlichen Entwicklung* (Leipzig: Stein Verlag, 1926), p. 143.

14 Quoted in Holzer, p. 282.

15 Review of *Das Pensionat* in *Rezensionen*, 24 November 1860. Quoted in Holzer, p. 283.

16 *Kikeriki*, 13 February 1879.

17 Schneidereit, *Suppé*, p. 166.

18 *Der Floh*, 21 July 1872. Adalbert Stifter (1805–68) served as Austrian minister of education and was a prolific novelist. He devotes loving attention to details of nature and the countryside in works such as *Der Nachsommer*.

19 Holzer, p. 335. See also Millöcker's accounting book in WSLB-HS, Ja 126.454.

20 Holzer, p. vi.

21 Indeed, this sharp wit was so associated with the Viennese that Marie, a character in Anton Langer's play "Strauß und Lanner" (I, x) exclaims: "I wouldn't be a real Viennese girl if I couldn't put four lines together from nothing."

22 Schneidereit, *Suppé*, p. 57. Comic Karl Schweighofer was once fined 20 fl. and sentenced to four days in jail for ignoring the censor's proscriptions (*Die Presse*, 21 February 1871).

23 Letter, Johann Strauss to Friedrich August Simrock, 17 March 1892, Coburg, MS 425. Strauss was writing in reference to a proposed premiere of his *Ritter Pásmán* in Prague.

24 Franz Hadamowsky, *Wien: Theater Geschichte von den Anfängen bis zum Ende des Ersten Weltkriegs* (Vienna and Munich: J & V, Edition Wien, Dachs-Verlag, 1994), p. 562.

25 Bauer, *150 Jahre*, p. 46.

26 "Eine Direction Jauner?," *Morgenpost*, 7 August 1883.

27 Attila E. Láng, *Das Theater an der Wien: Vom Singspiel zum Musical* (Munich: Jugend und Volk, 1976), p. 23.

28 Bauer, *150 Jahre*, p. 150.

29 *Der Floh*, 15 May 1870.

30 *Der Floh*, 13 March 1887.

31 *Der Floh*, 23 January 1887.

32 *Kikeriki*, 12 September 1889.

33 *Kikeriki*, 8 December 1889.

34 Holzer, p. 369.

35 *Ibid.*, p. 85.

36 *Kikeriki*, 1 September 1878.

37 *Kikeriki*, 21 November 1875.

38 Heinrich Laube, "Wiener Theater," *Deutsche Rundschau* June 1875, 471.

39 According to Heinz Gstrein, in 1880 there were 20,000 Jews in the Leopoldstadt alone (*Jüdisches Wien* [Vienna and Munich: Herold Verlag, 1984], p. 37), and Steven Beller calculated that the Jewish population of that district reached 34 percent by 1890 (*Vienna and the Jews, 1867–1938: A Cultural History* [Cambridge: Cambridge University Press, 1989], p. 44).

40 Letter, Johann Strauss to Max Kalbeck, n.d. Quoted in Strauss, p. 87.

41 Holzer, p. 80.

42 Bauer, *150 Jahre*, p. 85.

43 Anton Bauer, *Das Theater in der Josefstadt zu Wien* (Vienna and Munich: Manutiuspresse, 1957), p. 129.

44 The *Hammlet* parody was written by Julius Hopp, German translator of *Carmen* and other opera libretti. He also translated almost all the early Offenbach operettas for the German stage.

45 Text and music by Julius Hopp.

46 Quoted in Müller-Guttenbrunn, *Das Wiener Theaterleben*, p. 87.

47 Hadamowsky, *Wien*, p. 627.

48 Bauer, *150 Jahre*, p. 170 (Bauer's statistics).

49 Maximilian Steiner was the grandfather of émigré film composer Max Steiner.

50 *Kikeriki*, 26 March 1874.

51 *Der Floh*, 12 July 1873.

52 *Österreichische Musiker-Zeitung*, 16 June 1875.

53 During the period of their joint directorship, the theater's repertoire comprised 60 percent spoken works, 36 percent operetta, and 4 percent Italian opera. Bauer, *150 Jahre*, p. 185.

54 *Kikeriki*, 8 April 1875. "Brüderlein fein, Brüderlein fein, / Sieh', es muß geschieden sein! / Schreibt der Strauß auch noch so schön, / D'Leut' woll'n bloß Elefanten seh'n! / Brüderlein fein – / 's muß geschieden sein!"

55 "Feuilleton. Theaterkrisen," *Neues Wiener Tagblatt*, 22 March 1887.

56 Quoted in Holzer, p. 486.

57 Quoted in Holzer, p. 175.

58 The work became so popular that it merited a parody by Millöcker, *Die Reise durch Wien in 80 Stunden* [*The Trip through Vienna in 80 Hours*] (WSLB-MS, MH 11442).

59 Max Kuybensz, "Die einwirkungen der Börsenkatastrophe von 1873 auf das sociale Leben in Wien," *Deutsche Rundschau*, 3 (April 1875): 117.

60 *Neue Freie Presse*, 31 August 1875.

61 *Deutsche Rundschau*, January 1876.

62 Richard Wagner, *Briefe*, ed. Hans-Joachim Bauer (Stuttgart: Philipp Reclam jun., 1995), p. 399. See chapter 7 for more about Wagner in Vienna.

63 Heinrich Kralik, *Die Wiener Oper* (Wien: Verlag Brüder Rosenbaum, 1962), p. 57.

64 Boyer, *Political Radicalism*, pp. 200–1.

65 "Eine Direction Jauner?," *Morgenpost* (Vienna), 7 August 1883.

66 Holzer, p. 496.

67 *Ibid.*, p. 502.

68 Schnitzer, *Meister Johann*, vol. 2, p. 208.

69 Bauer, *150 Jahre*, p. 203.

70 It had been presented in Czech the previous year at Vienna's International Theater Exhibition. The Theater an der Wien presented it in Max Kalbeck's translation. Hanslick, *Am Ende des Jahrhunderts*, p. 40.

71 *Der Floh*, 12 January 1890.

72 Richard S. Geehr, *Karl Lueger: Mayor of Fin de Siècle Vienna* (Detroit: Wayne State University Press, 1990), p. 74.

73 *Österreichische Musik- und Theaterzeitung*, March 1891.

74 Bauer, *150 Jahre*, p. 218.

75 *Neues Wiener Abendblatt*, 2 December 1919.

76 Rudolf Holzer, ed., *Heinrich Laube, Der Theatercaesar* (Graz and Vienna: Stiasny Verlag, 1958), p. 65. Quoted from an essay by Laube entitled "Sprache und Kultur." Laube (1806–84) was an influential figure in Viennese theater life; he served as director of the Burgtheater (1848–67) and the Stadttheater (1872–74) before retiring to write theater criticism.

77 Holzer, p. 541.

78 František Salda, *Loutky i delníci bozi* (*Puppets and God's Workers*, 1918). Quoted in Robert P. Pynsent, ed., *Decadence and Innovation* (London: Weidenfeld and Nicolson, 1989), p. 119.

79 Ellen Rosand, *Opera in Seventeenth-Century Venice: The Creation of a Genre* (Berkeley, Los Angeles, and Oxford: University of California Press, 1991), p. 221.

80 Emil Pirchan, *Marie Geistinger: Die Königin der Operette* (Vienna: Verlag Wilhelm Frick, 1947), p. 12. To put her salary in perspective: it was not long after this that Strauss sold his "Blue Danube Waltz" to his publisher for 250 fl.

81 "Der neue Theaterdirektor an der Wien: Die Geistinger in einer neuen Hosenrolle." Pirchan, *Marie Geistinger*, n.p.

82 Hermann Bahr, *Austriaca* (Berlin: S. Fischer Verlag, 1911), p. 192.

83 Holzer, p. 292.

84 Letter, Lili Dietrich Strauss to Julius Bauer, 19 March 1884, ÖNB-HS, 583/49-3.

85 Mailer, vol. 3, pp. 74–75.

86 *Der Floh*, 19 February 1882. "Um sich die Haare auszuraufen, / Und an den Wänden hinzulaufen! / Bis in der Wohnung stillsten Ort, / Dringt dieses Liedlein fort und fort. / Und selbst im Traum noch hört man nur: / 'Nur für Natur." Another verse concludes: "Spät und Früh, als ob nie, / Aus den Gassen, Zimmern, Straßen / Schwände diese Melodie!"

87 *Kikeriki*, 9 April 1882.

88 *Kikeriki*, 31 August 1882.

89 WSLB-HS, IN 125.525, 4 October 1886.

90 Hadamowsky, *Wien*, p. 620.

91 Letter, Johann Strauss to Alexander Girardi, 9 September 1894, WSLB-HS, IN 135.802.

92 Letter, Johann Strauss to Alexander Girardi, 12 October 1894, WSLB-HS, IN 135.805.

93 Letter, Johann Strauss to Gustav Lewy, 15 July 1895, WSLB-HS, IN 121.600.

94 Millöcker's account book. WSLB-HS, Ja 126.454.

95 Müller-Guttenbrunn, *Wien war eine Theaterstadt*, p. 16.

96 Max Graf, *Legende einer Musikstadt* (Vienna: Österreichische Buchgemeinschaft, 1949), p. 339.

97 *Neues Wiener Tagblatt*, 16 January 1887.

98 Holzer, p. 613.

99 Alexander von Weilen, *Wiener Abendpost*, 23 April 1918.

100 *Radio Wien*, 10 February 1928 and 1 December 1933.

101 *Neue Freie Presse*, 21 April 1938.

102 Arthur Sullivan also died in 1900 in London.

103 Hadamowsky, *Wien*, pp. 621–22.

3 AUSTRIA PERSONIFIED

1 *Der Humorist*, February 1871. Quoted in Kobald, *Johann Strauß*, p. 64.

2 Quoted in Mailer, vol. 2, p. 79.

3 *Fremdenblatt*, 11 January 1893.

4 Mailer, vol. 1, p. 77.

5 Ilsa Barea, *Vienna* (London: Secker and Warburg, 1966), p. 203.

6 It remains unclear what exactly constituted "immoral" behavior. Perhaps it was a euphemism for "revolutionary," still punishing him for his behavior in 1848. After all, Strauss, Sr. had gained the title despite the fact that he had extramarital affairs and illegitimate children years before leaving his original family (including Johann and his siblings) and later divorcing his first wife.

7 Mailer, vol. 1, p. 230.

8 *Kikeriki*, 5 January 1879.

9 *Kikeriki*, 16 May 1886.

10 *Kikeriki*, 31 March 1872. Johann, on the other hand, felt that "A good musical thought is worth a Grand Cross. The adoration of thousands cannot create that . . . What good is a medal on my chest if my next operetta is a flop?" Strauss, p. 176.

11 *Kikeriki*, 7 February 1875.

12 Writing to Simrock, Strauss mentioned one of Eduard's upcoming tours of Germany: "Perhaps it is finally possible to make the Berlin conductors learn a *correct waltz tempo*. Success certainly depends very much on that." Letter, 31 March 1892, Pierpont Morgan Library.

13 The next day, Strauss wrote again to Simrock: "[Edi's] compositions are not bad – but they don't sell. If they did sell, then he would not play me any longer. He plays me – because he needs me. So it is." Letter, 1 April 1892, owned by Paul Pfändler, Zurich.

14 Linke, *Johann Strauß*, p. 159.

15 Although this destruction continues to impede scholarship on the bulk of Strauss's dance music, his operetta scores (to which Eduard did not have access) were unaffected.

16 See Franz Mailer, *Genie wider Willen* (Vienna and Munich: Jugend und Volk, 1977).

17 Eduard Strauss, *Erinnerungen* (Leipzig and Vienna: Franz Deuticke, 1906), p. 33.

18 F. R. Bridge, *The Habsburg Monarchy among the Great Powers, 1815–1918* (New York: St. Martin's Press, 1990), p. 93.

19 Letter, Johann Strauss to Eduard Strauss, n.d. Strauss, pp. 166–67.

20 Strauss Jubilee, 1884, Vienna.

21 *Fremdenblatt*, 12 October 1884.

22 *Neue Freie Presse*, 7 June 1891.

23 *Figaro*, October 1894.

24 Mailer, vol. 2, p. 48.

25 *Musikalisches Wochenblatt* 14 (1883): 528a. This journal reprinted the review originally published in the *Pester Lloyd*.

26 *Kikeriki*, 11 September 1873.

27 *Die Presse*, 7 April 1874.

28 *Kikeriki*, 7 January 1877.

29 *Kikeriki*, 11 September 1879.

30 Lindau, *Johann Strauß*, p. 18.

31 *Vossische Zeitung*, 5 October 1883.

32 *Ibid.*

33 *Die Presse*, 10 October 1883.

34 *Figaro*, 13 October 1883.

35 WSLB-DS, 172.817, Mappe 11. Unidentified newspaper, no date.

36 Lueger (1844–1910) was mayor of Vienna for almost thirteen years (1897–1910), longer than any other mayor of the city. His ideas for municipal improvements were combined with a flair for public speaking and a popularity with the low- to middle-income population often gained through use of anti-Semitic rhetoric. For more on this important Viennese figure, as well as on Georg von Schönerer, Lueger's political precursor and brother of Theater an der Wien director Alexandrine von Schönerer, see Schorske, pp. 116–80; and Geehr, *Karl Lueger*.

37 WSLB-DS, 172.817, Mappe 13, p. 48. Unidentified newspaper, 12 October 1894.

38 *Der Floh*, 22 December 1878.

39 *Neue Freie Presse*, 27 October 1885.

40 *Der Floh*, 10 January 1892.

41 *Wiener Tagblatt*, 2 January 1892.

42 The cartoon's caption reads: "The first operetta by Strauss outweighs all of Offenbach's operettas." Linke, *Johann Strauß*, p. 97.

43 See Johnston, p. 14.

44 *Neues Wiener Tagblatt*, 26 August 1928.

45 *Adaxel, unparteiische Zeitschrift für Heimatwesen*, Johann Strauss Festnummer, 9 (1925): 1.

46 *Neues Wiener Journal*, 14 October 1894.

47 *Neues Wiener Tagblatt*, 27 October 1885.

48 *Wiener Allgemeine Zeitung*, 6 October 1883.

49 See for example, Beller, *Vienna and the Jews*; Gstrein, *Jüdisches Wien*; Robert S. Wistrich, *The Jews of Vienna in the Age of Franz Joseph* (New York: Oxford University Press, 1989); Marsha L. Rozenblit, *The Jews of Vienna, 1867–1914: Assimilation and Identity* (Albany: State University of New York Press, 1983).

50 Beller, *Vienna and the Jews*, p. 216.

51 *Ibid.*, p. 23.

52 Bauer, *Theater in der Josefstadt*, p. 124.

53 Schneidereit, *Suppé*, p. 96.

54 NÖL, IN 135.038.

55 Marc A. Weiner, *Richard Wagner and the Anti-Semitic Imagination* (Lincoln and London: University of Nebraska Press, 1995), p. 8.

56 *Ibid.*, p. 8.

57 Mailer, vol. 4, p. 164.

58 *Alte Presse*, 4 March 1873.

59 Despite its title, Strauss's work includes only two minor Jewish characters (Mandelbaum and Feuerstein, "representatives from the city," who appear briefly in Act II), but the operetta acquired the nickname "the old Jew" for its biblical eponym.

60 Rozenblit, *The Jews of Vienna*, p. 78.

61 WSLB-MS, MH 7748/C.

62 Mailer, vol. 3, p. 57.

63 WSLB-DS, 172.817, Mappe 14, p. 50. Article by Max Schlesinger in the *Wiener Salonblatt*, no date but probably from early 1893.

64 Fred K. Prieberg, *Musik im NS-Staat* (Frankfurt: Fischer Taschenbuch Verlag, 1982), pp. 56–7. See also *Arbeiter Zeitung*, 8 June 1951; *Die Presse*, 28 May 1962; and "Goebbels und der Walzerkönig," *Welt und Sport*, 23 July 1962.

65 Letter, Johann Strauss to Josef Simon, December 1887, WSLB-HS, IN
    121.611.
66 Letter, Johann Strauss to Josef Simon, January 1889, WSLB-HS, IN
    121.822.
67 *Neue Freie Presse*, 26 June 1921.
68 *Radio Wien*, 31 May 1929.
69 *Radio Wien*, 8 September 1933.
70 *Neues Wiener Tagblatt*, 20 March 1938.
71 Evelyn Schreiner, "Nationalsozialistische Kulturpolitik in Wien
    1938–1945 unter spezieller Berücksichtigung der Wiener Theaterszene"
    (PhD dissertation, University of Vienna, 1980), pp. 307–8.
72 Erich Schenk, *Johann Strauß* (Potsdam: Akademische
    Verlagsgesellschaft Athenaion, 1940), p. 105.
73 Kurt Arnold Findeisen, *Das Leben ein Tanz, der Tanz ein Leben: Der
    Walzerkönig Johann Strauß und seine Zeit. Musikalisch-dichterisches
    Lebensbild in drei Teilen* (Leipzig: Hermann Eichblatt Verlag, 1941), p. 41.
74 See Benjamin M. Korstvedt, "Anton Bruckner in the Third Reich and
    After: An Essay on Ideology and Bruckner Reception," *Musical
    Quarterly* 80 (Spring 1996): 132–60; and Bryan Gilliam, "Bruckner's
    Annexation Revisited: A Response to Manfred Wagner," *Musical
    Quarterly* 80 (Spring 1996): 124–31.
75 Findeisen, *Das Leben ein Tanz*, p. 46.
76 Richard Traubner, "With a 1–2–3, 1–2–3, 1–2–3, Vienna Honors a King,"
    New York Times, Sunday, 27 June 1999, Arts and Leisure section.

4 FROM BALLROOM TO THEATER

1 *Morgen-Post*, 8 January 1883.
2 *Running with the Devil: Power, Gender, and Madness in Heavy Metal Music*
   (Hanover, NH and London: Wesleyan University Press, 1993),
   p. 128.
3 Letter, Johann Strauss to Ignaz Schnitzer, n.d. Quoted in Strauss, p. 187.
4 In the play *Strauß und Lanner*, Lanner reminds his nervous copyist that
   opera composers begin work on their overtures only when the ushers
   have admitted people to the balcony. Anton Langer, *Wiener Volks-Bühne*
   (Vienna: Jakob Dirnböck's Verlag, 1859).
5 Many of Strauss's harmony and figured-bass exercises are in the
   WSLB-MS, MH 12896/C.

6 Strauss, p. 102.

7 Whenever the violins and flutes shared material, instead of writing out both lines Strauss simply wrote "col violine" in the flute part, whereas Millöcker, a flutist, wrote "col flauto" in the violin line.

8 See for example, the second waltz from "Wiener Blut," op. 354.

9 *Neues Wiener Tagblatt*, 27 October 1885.

10 Hanslick reports in Strauss's obituary that Brahms turned to him at the premiere of *Waldmeister* (1895) and told him that "the Strauss orchestra reminded him of Mozart." *Aus dem Tagebuch eines Rezensenten: Gesammelte Musikkritiken*, ed. Peter Wapnewski (Kassel and Basel: Bärenreiter Verlag, 1989), p. 310.

11 Letter, Johann Strauss to Gustav Lewy, n.d. Quoted in Strauss, pp. 106–7.

12 Fred Hennings, *Ringstrassensymphonie, 1. Satz 1857–1870* (Vienna and Munich: Verlag Herold, 1963), p. 59. "Hier singen wir und musizieren wir, gehen ins Theater und zu Strauß und stecken mit ihm den Kopf in den Sand unserer Gemütlichkeit." Billroth makes a pun on the word "Strauß," German for "ostrich."

13 *Die Presse*, 12 February 1871. Schwender's was a popular Viennese establishment where patrons could eat, drink, and dance.

14 *Neue Freie Presse*, 13 February 1871.

15 WSLB-HS, Ja 126.454.

16 Mailer, vol. 2, p. 190.

17 Franz von Suppé made a more grievous business miscalculation yet, when, in 1846, he sold the rights to his *Poet and Peasant* overture to a Munich publisher for 8 fl.! Schneidereit, *Suppé*, p. 44.

18 Strauss, pp. 92–93.

19 The libretto is in the WSLB-HS (Jb 171.922).

20 *Fremdenblatt*, 19 June 1870.

21 *Fremdenblatt*, 3 July 1870.

22 Mailer, vol. 2, p. 186.

23 Quoted in Kobald, *Johann Strauss*, p. 64.

24 *Mein Kampf*, trans. Ralph Manheim (Boston: Houghton Mifflin, 1943). Quoted in Schorske, p. 46.

25 See Appendix for plot synopsis.

26 Margaret Ross Griffel's dissertation "'Turkish' Opera from Mozart to Cornelius" (Columbia University, 1975) offers a useful survey of works. Her discussion of "'Turkish" characteristics in western European

operas mentions the same signifiers operating in Strauss's operetta, though her work stops with Cornelius's *Barbier von Bagdad* (1858), which she claims marks the end of "Turkish" opera.

27 *Fremdenblatt*, 12 February 1871.

28 Jean-Paul Bled, *Franz Joseph*, trans. Teresa Bridgeman (Cambridge, MA and Oxford: Blackwell, 1992), p. 173.

29 Rev. Robert Walsh, *Constantinople and the Scenery of the Seven Churches of Asia Minor* (London, 1838).

30 See Mary Hunter, "The *Alla Turca* Style in the Late Eighteenth Century: Race and Gender in the Symphony and the Seraglio," in *The Exotic in Western Music*, ed. Jonathan Bellman (Boston: Northeastern University Press, 1998), pp. 43–73.

31 Hunter, "The *Alla Turca* Style," p. 68.

32 See also Rameau's *Les Indes galantes*.

33 Hunter, "The *Alla Turca* Style," p. 58.

34 Griffel, "Turkish Opera," p. 172.

35 Rossini's opera was frequently performed both at the Vienna Court Opera and by visiting Italian opera troupes at the Theater an der Wien.

36 McGrath, p. 45.

37 Hennings, *Ringstrassensymphonie, 1. Satz*, p. 28.

38 Bled, *Franz Joseph*, p. 79.

39 *Die Presse*, 19 February 1871.

40 See Julius Jakob, *Wörterbuch des Wiener Dialektes* (Vienna and Leipzig: Gerlach and Wiedling, 1929).

41 Note the striking similarity of this harmonic progression with that found in Ravel's *La Valse* (1919–20).

42 Janio wants to spend the night with her in the woods (a foretaste of *Der Zigeunerbaron*), but Fantasca chases him away, reminding him not to pull his sword too quickly when he finds the robbers. Fantasca warns him to keep his "weapon" in check immediately after she rebuffs his seduction. Perhaps jokes such as these, which could slip by the censors but be heightened in performance, exemplify what Hanslick and other music critics denounced as lascivious.

5 *DIE FLEDERMAUS* AND THE ILLUSION OF CARNIVAL IN VIENNA

1 Ludwig Eisenberg, *Johann Strauß: Ein Lebensbild* (Leipzig: Breitkopf und Härtel, 1894), p. 82.

2 See Appendix for plot synopsis.

3 *Johann Strauß (Sohn) Gesamtausgabe, Series II . . . Die Fledermaus*, ed. Fritz Racek (Vienna: Doblinger and Universal Edition, 1974), p. 500.

4 As required by tradition in Vienna, all proceeds from performances on Easter Sunday were given to charity; the Theater an der Wien donated its gross income of 1550 fl. to the Emperor Franz Joseph Foundation for the Advancement of Small Business (Kaiser-Franz-Joseph-Stiftung zur Förderung des Kleingewerbes). *Ibid.*, p. 502.

5 Keller, *Die Operette*, p. 420.

6 Kuybensz, "Börsenkatastrophe," p. 104.

7 Act II, No. 12.

8 Act I, No. 5.

9 Act III, Finale.

10 *Johann Strauß . . . Die Fledermaus*, ed. Racek, p. 501.

11 Kuybensz, "Börsenkatastrophe," p. 109.

12 *Ibid.*, p. 104.

13 See Friedrich Schlögl, "Sonderbare Käuze" (1872), in *Wiener Blut und Wiener Luft: Skizzen aus dem alten Wien*, ed. Karlheinz Rossbacher and Ulrike Tanzer (Salzburg and Vienna: Residenz Verlag, 1997), pp. 191–96.

14 Holzer, p. 590.

15 Mikhail Bakhtin, *Rabelais and His World*, trans. Hélène Iswolsky (Bloomington: Indiana University Press, 1984), pp. 11–12.

16 Beller, *Vienna and the Jews*, p. 37.

17 "Ein zischender, schrillender, summsender und murksender Lautausdruck." Richard Wagner, *Judaism in Music* (1850, appendix 1869), trans. William Ashton Ellis, *Judaism in Music and Other Essays* (Lincoln and London: University of Nebraska Press, 1995), p. 85.

18 See chapter 1 for more about breeches roles in operetta.

19 Marjorie Garber, *Vested Interests: Cross-Dressing and Cultural Anxiety* (New York: Routledge, 1992), p. 17.

20 Much of the information on Hungarian style comes from Jonathan Bellman's article "Toward a Lexicon for the *Style hongrois*," *Journal of Musicology* 9, no. 2 (1991): 214–37; and his book, *The Style hongrois in the Music of Western Europe* (Boston: Northeastern University Press, 1993). See also chapter 6 for more on the Hungarian topos in Strauss's music.

21 Liszt uses a similar bipartite form in several of his Hungarian Rhapsodies, and in No. 2 he labels the two parts following the introduction "Lassan" and "Friska."

22 Bellman, *The* Style hongrois, cites the third movement of Brahms' Clarinet Quintet, op. 115, as an example of *hallgató* style in chamber music.

23 The short-long rhythmic pattern alone would not necessarily indicate a Hungarian association; the gesture is also known, after all, by the names "Lombard rhythm" and "Scotch snap." However, its appearance within the context of so many other Hungarian musical traits makes its national affiliation unmistakable.

24 Other nineteenth-century composers used similar cadential formulae in "Hungarian" works. See Brahms' Hungarian Dance No. 5, Berlioz's *Damnation of Faust*, or Liszt's Hungarian Rhapsodies Nos. 2 and 3.

25 Bálint Sárosi, *Gypsy Music*, trans. Fred Macnicol (Budapest: Franklin Publishing House, 1970), p. 122.

26 Karl Westermeyer, *Die Operette im Wandel des Zeitgeistes von Offenbach bis zur Gegenwart* (Munich: Drei Masken Verlag, 1930), p. 74.

27 Dissolving the Concordat, which had been signed with the Catholic church in 1855, headed the Liberal agenda until they accomplished it in 1868.

28 *FleZiWiCsá & Co.: Die Wiener Operette*. Exhibition Catalogue for Historisches Museum der Stadt Wien (Vienna: Eigenverlag der Museen der Stadt Wien, 1985), p. 91.

29 In German and other European languages, the shift from the formal mode of address (Sie) to the familiar (Du) is a ceremonial event ("die Du-Bruderschaft schliessen").

30 Norbert Rubey, "Unterhaltung und Aktualität: Musikzitate bei Johann Strauss," *Österreichische Musikzeitschrift* 1–2 (1999): 51–57.

31 See Daniel Heartz, "Citation, Reference, and Recall in *Così fan tutte*," in *Mozart's Operas*, ed., with contributing essays, Thomas Bauman (Berkeley, Los Angeles and Oxford: University of California Press, 1990), pp. 229–53.

32 Strauss's *Fledermaus* also resembles Mozart's opera in the characterization and imitation of the lawyer; Despina disguises herself as a notary in Act II, a disguise that includes singing legal-sounding nonsense on a monotone with a nasal voice, just as Blind does in Act I. Eisenstein, unlike Despina, is too upset at the turn of events to maintain that subtlety when he disguises himself as the lawyer in Act III.

33 For more about the reception of *Così fan tutte* in Vienna, see Hanslick's

"Mozart" in *Die moderne Oper: Kritiken und Studien* (Berlin: Allgemeiner Verein für Deutsche Litteratur, 1885), pp. 29–60.

34 Otto Schenk production at the Bavarian State Opera in Munich, 1988.

35 Bakhtin, *Rabelais*, p. 10.

36 See William M. Johnston's discussion of "Therapeutic Nihilism in the Medical Faculty at Vienna" in Johnston, pp. 223–29.

37 Franz Tomandl, "Die Operetten von Johann Strauß und die Geschichte ihrer Aufführungen in Wien von 1871–1914" (Ph.D. dissertation, University of Vienna, 1985), p. 447.

38 Wilhelm Beetz, *Das Wiener Opernhaus, 1869 bis 1945* (Zurich: The Central European Times Verlag, 1949).

39 *Radio Wien*, 13 February 1931.

40 *Radio Wien*, 1 June 1934.

41 ÖNB-DS, B147.672. Published by the *Theater-Tagblatt*, Berlin, 15 November 1933, in anticipation of the 60th anniversary.

42 Beetz, *Wiener Opernhaus*.

43 Handbills for each night's performance are collected in the WSLB-DS, 71.115.

44 Anja Gewalt, "Aufführungtradition und Bearbeitungsfragen bei Strauß-Operetten an der Wiener Volksoper seit 1945" (Diplomarbeit, Wien, 1986), p. 109.

6 AUSTRO-HUNGARIAN RELATIONS AND *DER ZIGEUNERBARON*

1 *Das Vaterland*, 27 December 1910.

2 As biographer H. E. Jakob wrote, "All [Strauss] wanted to compose was the reconciliation between the two halves of the Empire, between Austria and Hungary." *Johann Strauss, Father and Son*, trans. Marguerite Wolff (Richmond, VA: The Greystone Press, 1940), p. 314. A decade later, Rudolf Holzer expressed a similar sentiment (Holzer, p. 312). More recently, operetta scholar Moritz Csáky has reiterated these views, describing *Der Zigeunerbaron* as "a contribution to the reconciliation of the 'Austrian' with the 'Magyar' element in the post-1867 dualistic monarchy." See *Johann Strauß: Zwischen Kunstanspruch und Volksvergnügen*, ed. Ludwig Finscher and Albrecht Riethmüller (Darmstadt: Wissenschaftliche Buchgesellschaft, 1995), pp. 28–65. And Péter Hanák insists, "The Viennese-Budapest operetta [including *Der Zigeunerbaron*] definitely contributed to the formation of a common

mass culture in the Monarchy, thereby contributing to cultural integration." See *The Garden and the Workshop: Essays on the Cultural History of Vienna and Budapest* (Princeton: Princeton University Press, 1998), p. 140.

3 Ernst Decsey, *Johann Strauß* (Stuttgart and Berlin: Deutsche Verlags-Anstalt, 1922), p. 212.

4 See Good, *The Economic Rise*, p. 96.

5 *Das bedrängte Wien. Eine politisch-finanzielle Studie* (Vienna, 1885).

6 *Kikeriki*, 22 February 1883. Front-page article entitled "Fort von Wien!" "Krähwinkel" was an Austrian term for a small, provincial village. The term entered common parlance after Nestroy's 1848 comedy *Freiheit im Krähwinkel*.

7 *Das bedrängte Wien*, p. 74.

8 *Das bedrängte Wien*, p. 75.

9 Prince Rudolf was a devoted friend of the Hungarians, and even spoke their language, in the words of Jókai, like a peasant. Johnston, p. 35. See Jókai's "Denkrede auf Kronprinz Rudolf," *Ungarische Revue* 9 (1889): 385–406.

10 See Appendix for synopsis of the operetta.

11 Johnston, p. 347.

12 Eduard Hanslick, *Aus meinem Leben*, 2 vols. (Berlin: Hermann Paetel Verlag 2nd edn, 1911), vol. 2, p. 241.

13 *Der Floh*, 1 March 1885.

14 *Der Goldmensch* was a "dramatic novel in 7 scenes" with music by Adolf Müller, Jr. (premiere: 28 February 1885, Theater an der Wien). It also dealt with a Hungarian subject, and Müller contributed music accordingly: minor keys, much percussion, accented syncopation, quick ornamental runs into downbeats (WSLB-MS, MH 6050/C).

15 Johann Strauss to Gustav Lewy, 1 August 1884. Quoted in Mailer, vol. 3, p. 239.

16 Franz Jauner to Ignaz Schnitzer, 26 August 1885, WSLB-HS, IN 211.305.

17 Johann Strauss to Ignaz Schnitzer, n.d., WSLB-HS, IN 121.918.

18 Johann Strauss to Ignaz Schnitzer, n.d., WSLB-HS, IN 121.582.

19 Johann Strauss to Ignaz Schnitzer, n.d., WSLB-HS, IN 121.918.

20 Eric Hobsbawm, "Introduction: Inventing Tradition," in *The Invention of Tradition*, ed. Eric Hobsbawm and Terence Ranger (Cambridge: Cambridge University Press, 1983), pp. 1–2.

21 See Schorske, pp. 24–115.

22 See Johnston, pp. 141–42.

23 James H. Johnson, *Listening in Paris: A Cultural History* (Berkeley, Los Angeles, and London: University of California Press, 1995), p. 121.

24 See Rudolph Angermüller, "Zigeuner und Zigeunerisches in der Oper des 19. Jahrhundert," in *Die* Couleur locale *in der Oper des 19. Jahrhundert*, ed. Heinz Becker (Regensburg: Gustav Bosse Verlag, 1976), pp. 131–59.

25 The Gypsy Lore Society was founded in England in 1888. See David Mayall, *Gypsy-Travellers in Nineteenth-Century Society* (Cambridge: Cambridge University Press, 1988), p. 4.

26 Johann Strauss to Carl Haslinger, 7 June 1863. Published in Strauss, p. 15.

27 The censor's copy of the libretto is housed in the NÖL in St. Pölten.

28 WSLB-MS, MH 13000.

29 Possible reasons for Zsupán's original inclusion in the opening scene will be discussed below.

30 Gewalt, "Aufführungstradition," p. 45.

31 Libretto, NÖL.

32 Strauss, perhaps leaving the trace of an inside joke, labels Barinkay's staff in the full score with a slightly different name each time it appears: Bochinskay, Postinzkay, Bosthinkay, Pontinskay, Postinskay, Poschkay, Bo-Kay, Postrinskay, then finally, Barinkay. The differences are too varied and subtle for his mislabeling to be accidental. It might also reveal something of his cultural chauvinism, as if all Hungarian/ Gypsy names sound alike.

33 Libretto, NÖL.

34 Inheritance disputes were quite common in nineteenth-century Hungary and a matter of intense public attention and interest. In the same year that *Der Zigeunerbaron* premiered, *Ein wahrer Teufel* appeared by József Konti, Kapellmeister of the Népszínház (the Hungarian national theater troupe), which also dealt with an inheritance dispute. Batta, *Träume sind Schäume*, p. 79.

35 Libretto, NÖL.

36 Johann Strauss to Lili Dietrich Strauss, ÖNB-HS, MS 146/60–18.

37 Letter, Johann Strauss to Lili Dietrich Strauss, ÖNB-HS, MS 146/60–39.

38 The conflation of "Oriental" with "Jewish" was widespread, especially in France, in the nineteenth century. See Susan McClary, *Carmen* (Cambridge: Cambridge University Press, 1992), pp. 34–35.

39 Boyer, *Political Radicalism*, p. 77.

40 Pynsent, *Decadence and Innovation*, p. 125.

41 Hans F. K. Günther, *Rassenkunde des jüdischen Volkes* (2nd edn Munich, 1931; 1st edn 1922), p. 251.

42 Geehr, *Karl Lueger*, pp. 61, 68–69.

43 *Judaism in Music*, p. 84.

44 WSLB-MS, MH 14865/C. As was his habit, Strauss wrote the key name in the margin next to the staff, rather than include a key signature.

45 See chapter 3 for a discussion of Strauss and anti-Semitism.

46 Holzer, p. 596.

47 *Kikeriki*, 30 July 1885.

48 Chris Priewalder, "Operette und Folklorismus: Eine Untersuchung des Folklorismusproblems in den klassischen Operetten des 19. Jahrhundert an den Beispielen *Die Fledermaus, Eine Nacht in Venedig* und *Der Zigeunerbaron* von Johann Strauß" (Diplomarbeit, University of Vienna, 1987), p. 118.

49 Benedict Anderson, *Imagined Communities: Reflections on the Origin and Spread of Nationalism* (London and New York: Verso, rev. edn 1991), p. 20.

50 See chapter 1 for more about the Schrammel brothers and their music.

51 Although this scene seems sentimental and romantic in the context of the operetta genre, it actually perpetuated a contemporary stereotype, for it was commonly held that Gypsies were promiscuous and took marriage vows lightly. See Bellman, *The* Style hongrois, p. 84. Opera devotees may also have recalled the second part of *Götterdämmerung*'s prologue when Siegfried and Brünnhilde awaken after a night spent together; much of their duet is also in E-flat major and includes triplet subdivision of the beat in more tender moments.

52 This *Schatzwalzer* became one of the most popular and frequently excerpted dances from the operetta. When Anton Webern chose to arrange it for small ensemble, it was performed and auctioned at a benefit concert of the *Verein für musikalische Privataufführungen* (17 May 1921).

53 Boyer, *Political Radicalism*, p. 137.

54 The practice occurred frequently enough to be taken for common knowledge in Anzengruber's *Das vierte Gebot* (1877). The wealthy Stolzenthaler imagines he can find a woman to run off to Hungary

with him and convert: "kann man a jede bereden, daß s' mit ein nach Ungarn abirennt und unitarisch wird, wann ihr etwa vor derer Prozedur graust!?" (II, xi).

55 NÖL.

56 NÖL. The censor added the parentheses and crossed through the words as shown here.

57 Bridge, *The Habsburg Monarchy*, p. 195.

58 Joseph Lanner's waltz *Die Werber*, op. 103 (1835) includes many of the Hungarian musical traits found here: dotted and *alla zoppa* rhythms, upper grace notes, and pizzicato string accompaniment.

59 In the Hungarian language the emphasis is always on the first syllable. "The invariable ictus on the leading syllable sets up a kind of dactylic or anaepaestic canter which, to a new ear, gives Magyar a wild and most unfamiliar ring." Patrick Leigh Fermor, *Between the Woods and the Water* (London: John Murray, 1986), p. 33.

60 *Fremdenblatt*, 19 June 1885.

61 Op. 333 (1869), dedicated to Vienna Court Opera director Johann Herbeck.

62 Like Azucena in *Il trovatore*, Czipra has raised a noble child as her own, a Gypsy.

63 The first translation of *Zigeunerbaron* into Hungarian made Barinkay's decision to join the army a reenactment of the freedom fighter for Hungary in 1848: "To battle! We fight for the Fatherland! The *Hungarian* must be victorious! Now the weapons will speak! To battle to defend our beautiful Fatherland." Batta, *Träume sind Schäume*, p. 121.

64 Johann Strauss to Ignaz Schnitzer, 13 March 1885, WSLB-HS, IN 121.881.

65 Schnitzer, *Meister Johann*, vol. 2, p. 63.

66 *Neue Freie Presse*, 27 October 1885. Reprinted in *Musikalisches Skizzenbuch (Der "Modernen Oper" IV. Teil)* (Berlin, 1888). A translation of this review appears in Appendix B of my "Viennese Musical Life and the Operettas of Johann Strauss" (Ph.D. dissertation, Duke University, 1997), pp. 388–91.

67 Johann Strauss to Ignaz Schnitzer, 26 July 1885, WSLB-HS, IN 121.929.

68 Hanslick, *Aus meinem Leben*, p. 98.

69 Mailer, vol. 3, p. 302.

70 Alan Sked, *The Decline and Fall of the Habsburg Empire 1815–1918* (London and New York: Longman, 1989), p. 195.

71 Boyer, *Political Radicalism*, p. 58.

72 *Ibid.*, p. 62.

73 *Der Floh* (19 October 1879) devoted its front-page cartoon to the troupe when it came to Vienna in October 1879. The explanatory text inside the first page read: "In front of the Ring Theater. – My Lord, what a crowd! The public is really storming the theater! – Public? But that crowd of people is the performers."

74 Tomandl, "Die Operetten von Johann Strauß," p. 309.

75 See for example the review by Ludwig Speidl, "Die Meininger in Wien" in the *Neue Freie Presse*, 29 September 1875: "Directors and actors could learn from the Meiningen troupe, at least in details; to imitate their methods in their entirety, however, would not occur to any theater director who values the artist above the statisticians and stands at least half-way on the side of the author as opposed to the decorators and tailors."

76 Tomandl, "Die Operetten von Johann Strauß," p. 312.

77 Rudolf Klein, *Die Wiener Staatsoper* (Vienna: Verlag Elisabeth Lafite, 1969), p. 11.

78 Postcard, Franz Jauner to Johann Strauss, n.d., WSLB-HS, IN 211.304: "Dear friend! Our costumer found the necessary sheepskin for the Gypsy Baron today. Perhaps you will find a source in Pest for the magnate's costume . . . In any case, please bring photographs with you of Hungarian national dress."

79 Batta, *Träume sind Schäume*, p. 63.

80 "Wohl ein dem Walzer aufgepfropfter dualistischer Csárdás!" Batta, *Träume sind Schäume*, p. 65.

81 *Neue Freie Presse*, 25 October 1885: "But the masquerade did not last long, soon the Viennese dialect broke through victoriously. And so the *Zigeunerbaron* remains an Austrian operetta, although only the last act takes place in the shadow of St. Stephen's."

82 *Fremdenblatt*, 25 October 1885.

83 *Der Floh*, 25 October 1885.

84 *Neues Wiener Tagblatt*, 25 October 1885.

85 *Vorstadtzeitung*, 25 October 1885. The reviewer conveniently miscounted – *Der Zigeunerbaron* is actually Strauss's tenth operetta.

86 Eduard Hanslick to Johann Strauss, 18 October 1885, WSLB-HS, IN 201.795.

87 Franz Jauner to Ignaz Schnitzer, 18 November 1885, WSLB-HS, IN 211.306.

88 Hanák, *The Garden and the Workshop*, p. 138.

89 Clipping from an unidentified Hungarian newspaper, WSLB-DS, 172.817L, Mappe 12.

90 Keller, *Die Operette*, p. 420.

91 Schnitzer, *Meister Johann*, vol. 2, p. 92.

92 Tomandl, "Die Operetten von Johann Strauß," p. 382.

93 26 December 1910 under Felix Weingartner. Klein, *Die Wiener Staatsoper*, p. v.

94 Strauss conducted this performance, 29 December 1885. Mailer, vol. 3, p. 313.

7 WALTZING BRÜNNHILDE

1 "Germany, Austria" s.v. *New Grove Opera*, vol. 2 (New York: Macmillan, 1992), p. 389.

2 McGrath, p. 22.

3 McGrath, p. 79.

4 See McGrath for more on the *Sagengesellschaft* and the Pernerstorfer Circle.

5 Hermann Bahr, *Selbstbildnis* (Berlin, 1923), p. 139.

6 See William A. Jenks, *Austria under the Iron Ring: 1879–1893* (Charlottesville: The University Press of Virginia, 1965), pp. 60–118.

7 Botstein, "Music and Its Public," p. 893.

8 Linhardt, *Inszenierung der Frau*, p. 205.

9 Hugo Wolf, *The Music Criticism of Hugo Wolf*, trans. and ed. Henry Pleasants (New York and London: Holmes and Meier Publishers, Inc., 1978), p. 113.

10 Wolf, *Music Criticism*, p. 66.

11 *Der Floh*, 21 November 1886. Hermann Winkelmann (1849–1912) created the role of Parsifal at Bayreuth (1882) and was engaged by the Vienna Court Opera from 1883 until his retirement in 1906. Alexander Girardi (1850–1918) was the leading comic actor at the Theater an der Wien (see previous chapters).

12 See Max Morold, *Wagners Kampf und Sieg dargestellt in seinen Beziehungen zu Wien* (Zurich, Leipzig, and Vienna: Amalthea Verlag, 1930).

13 Martin Gregor-Dellin, *Richard Wagner: His Life, His Work, His Century*, trans. J. Maxwell Brownjohn (San Diego, New York, and London: Harcourt Brace Jovanovich, 1983), p. 321.

14 *Der Floh*, 12 May 1872. "Wagners Einzug in Wien."

15 Alexander Witeschnik, *Wiener Opernkunst von den Anfängen bis zu Karajan* (Vienna: Buchgemeinschaft Donauland, 1959), p. 139.

16 *Kikeriki*, 12 May 1872.

17 Witeschnik, *Wiener Opernkunst*, p. 148.

18 The correspondence between Wagner and Richter illuminates much about the process of mounting these operas in Vienna and the personal dynamics involved. See Richard Wagner, *Briefe an Hans Richter*, ed. Ludwig Karpath (Berlin, Vienna, and Leipzig: Paul Zsolnay Verlag, 1924), pp. 129–70.

19 *Das Lachende Wien. Organ für das locale Leben, Kunst, Literatur, Theater und Vergnügen* 1 (14 October 1887). "Jemandem über die Achsel anschauen" is similar to the English expression "to look down one's nose at someone."

20 The *Österreichische Musik- und Theaterzeitung* (15 April 1890) reported that the income of the museum in 1889 was almost double that of the previous year.

21 *Kikeriki*, 7 February 1886.

22 *Der Floh*, 7 February 1886.

23 Schönau, the name of the Freiherr in *Der Trompeter von Säkkingen*, was also the name of Strauss's summer residence.

24 Hanslick, *Aus meinem Leben*, vol. 2, p. 4.

25 For the texts to these and other Wagner parodies see Dieter Borchmeyer and Stephen Kohler, eds., *Wagner Parodien* (Frankfurt am Main: Insel Verlag, 1983).

26 *Fremdenblatt*, 6 January 1877.

27 WSLB-MS, MH 2834.

28 Off-stage hunting horn calls appeared also in spoken stage works, such as Anzengruber's *Der Pfarrer von Kirchfeld* (end of Act IV).

29 *Der Floh*, 9 October 1887.

30 Quoted in Mailer, vol. 1, p. 97.

31 It seems Strauss failed to read even his own biography (Eisenberg, *Johann Strauß*, 1894). Writing to his biographer, Strauss based his congratulations on favorable reviews published in domestic and foreign

newspapers, for he had not taken time to read the book himself.
Strauss, p. 180.

32 Schnitzer, *Meister Johann*, vol. 2, p. 102.

33 Schnitzer's libretto, *Der Schelm von Bergen*, involved a merry execu-
tioner. When Strauss heard that a similar character appears in Gilbert
and Sullivan's *Mikado* (which enjoyed tremendous success at the
Theater an der Wien from its Viennese premiere there in September
1886), he stopped composing at once.

34 18 February 1887. This is the question Elsa is proscribed from asking
Lohengrin.

35 McGrath, p. 6.

36 Josef Priester (1836–1904) was a Viennese businessman and close friend
of the Strauss family.

37 Victor Léon to Johann Strauss, 29 June 1887, WSLB-HS, IN 119.456.

38 The manuscript orchestral score (WSLB-MS, MH 12200) is disorganized
despite its attractive binding. Missing pages, parts of songs and
choruses separated from each other, and miscellaneous pages bound
randomly in the back attest to the work's complicated history of performance and revision. The autograph's confused state also demonstrates the uncertainty about the work's structure and character. The
published libretto of song texts (WSLB-DS, A68045; published by Aug.
Cranz, Hamburg) and the published director's handbook to the
operetta (WSLB-DS, B172.832; Regiebuch, edited by Hugo Benedix,
Oberregisseur of the Theater an der Wien) correspond to Léon's original book and follow Strauss's score. The published piano reduction and
the surviving promptbook (ÖNB-TS, MS 547–B), however, include subsequent revisions and thus only partially match Strauss's original score.

39 Harald Bachmann, ed., *Johann Strauß und Coburg* (Coburg: Historische
Gesellschaft Coburg e. V., 1990), p. 22.

40 "Germany, Austria" s.v. *New Grove Opera*, 2, p. 389.

41 A caricature of Duke Ernst appeared on the cover of *Der Floh* during
the Franco-Prussian War (30 October 1870). He is portrayed with a
German cross around his neck and riding a winged horse. In a mock
letter to his wife, printed in *Der Floh*, he writes: "I have composed a
great War Symphony of military significance. Bismarck believes one
could bombard Paris with it; since the Parisians are very musical, they
would not hold out long."

42 Victor Léon to Johann Strauss, 20 June 1887, WSLB-HS, IN 119.454.

43 Victor Léon to Johann Strauss, 27 August 1887, WSLB-HS, IN 119.458.

44 Victor Léon to Joseph Priester, 27 August 1887, WSLB-HS, IN 119.462.

45 *Das lachende Wien. Organ für das locale Leben, Kunst, Literatur, Theater und Vergnügen*, 6 January 1888.

46 Adolf Wilbrandt, *Erinnerungen* (Stuttgart and Berlin: J. G. Cotta'sche Buchhandlung Nachfolger, 1905), p. 45.

47 A cynical critic praised his choice of construction, commenting that since the third act of any Viennese operetta is always the weakest, his reform deserves to be emulated. *Fremdenblatt*, 18 December 1887.

48 *Das Rheingold* is described as a "Vorabend," a prologue to the remaining three operas of the cycle. The popularity of a dramatic *Vorspiel* continued in the 1890s with Adolf Müller's *Die Kammerjungfer* (1891), an operetta in a prologue and two acts (WSLB-MS, MH 3510). Müller listed no author on the operetta's title page as was his custom. However, Léon's hand appears on revisions in the sketches where he wrote: "Honored Sir! I texted it in such a hurry that I truly do not know if everything has come out right and fits your wishes! . . . Best greetings! Léon." Whether Léon was the sole librettist or not, his ideas may have informed the operetta's structure as well as other details.

49 *Fremdenblatt*, 18 December 1887.

50 WSLB-DS, 172.817, Mappe 12, p. 39. The source of the clipping is unidentified; however the reviewer's initials (W. Fr.) suggest that it may have been Wilhelm Frey, a writer for the *Neues Wiener Tagblatt*.

51 Libretto, ÖNB-MS, Sm. 3570.

52 In later revisions, Simplicius becomes more like Parsifal in that he admires rather than fears the knights on horseback and, like Parsifal, wants to join them (see the piano-vocal score).

53 *Wiener Tagblatt*, 18 December 1887. "Textliche Umdichtung des Erlkönigs."

54 Parallel passages of Goethe's poem are as follows: "Siehst, Vater du den Erlkönig nicht? . . . Mein Vater, mein Vater, und hörest du nicht . . . Mein Vater, mein Vater, jetzt fasst er mich an! Erlkönig hat mir ein Leids gethan!"

55 *Illustriertes Wiener Extrablatt*, n.d. (WSLB-DS, 172.817, Mappe 12).

56 Victor Léon to Johann Strauss, 27 August 1887, WSLB-HS, IN 119.458.

57 Writings by Heinrich Schenker and Anton Webern, among others,

apply Goethe's ideas of organicism to music composition. See also Ruth A. Solie, "The Living Work: Organicism and Musical Analysis," *19th-Century Music 4* (Fall 1980): 147–56.

58 In an undated letter to Franz Jauner, Strauss explained, "The choruses are more difficult to study than those in my earlier operettas. In addition, there are many instrumental rearrangements, melodramatic insertions, etc." Strauss, p. 177.

59 WSLB-HS, IN 127.592/2.

60 This choice of instrumentation may also have been inspired by Brahms' op. 17 (1862) for women's chorus with harp and horn accompaniment.

61 Victor Léon to Johann Strauss, 20 June 1887, WSLB-HS, IN 119.454. Léon perhaps had in mind the end of *Parsifal's* first scene when Gurnemanz and Parsifal walk to the Grail ("zum Raum wird hier die Zeit"); as they silently cross the stage, the scene changes while the orchestra plays the various Grail motives and the "sinful world" motive.

62 WSLB-DS, 172.817, Mappe 12. *Illustriertes Wiener Extrablatt*, n.d.

63 *Kikeriki*, 25 December 1887.

64 *Der Floh*, 25 December 1887.

65 WSLB-DS, 172.817, Mappe 12, p. 44.

66 See Appendix for a more detailed synopsis.

67 Highly decorative autograph copies of orchestral reductions for both operas were sent to the Duke and remain in Coburg. See Harald Bachmann, ed., *Johann Strauß und Coburg* (Coburg: Historische Gesellschaft Coburg e. V., 1990), p. 43.

68 Klingsor calls to her at the beginning of Act II: "Gundryggia dort, Kundry hier!"

69 Insert to No. 4113, January 1892, of the *Wiener Allgemeine Zeitung*, Theater, Art and Literature section.

70 The "Spinning Song" is a recurring genre among Austro-German composers in the nineteenth century. Precedents to Wagner's spinning chorus include Haydn's song for Hanna and women's choruses in *Die Jahreszeiten*, Schubert's "Gretchen am Spinnrade," and Mendelssohn's spinning song for piano. The genre was also a local Viennese favorite: the opening of Anzengruber's *Pfarrer von Kirchfeld*, Act II features two maids singing as they spin.

71 The popularity of the spinning wheel as an icon of domesticity carried over into Viennese bourgeois home furnishings. By the late 1880s many of the fashionable houses on the Ring boasted "authentic" spinning wheels. See Otto Schneidereit, *Johann Strauß und die Stadt an der schönen blauen Donau* (Berlin, VEB Lied der Zeit, Musikverlag, 1972), p. 228.

72 Patrick McCreless has noted the special significance of this particular chord (F / A-flat / C-flat / E-flat) for the third Norn's prophecies of doom in the Vorspiel to Wagner's *Götterdämmerung*. See "Schenker and the Norns," in *Analyzing Opera: Verdi and Wagner*, ed. Carolyn Abbate and Roger Parker (Berkeley, Los Angeles, and London: University of California Press, 1989), pp. 276–97.

73 Carl Millöcker to Hugo Wittman, 27 September 1889, WSLB-HS, IN 165.856.

74 Victor Léon to Johann Strauss, WSLB-HS, 20 June 1887, IN 119.454.

75 Johann Strauss to Friedrich August Simrock, 10 November 1891, Coburg, MS 425.

76 Ludwig Dóczi to Johann Strauss, n.d., WSLB-HS, IN 118.812.

77 Ludwig Dóczi to Johann Strauss, 25 August 1891, WSLB-HS, IN 127.536.

78 Johann Strauss to Friedrich August Simrock, 9 January 1892, WSLB-HS, IN 164.397.

79 Friedrich August Simrock to Johann Strauss, 17 March 1892, Coburg, MS 425.

80 Johann Strauss to Josef Simon, n.d., WSLB-HS, IN 127.597. Muck (1859–1940) was director of the Berlin Royal Opera from 1892 to 1912 and conducted at Bayreuth until 1931. As conductor of the Boston Symphony Orchestra (1912–17) he gave the American premiere of Schoenberg's Five Pieces for Orchestra, op. 16.

81 Mailer, vol. 4, p. 246.

82 *Fremdenblatt*, 1 January 1892. "The 'Strauss'-Premiére in the Opera awakened an interest in the [Imperial] Residence like few opera events have in years. This expressed itself most clearly in the stampede at the bureaus and box offices, where one tried for months to request reservations for the significant day. So the present day was sold-out 'times six.'"

83 *Wiener Tagblatt*, 2 January 1892.

84 *Fremdenblatt*, 2 January 1892.

85 *Ibid.*, 3 January 1892.

86 *Deutsche Zeitung*, 2 January 1892; *Neues Wiener Tagblatt*, 2 January 1892.

87 Brahms had written to his (and Strauss's) publisher Simrock already on 2 November 1891, requesting a vocal score of the work. Brahms wrote: "The whole affair interests me quite dearly, and I hope the good Strauss comes through it well." Quoted in Eberhard Würzl, "Johann Strauß: Höhen und Tiefen der Meisterjahre, 1884–1894" (Ph.D. dissertation, University of Vienna, 1987), p. 286.

88 *Die Presse*, 2 January 1892.

89 WSLB-HS, IN 119.460, 31 December 1891.

90 *Wiener Tagblatt*, 2 January 1892.

91 *Illustriertes Wiener Extrablatt*, 2 January 1892.

92 *Wiener Abendpost*, 2 January 1892.

93 Strauss wrote to a friend at this time (8 August 1891) that "instrumentation demands even more time than composition." Strauss, p. 56.

94 *Wiener Tagblatt*, 2 January 1892.

95 *Neue Zeitschrift für Musik*, 3 February 1892.

96 *Ibid.*

97 *Ibid.*

98 Johann Strauss to Friedrich August Simrock, 12 January 1892, in the possession of Paul Pfändler, Zurich.

99 Friedrich August Simrock to Johann Strauss, 22 January 1892, Coburg, MS 425.

100 "Johann Strauß (†1899)," in *Aus dem Tagebuch eines Rezensenten*, pp. 307–12.

101 Quoted in Mailer, vol. 4, p. 319.

102 Johann Strauss to Eduard Strauss, 22 April 1892, Strauss, p. 122.

103 See the *Wiener Allgemeine Zeitung*, 21 November 1891.

104 *Aus meinem Leben*, vol. 2, pp. 275–76.

105 "Doch werd' ich mit dem Pásmán erst fertig sein, dann kommen die abscheulichen Geburtswehen, die ohne Kaiserschnitt nicht denkbare Überlieferung des corpus delicti, welches schon nach dem ersten Bade zu ersaufen das Mißgeschick haben wird." Strauss's metaphor is more amusing in German where "Kaiserschnitt" (cesarean section) implies also the necessary stage "cuts." Strauss, p. 57.

106 Johann Strauss to Josef Simon, n.d., WSLB-HS, IN 127.597.

107 *Ibid.*

108 Johann Strauss to Eduard Strauss, 22 April 1892, Strauss, p. 122.

EPILOGUE

1 *Illustriertes Wiener Extrablatt*, 7 June 1899. *Neues Wiener Tagblatt*, 7 June 1899.

2 *Morgenblatt*, 7 June 1899.

3 *Illustriertes Wiener Extrablatt*, 4 June 1899.

4 *Fremdenblatt*, 4 June 1899.

5 *Neues Wiener Journal*, 7 June 1899.

6 *Neues Wiener Journal*, 5 June 1899.

7 Lueger's graveside speech, *Neues Wiener Tagblatt*, 7 June 1899.

8 "Musik als eigene Sprache: Zur Aufführung der *Fledermaus* von Johann Strauss," interview with Manfred Wagner, *Österreichische Musikzeitschrift* 5 (1999): 4–10.

9 Edwin McDowell, "Business Travel," *New York Times*, 3 March 1999, C6.

10 See Allen Forte, *The American Popular Ballad of the Golden Era, 1924–1950* (Princeton: Princeton University Press, 1995); articles by Alexander Ringer and William Kindermann in Ludwig Finscher and Albrecht Riethmüller, eds., *Johann Strauß: Zwischen Kunstanspruch und Volksvergnügen* (Darmstadt: Wissenschaftliche Buchgesellschaft, 1995); and Bryan Gilliam's "A Viennese Composer in Hollywood: Korngold's Double Exile in America," in *"Driven into Paradise": The Musical Migration from Nazi Germany to the United States*, ed. Reinhold Brinkman (Los Angeles and Berkeley: University of California Press, 1999).

11 Letter, Johann Strauss to Josef Simon, March 1892, WSLB-HS, 127.597.

12 Arnold Schoenberg, *Style and Idea* (Berkeley: University of California Press, 1975), p. 415.

13 Richard Specht, *Johann Strauß* (Berlin: Verlag von Marquardt and Co., 1909), p. 89.

SELECT BIBLIOGRAPHY

PRIMARY SOURCES

Anonymous. *Wien und die Wiener: Ungeschminkte Schilderungen eines fahrenden Gesellen*. Berlin: Verlag von Eduard Rentzel, 1892.

Anzengruber, Ludwig. *Ausgewählte Werke*. Introduced by Erwin Heinzel. Vienna: Verlag Kremayr and Scheriau, 1966.

Bahr, Hermann. *Austriaca*. Berlin: S. Fischer Verlag, 1911.

   Wien. Vienna: n.p., 1906.

   Wiener Theater. Berlin: S. Fischer Verlag, 1899.

   Das bedrängte Wien. Eine politisch-finanzielle Studie. Vienna, 1885.

Billroth, Theodor. *Wer ist musikalisch?* Edited by Eduard Hanslick. Berlin: Verlag von Gebrüder Paetel, 3rd edn, 1898.

Eisenberg, Ludwig. *Johann Strauß: Ein Lebensbild*. Leipzig: Breitkopf und Härtel, 1894.

Hanslick, Eduard. *Aus dem Tagebuch eines Rezensenten: Gesammelte Musikkritiken*. Edited by Peter Wapnewski. Kassel and Basel: Bärenreiter Verlag, 1989.

   Geschichte des Concertwesens in Wien, vol. 1. Vienna: Wilhelm Braumüller, 1869.

   Die moderne Oper: Kritiken und Studien. Berlin: Allgemeiner Verein für Deutsche Litteratur, 1885.

   Musikalisches Skizzenbuch (Der "Modernen Oper" IV. Teil). Berlin: Allgemeiner Verein für Deutsche Litteratur, 1888.

   Fünf Jahre Musik (Der "Modernen Oper" VII. Teil). Berlin: Allgemeiner Verein für Deutsche Litteratur, 2nd edn. 1896.

   Am Ende des Jahrhunderts (Der "Modernen Oper" VIII. Teil). Berlin: Allgemeiner Verein für Deutsche Litteratur, 1899.

   The Beautiful in Music. Translated by Gustav Cohen. Indianapolis: Bobbs-Merrill Co., Inc., 1957.

   Aus dem Opernleben der Gegenwart. Berlin: Allgemeiner Verein für Deutsche Litteratur, 4th edn, 1901.

Aus meinem Leben. 2 vols. Berlin: Hermann Paetel Verlag, 2nd edn, 1911.

Hanslick's Music Criticisms. Translated and edited by Henry Pleasants. New York: Dover Publications, Inc., 1950.

Lindau, Paul. *Johann Strauß.* Breslau and Berlin: S. Schottlaender, 1885.

Mailer, Franz, editor. *Johann Strauß (Sohn): Leben und Werk in Briefen und Dokumenten. Bd. 1, 1825–1863.* Tutzing: Hans Schneider, 1983.

Johann Strauß (Sohn): Leben und Werk in Briefen und Dokumenten. Bd. 2, 1864–1877. Tutzing: Hans Schneider, 1986.

Johann Strauß (Sohn): Leben und Werk in Briefen und Dokumenten. Bd. 3, 1878–1886. Tutzing: Hans Schneider, 1990.

Johann Strauß (Sohn): Leben und Werk in Briefen und Dokumenten. Bd. 4, 1887–1889. Tutzing: Hans Schneider, 1992.

Johann Strauß (Sohn): Leben und Werk in Briefen und Dokumenten. Bd. 5, 1890–1891. Tutzing: Hans Schneider, 1996.

Johann Strauß (Sohn): Leben und Werk in Briefen und Dokumenten. Bd. 6, 1892–1893. Tutzing: Hans Schneider, 1996.

Johann Strauß (Sohn): Leben und Werk in Briefen und Dokumenten. Bd. 7, 1894. Tutzing: Hans Schneider, 1998.

Müller-Guttenbrunn, Adam. *Wien war eine Theaterstadt.* Vienna: Verlag von Carl Graeser, 1885.

Das Wiener Theaterleben. Leipzig: Verlag und Druck von Otto Spamer, 1890.

Nestroy, Johann. *Nestroys Werke.* 2 volumes. Edited and introduced by Paul Reimann. Berlin and Weimar: Aufbau-Verlag, 1969.

Neuester Plan und Führer durch Wien und nächste Umgebung. Vienna: R. Lechner's k.k. Hof- und Universitäts-Buchhandlung, 1883.

Schlögl, Friedrich. *Wiener Blut und Wiener Luft: Skizzen aus dem alten Wien.* Edited by Karlheinz Rossbacher and Ulrike Tanzer. Salzburg and Vienna: Residenz Verlag, 1997.

Speidel, Ludwig. *Wiener Feuilletons.* Edited by Joachim Schreck. Vienna and Cologne: Böhlau Verlag, 1989.

Wiener Frauen und anderes Wienerische. Berlin: Meyer und Jessen, 1910.

Spitzer, Daniel. *Hereinspaziert ins alte Wien: Heiter-Satirisches aus der Donaumonarchie.* Edited by Hermann Hakel. Herrenalb / Schwarzwald: Horst Erdmann Verlag, 1967.

Meisterfeuilletons. Edited by Walter Obermaier. Vienna: J and V Edition, 1991.

Strauss, Eduard. *Erinnerungen*. Leipzig and Vienna: Franz Deutike, 1906.

Strauss, Johann. *Johann Strauss schreibt Briefe*. Edited by Adele Strauss. Berlin: Verlag für Kulturpolitik, 1926.

Sydacoff, Bresnitz von. *Ein halbes Jahrhundert österreichischen Hof- und Staatslebens*. Leipzig and Berlin: Verlag von Friedrich Luckhardt, 1899.

Wagner, Richard. *Briefe*. Edited by Hans-Joachim Bauer. Stuttgart: Philipp Reclam jun., 1995.

   Briefe an Hans Richter. Edited by Ludwig Karpath. Berlin, Vienna, and Leipzig: Paul Zsolnay Verlag, 1924.

   Judaism in Music and Other Essays. Translated by William Ashton Ellis. Lincoln and London: University of Nebraska Press, 1995.

Weilen, Alexander von, editor. *Charlotte Birch-Pfeiffer und Heinrich Laube im Briefwechsel*. Berlin: Selbstverlag der Gesellschaft für Theatergeschichte, 1917.

Wilbrandt, Adolf. *Erinnerungen*. Stuttgart and Berlin: J. G. Cotta'sche Buchhandlung Nachfolger, 1905.

Wolf, Hugo. *The Music Criticism of Hugo Wolf*. Translated and edited by Henry Pleasants. New York and London: Holmes and Meier Publishers, Inc., 1978.

PERIODICALS AND NEWSPAPERS

Arbeiter Zeitung
Deutsche Rundschau
Deutsche Zeitung
Der Floh
Fremdenblatt
Illustriertes Wiener Extrablatt
Kikeriki
Das Lachende Wien. Organ für das locale Leben, Kunst, Literatur, Theater und Vergnügen
Musikalisches Wochenblatt
Neue Freie Presse
Neue Zeitschrift für Musik
Neues Wiener Journal
Neues Wiener Tagblatt
Österreichische Musik- und Theaterzeitung

Die Presse
Theater Tagblatt
Vorstadtzeitung
Wiener Abendpost
Wiener Extrablatt
Wiener Salonblatt
Wiener Zeitung

SECONDARY SOURCES

Abbate, Carolyn and Roger Parker, editors. *Analyzing Opera: Verdi and Wagner*. Berkeley, Los Angeles, and London: University of California Press, 1989.

Anderson, Benedict. *Imagined Communities: Reflections on the Origin and Spread of Nationalism*. London and New York: Verso, rev. edn 1991.

Angermüller, Rudolph. "Zigeuner und Zigeunerisches in der Oper des 19. Jahrhundert." In *Die Couleur locale in der Oper des 19. Jahrhundert*, edited by Heinz Becker. Regensburg: Gustav Bosse Verlag, 1976.

Bachmann, Harald, editor. *Johann Strauß und Coburg*. Coburg: Historische Gesellschaft Coburg e. V., 1990.

Bakhtin, Mikhail. *Rabelais and His World*. Translated by Hélène Iswolsky. Bloomington: Indiana University Press, 1984.

Banks, Paul. "Vienna: Absolutism and Nostalgia" and "Fin-de-siècle Vienna: Politics and Modernism." In *Music and Society: The Late Romantic Era*, edited by Jim Samson. Englewood Cliffs, NJ: Prentice Hall, 1991.

Barea, Ilsa. *Vienna*. London: Secker and Warburg, 1966.

Batta, András. *Träume sind Schäume: Die Operette in der Donaumonarchie*. Translated from Hungarian by Maria Eisenreich. Budapest: Corvina, 1992.

Bauer, Anton. *150 Jahre Theater an der Wien*. Zurich, Leipzig, and Vienna: Amalthea Verlag, 1952.

   Das Theater in der Josefstadt zu Wien. Vienna and Munich: Manutiuspresse, 1957.

Becker, Heinz, editor. *Die Couleur locale in der Oper des 19. Jahrhundert*. Regensburg: Gustav Bosse Verlag, 1976.

Beetz, Wilhelm. *Das Wiener Opernhaus, 1869 bis 1945*. Zurich: The Central European Times Verlag, 1949.

Beller, Steven. *Vienna and the Jews, 1867–1938: A Cultural History*. Cambridge: Cambridge University Press, 1989.

Bellman, Jonathan, editor. *The Exotic in Western Music*. Boston: Northeastern University Press, 1998.

The Style hongrois *in the Music of Western Europe*. Boston: Northeastern University Press, 1993.

"Toward a Lexicon for the *Style hongrois*." *Journal of Musicology* 9, no. 2 (1991): 214–37.

Bled, Jean-Paul. *Franz Joseph*. Translated by Teresa Bridgeman. Cambridge, MA and Oxford: Blackwell, 1992.

Borchmeyer, Dieter. "Wagner and Nietzsche." In *Wagner Handbook*, edited by Ulrich Müller and Peter Wapnewski. Cambridge, MA: Harvard University Press, 1992.

Borchmeyer, Dieter and Stephen Kohler, editors. *Wagner Parodien*. Frankfurt am Main: Insel Verlag, 1983.

Botstein, Leon. "Music and Its Public: Habits of Listening and the Crisis of Musical Modernism in Vienna, 1870–1914." Ph.D. dissertation, Harvard University, 1985.

"Wagner and Our Century." *19th-Century Music* 11, no. 1 (1987): 92–104.

Botstein, Leon and Linda Weintraub, editors. *Pre-Modern Art of Vienna, 1848–1898*. Annandale-on-Hudson, NY: Edith C. Blum Art Institute, 1987.

Boyer, John W. *Political Radicalism in Late Imperial Vienna: Origins of the Christian Social Movement, 1848–1897*. Chicago and London: University of Chicago Press, 1981.

Bridge, F. R. *The Habsburg Monarchy among the Great Powers, 1815–1918*. New York: St. Martin's Press, 1990.

Broch, Hermann. *Hugo von Hofmannsthal and His Time: The European Imagination, 1860–1920*. Translated and edited by Michael P. Steinberg. Chicago and London: University of Chicago Press, 1984.

Bruckmüller, Ernst. *Sozialgeschichte Österreichs*. Vienna and Munich: Herold Verlag, 1985.

Bujic, Bojan, editor. *Music in European Thought, 1851–1912*. Cambridge: Cambridge University Press, 1988.

Bullough, Vern L. and Bonnie Bullough. *Cross Dressing, Sex, and Gender*. Philadelphia: University of Pennsylvania Press, 1993.

Burkholder, J. Peter. "Berg and the Possibility of Popularity." In *Alban Berg:*

Historical and Analytical Perspectives, edited by David Gable and Robert P. Morgan. Oxford: Clarendon Press, 1991.

Carner, Mosco and Max Schönherr. "Strauss Family." *New Grove Dictionary of Music and Musicians*, vol. 18 (1980), 205–17.

Crittenden, Camille. "Viennese Musical Life and the Operettas of Johann Strauss." Ph.D. dissertation, Duke University, 1997.

Csáky, Moritz. *Ideologie der Operette und Wiener Moderne: Ein kulturhistorischer Essay zur österreichischen Identität.* 2nd edn. Vienna: Böhlau Verlag, 1998.

Dahlhaus, Carl. "Wagner's Place in the History of Music." In *Wagner Handbook*, edited by Ulrich Müller and Peter Wapnewski. Cambridge, MA: Harvard University Press, 1992.

Dahlhaus, Carl, editor. *Studien zur Trivialmusik des 19. Jahrhunderts.* Regensburg: Bosse, 1967.

Daviau, Donald, editor. *Österreichische Tagebuchschriftsteller.* Vienna: Edition Atelier, 1994.

Decsey, Ernst. *Johann Strauß.* Stuttgart and Berlin: Deutsche Verlags-Anstalt, 1922.

Decsy, János. *Prime Minister Gyula Andrássy's Influence on Habsburg Foreign Policy.* New York: Columbia University Press, 1979.

Döbler, Erika. "Josefine Gallmeyer. Der Ausklang des Wiener Volksstücks." Ph.D. dissertation, University of Vienna, 1935.

Dressler, Robert. "Die Figuren der Wiener Operette als Spiegel ihrer Gesellschaft." Ph.D. dissertation, University of Vienna, 1986.

Dyer, Richard. "Entertainment and Utopia." In *Genre: The Musical*, edited by Rick Altman. London: Routledge and Kegan Paul, 1981.

Egger, Margarethe. *Die "Schrammeln" in ihrer Zeit.* Vienna: Österreichischer Bundesverlag, 1989.

Ehalt, Hubert Ch., Gernot Heiß, and Hannes Stekl, editors. *Glücklich ist, wer vergißt . . . ? Das andere Wien um 1900.* Vienna: Hermann Böhlaus Nachfolger, 1986.

Faris, Alexander. *Jacques Offenbach.* New York: Charles Scribner's Sons, 1980.

Fermor, Patrick Leigh. *Between the Woods and the Water.* London: John Murray, 1986.

Findeisen, Kurt Arnold. *Das Leben ein Tanz, der Tanz ein Leben: Der Walzerkönig Johann Strauß und seine Zeit. Musikalisch-dichterisches Lebensbild in drei Teilen.* Leipzig: Hermann Eichblatt Verlag, 1941.

Finscher, Ludwig and Albrecht Riethmüller, editors. *Johann Strauss: Zwischen*

Kunstanspruch und Volksvergnügen. Darmstadt: Wissenschaftliche Buchgesellschaft, 1995.

FleZiWiCsá & Co.: Die Wiener Operette. Exhibition Catalogue for Historisches Museum der Stadt Wien. Vienna: Eigenverlag der Museen der Stadt Wien, 1985.

Flinn, Caryl. *Strains of Utopia: Gender, Nostalgia, and Hollywood Film Music*. Princeton: Princeton University Press, 1992.

Freyenfels, Jodok. "Johann Strauß in Rußland." *Neue Zeitschrift für Musik* 134 (1973): 691–702.

Garber, Marjorie. *Vested Interests: Cross-Dressing and Cultural Anxiety*. New York: Routledge, 1992.

Gartenberg, Egon. *Johann Strauss: The End of an Era*. University Park, PA and London: The Pennsylvania State University Press, 1974.

Geehr, Richard S. *Adam Müller-Guttenbrunn and the Aryan Theater of Vienna, 1898–1903: The Approach of Cultural Fascism*. Göppingen: Verlag Alfred Kummerle, 1973.

Karl Lueger: Mayor of Fin de Siècle Vienna. Detroit: Wayne State University Press, 1990.

Gerhard, Anselm. *Die Verstädterung der Oper: Paris und das Musiktheater des 19. Jahrhunderts*. Stuttgart: Verlag J. B. Metzler, 1992.

Gewalt, Anja. "Aufführungstradition und Bearbeitungsfragen bei Strauß-Operetten an der Wiener Volksoper seit 1945." Diplomarbeit, Vienna, 1986.

Glanz, Christian. "Popularmusik: Ein Brennspiegel für Identität und Gemeinschaft." *Österreichische Musikzeitschrift* 10–11 (1996): 718–27.

Good, David F. *The Economic Rise of the Habsburg Empire, 1750–1914*. Berkeley: University of California Press, 1984.

Graf, Max. *Legende einer Musikstadt*. Vienna: Österreichische Buchgemeinschaft, 1949.

Griffel, Margaret Ross. "'Turkish' Opera from Mozart to Cornelius." Ph.D. dissertation, Columbia University, 1975.

Grossberg, Mimi. *Die k. u. k. Armee in der österreichischen Satire*. Vienna: Bergland Verlag, 1974.

Grun, Bernard. *Kulturgeschichte der Operette*. Munich: Albert Langen-Georg Müller Verlag, 1961.

Gstrein, Heinz. *Jüdisches Wien*. Vienna and Munich: Herold Verlag, 1984.

Hadamowsky, Franz. *Wien: Theater Geschichte von den Anfängen bis zum Ende des Ersten Weltkriegs*. Vienna and Munich: J and V, Edition Wien, Dachs-Verlag, 1994.

Hailey, Christopher. "Between Instinct and Reflection: Berg, Opera and the Viennese Dichotomy." In *The Berg Companion*, edited by Douglas Jarman. London: Macmillan, 1989.

Hamm, Charles. "Genre, Performance, and Ideology in the Early Songs of Irving Berlin." In *Putting Popular Music in its Place*. Cambridge: Cambridge University Press, 1995.

Hanák, Péter. *The Garden and the Workshop: Essays on the Cultural History of Vienna and Budapest*. Princeton: Princeton University Press, 1998.

Heartz, Daniel. *Mozart's Operas*. Edited, with contributing essays, by Thomas Bauman. Berkeley, Los Angeles, and Oxford: University of California Press, 1990.

Hennings, Fred. *Ringstrassensymphonie, 1. Satz 1857–1870*. Vienna and Munich: Verlag Herold, 1963.

Ringstrassensymphonie, 2. Satz 1870–1884. Vienna and Munich: Verlag Herold, 1963.

Ringstrassensymphonie, 3. Satz 1884–1899. Vienna and Munich: Verlag Herold, 1964.

Hobsbawm, Eric and Terence Ranger, editors. *The Invention of Tradition*. Cambridge: Cambridge University Press, 1983.

Hoffmann, Niels Frédéric. "Die Operette, Musik der Halbwelt." *Musica* 41 (Fall 1987): 407–13.

Holzer, Rudolf, editor. *Heinrich Laube, Der Theatercaesar*. Graz and Vienna: Stiasny Verlag, 1958.

Die Wiener Vorstadtbühnen, Alexander Girardi und das Theater an der Wien. Vienna: Druck und Verlag der österreichischen Staatsdruckerei, 1951.

Jacob, P. Walter. *Jacques Offenbach in Selbstzeugnissen und Bilddokumenten*. Reinbek bei Hamburg: Rowohlt Taschenbuch Verlag, 1969.

Jakob, H. E. *Johann Strauss, Father and Son*. Translated by Marguerite Wolff. Richmond, VA: The Greystone Press, 1940.

Jakob, Julius. *Wörterbuch des Wiener Dialektes*. Vienna and Leipzig: Gerlach and Wiedling, 1929.

Jameson, Frederic. "Towards a New Awareness of Genre." *Science Fiction Studies* 9 (1982): 322–24.

Janik, Allan and Stephen Toulmin. *Wittgenstein's Vienna*. New York: Simon and Schuster, 1973.

Jaspert, Werner. *Johann Strauss: Sein Leben, sein Werk, seine Zeit*. Lindau-Bodensee: Werk-Verlag/Frisch and Perneder, n.d.

Jenks, William A. *Austria under the Iron Ring: 1879–1893*. Charlottesville: The University Press of Virginia, 1965.

Johnson, James H. *Listening in Paris: A Cultural History*. Berkeley, Los Angeles, and London: University of California Press, 1995.

Johnston, William M. *The Austrian Mind: An Intellectual and Social History, 1848–1938*. Berkeley: University of California Press, 1972.

Kallberg, Jeffrey. *Chopin at the Boundaries: Sex, History, and Musical Genre*. Cambridge, MA: Harvard University Press, 1996.

Keller, Otto. *Die Operette in ihrer Geschichtlichen Entwicklung*. Leipzig: Stein Verlag, 1926.

Klein, Rudolf. *Die Wiener Staatsoper*. Vienna: Verlag Elisabeth Lafite, 1969.
"Das Zweite 'Wiedner' Theater." *Österreichische Musikzeitschrift* 17 (June–July 1962): 262–325.

Klotz, Volker. *Bürgerliches Lachtheater: Komödie–Posse–Schwank–Operette*. Reinbek bei Hamburg: Rowohlts Enzyklopädie, 1987.
Operette: Porträt und Handbuch einer unerhörten Kunst. Munich: Piper Verlag, 1991.

Kobald, Karl. *Johann Strauß*. Vienna: Österreichischer Bundesverlag, 1925.

Koller, Folkmar. "Das Theaterpublikum Wiens." Ph.D. dissertation, University of Vienna, 1968.

Kracauer, Siegfried. *Jacques Offenbach und das Paris seiner Zeit*. Frankfurt am Main: Suhrkamp Verlag, 1976.

Kralik, Heinrich. *Die Wiener Oper*. Vienna: Verlag Brüder Rosenbaum, 1962.

Krenek, Ernst. "Ein Paar Worte über Johann Strauß (1929)" and "Operette und Revue (1929)." In *Zur Sprache gebracht*. Munich: Albert Langen-Georg Müller Verlag, 1958.

Láng, Attila E. *Das Theater an der Wien: Vom Singspiel zum Musical*. Munich: Jugend und Volk, 1976.

Langer, Anton. *Wiener Volks-Bühne*. Vienna: Jakob Dirnböck's Verlag, 1859.

Linhardt, Marion. *Inszenierung der Frau – Frau in der Inszenierung: Operette in Wien zwischen 1865 und 1900*. Tutzing: Hans Schneider, 1997.

Linke, Norbert. *Johann Strauß (Sohn) in Selbstzeugnissen und Bilddokumenten*. Reinbek bei Hamburg: Rowohlt Taschenbuch Verlag, 1982.

Locke, Ralph P. "Constructing the Oriental 'Other': Saint-Saëns's *Samson et Dalila*." *Cambridge Opera Journal* 3, no. 3 (1991): 261–302.

Loewy, Siegfried. *Johann Strauß, der Spielmann von der blauen Donau: Lebensfragmente*. Vienna and Leipzig: Wiener Literarische Anstalt Aktiengesellschaft, 1924.

Lothar, Rudolph. *Das Wiener Burgtheater*. Berlin and Leipzig: Schuster und Loeffler, n.d. [pre-1927].

McClary, Susan. *Carmen*. Cambridge: Cambridge University Press, 1992.

McGrath, William. *Dionysian Art and Populist Politics in Austria*. New Haven and London: Yale University Press, 1974.

McRobbie, Angela. "Dance and Social Fantasy." In *Gender and Generation*, edited by Angela McRobbie and Mica Nava. London: Macmillan, 1984.

Mahling, Christoph-Hellmut. "Zum Problem fiktiver Nationalstile in der Oper des 19. Jahrhunderts." In *Die* Couleur locale *in der Oper des 19. Jahrhundert*, edited by Heinz Becker. Regensburg: Gustav Bosse Verlag, 1976.

Mailer, Franz. *Genie wider Willen*. Vienna and Munich: Jugend und Volk, 1977.

"'Man tut mir zuviel Ehre an.' Gedanken zum Persönlichkeit von Johann Strauss." *Österreichische Musikzeitung* 30 (1975): 257–60.

May, Arthur J. *Vienna in the Age of Franz Joseph*. Norman: University of Oklahoma Press, 1966.

Mayall, David. *Gypsy-Travellers in Nineteenth-Century Society*. Cambridge: Cambridge University Press, 1988.

Morold, Max. *Wagners Kampf und Sieg dargestellt in seinen Beziehungen zu Wien*. Zurich, Leipzig and Vienna: Amalthea Verlag, 1930.

Mukerji, Chandra and Michael Schudson, editors. *Rethinking Popular Culture: Contemporary Perspectives in Cultural Studies*. Berkeley: University of California Press, 1991.

Musgrave, Michael. "The Cultural World of Brahms." In *Brahms: Biographical, Documentary and Analytical Studies*, edited by Robert Pascall. Cambridge: Cambridge University Press, 1983.

Nick, Edmund. "Strauß, familie." *Musik in Geschichte und Gegenwart* 12 (1965): 1450–74.

Nietzsche, Friederich. *The Birth of Tragedy*. Translated by Francis Golffing. Garden City, NY: Doubleday, 1956.

Nischkauer, Norbert. "Bemerkungen zum Thema Johann Strauß und die Zensur." *Die Fledermaus* 4 (1992): 10–16.

Nowak, K. F. *Alexander Girardi: Sein Leben und sein Wirken*. Berlin: Concordia Deutsche Verlags Anstalt, Hermann Ehbock, 1908.

Palmer, Alan. *Twilight of the Habsburgs: The Life and Times of Emperor Francis Joseph*. London: Weidenfeld and Nicolson, 1994.

Pirchan, Emil. *Marie Geistinger: Die Königin der Operette*. Vienna: Verlag Wilhelm Frick, 1947.

Unsterbliches Wien. Berlin: Gustav Kiepenheuer Verlag, 1939.

Prawy, Marcel. *Johann Strauß*. Vienna: Ueberreuter, 1991.

Prieberg, Fred K. *Musik im NS-Staat*. Frankfurt: Fischer Taschenbuch Verlag, 1982.

Priewalder, Chris. "Operette und Folklorismus: Eine Untersuchung des Folklorismusproblems in den klassischen Operetten des 19. Jahrhundert an den Beispielen *Die Fledermaus, Eine Nacht in Venedig* und *Der Zigeunerbaron* von Johann Strauß." Diplomarbeit, University of Vienna, 1987.

Pynsent, Robert B., editor. *Decadence and Innovation*. London: Weidenfeld and Nicolson, 1989.

Rabenalt, Arthur Marie. *Operette als Aufgabe*. Berlin: Heinz Menge Verlag, 1948.

Radway, Janice A. *Reading the Romance: Women, Patriarchy, and Popular Literature*. Chapel Hill and London: The University of North Carolina Press, 1984.

Reiss, Gunter. "Das verweigerte Einverständnis: Versuch zur Geschichte der Musikkomödie von Mozart bis Brecht." In *Oper und Operntext*, edited by Jens Malte Fischer. Heidelberg: Carl Winter-Universitätsverlag, 1985.

Rosand, Ellen. *Opera in Seventeenth-Century Venice: The Creation of a Genre*. Berkeley, Los Angeles, and Oxford: University of California Press, 1991.

Rozenblit, Marsha L. *The Jews of Vienna, 1867–1914: Assimilation and Identity*. Albany: State University of New York Press, 1983.

Rubey, Norbert. "Unterhaltung und Aktualität: Musikzitate bei Johann Strauss." *Österreichische Musikzeitschrift* 1–2 (1999): 51–57.

Said, Edward. *Orientalism*. New York: Vintage Books, 1979.

Sárosi, Bálint. *Gypsy Music*. Translated by Fred Macnicol. Budapest: Franklin Publishing House, 1970.

Schenk, Erich. *Johann Strauß*. Potsdam: Akademische Verlagsgesellschaft Athenaion, 1940.

Schmidt, Harro. *Musikerziehung und Musikwissenschaft im 19. Jahrhundert.* Hamburg: Verlag der Musikalienhandlung Karl Dieter Wagner, 1979.

Schneidereit, Otto. *Franz von Suppé: Der Wiener aus Dalmatien.* Berlin: VEB, Lied der Zeit, Musikverlag, 1977.

Johann Strauß und die Stadt an der schönen blauen Donau. Berlin: VEB, Lied der Zeit, Musikverlag, 1972.

Schnitzer, Ignaz. *Meister Johann: Bunte Geschichten aus der Johann-Strauß-Zeit.* 2 vols. Vienna and Leipzig: Halm und Goldmann, 1920.

Schorske, Carl E. *Fin-de-siècle Vienna: Politics and Culture.* New York: Vintage Books, 1980.

Sked, Alan. *The Decline and Fall of the Habsburg Empire, 1815–1918.* London and New York: Longman, 1989.

Smith, Barbara Herrnstein. *Contingencies of Value: Alternative Perspectives for Critical Theory.* Cambridge, MA: Harvard University Press, 1988.

Solie, Ruth A. "The Living Work: Organicism and Musical Analysis." *19th-Century Music* 4 (Fall 1980): 147–56.

Specht, Richard. *Johann Strauß.* Berlin: Verlag von Marquardt and Co., 1909.

Steinberg, Michael P. *The Meaning of the Salzburg Festival: Austria as Theater and Ideology, 1890–1938.* Ithaca and London: Cornell University Press, 1990.

Strauss, Johann. *Johann Strauß (Sohn) Gesamtausgabe, Serie II: Bühnen- und Vokalwerke: Band 3: Die Fledermaus.* Edited by Fritz Racek. Vienna: Doblinger and Universal Edition, 1974.

Johann Strauß (Sohn) Gesamtausgabe, Serie II: Bühnen- und Vokalwerke: Band 9: Eine Nacht in Venedig. Edited by Fritz Racek. Vienna: Doblinger and Universal Edition, 1970.

Stuckenschmidt, Hans Heinz. "Das Banale in der Musik (1929)." In *Die Musik eines halben Jahrhunderts: 1925–1975, Essay und Kritik.* Munich and Zurich: R. Piper and Co. Verlag, 1976.

Tanner, Marie. *The Last Descendant of Aeneas: The Hapsburgs and the Mythic Image of the Emperor.* New Haven: Yale University Press, 1993.

Todorov, Tzvetan. *Genres in Discourse.* Translated by Catherine Porter. Cambridge: Cambridge University Press, 1990.

Tomandl, Franz. "Die Operetten von Johann Strauß und die Geschichte ihrer Aufführungen in Wien von 1871–1914." Ph.D. dissertation, University of Vienna, 1985.

Tomlinson, Gary. "The Web of Culture." *19th-Century Music* 7, no. 3 (1984): 350–62.

Traubner, Richard. *Operetta: A Theatrical History*. Garden City, NY: Doubleday, 1983.

Van der Merwe, Peter. *Origins of the Popular Style*. Oxford: Clarendon Press, 1989.

Wagner, Manfred, editor. *Die Geschichte der österreichischen Musikkritik in Beispielen*. Tutzing: Hans Schneider, 1979.

Walser, Robert. *Running with the Devil: Power, Gender, and Madness in Heavy Metal Music*. Hanover, NH and London: Wesleyan University Press, 1993.

Weber, William. *Music and the Middle Class: The Social Structure of Concert Life in London, Paris and Vienna*. New York: Holmes and Meier Publishers, Inc., 1975.

Wechsberg, Joseph. *The Waltz Emperors: The Life and Times and Music of the Strauss Family*. New York: G. P. Putman's Sons, 1973.

Weiner, Marc A. *Richard Wagner and the Anti-Semitic Imagination*. Lincoln and London: University of Nebraska Press, 1995.

Werba, Christine. "Das Wiener Kabarett im Zeichen des Jugendstils." Ph.D. dissertation, University of Vienna, 1976.

Westermeyer, Karl. *Die Operette im Wandel des Zeitgeistes von Offenbach bis zur Gegenwart*. Munich: Drei Masken Verlag, 1930.

Wheatcroft, Andrew. *The Habsburgs: Embodying Empire*. London: Viking, 1995.

Wistrich, Robert S. *The Jews of Vienna in the Age of Franz Joseph*. New York: Oxford University Press, 1989.

Witeschnik, Alexander. *Wiener Opernkunst von den Anfängen bis zu Karajan*. Vienna: Buchgemeinschaft Donauland, 1959.

Würzl, Eberhard. "Johann Strauß: Höhen und Tiefen der Meisterjahre, 1884–1894." Ph.D. dissertation, University of Vienna, 1987.

Wutzky, Anna Charlotte. *Girardi*. Vienna: Wilhelm Frick Verlag, 1943.

Yates, W. E. *Theatre in Vienna: A Critical History, 1776–1995*. Cambridge: Cambridge University Press, 1996.

Ziak, Karl, editor. *Unvergängliches Wien*. Vienna: Europa-Verlag, 1964.